FOR JERUSALEM

FOR JERUSALEM

A Life by Teddy Kollek

with his son, Amos Kollek

Random House New York

First American Edition
Copyright © 1978 by Teddy Kollek
All rights reserved under International and Pan-American
Copyright Conventions. Published in the United States by
Random House, Inc., New York.

Library of Congress Cataloging in Publication Data
Kollek, Teddy, 1911-
For Jerusalem.
Includes index.
1. Kollek, Teddy, 1911-   2. Jerusalem—
Mayors—Biography. I. Kollek, Amos, joint author.
II. Title.
DS109.86.K64A33 1978   956.94′4′050924   [B]
ISBN 0-394-49296-X   77-90301
ISBN 0-394-50145-4 lib. bdg.

A limited edition of this book has been privately printed.

Manufactured in United States of America
24689753

To Tamar and all who hold Jerusalem dear and have given of themselves to make it a better and more beautiful city.

Contents

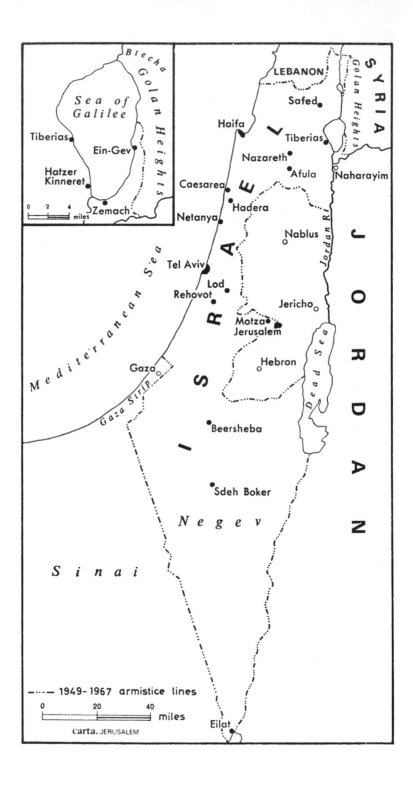

Inset map labels:
Btecha
Golan Heights
Sea of Galilee
Tiberias
Ein-Gev
Hatzer Kinneret
Zemach
0 2 4 miles

Main map labels:
LEBANON
Golan Heights
SYRIA
Safed
Haifa
Tiberias
Nazareth
Afula
Naharayim
Caesarea
Hadera
Netanya
Jordan R.
Nablus
I S R A E L
Tel Aviv
Lod
Rehovot
Jericho
Motza
Jerusalem
Dead Sea
J O R D A N
Mediterranean Sea
Hebron
Gaza
Gaza Strip
Beersheba
Sdeh Boker
N e g e v
S i n a i

----···— 1949–1967 armistice lines
0   20   40 miles
Carta. JERUSALEM
Eilat

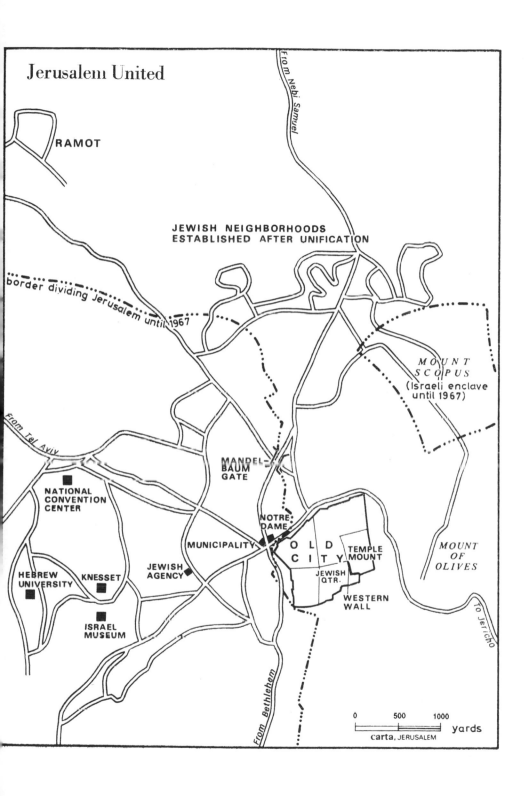

Jerusalem United

RAMOT

JEWISH NEIGHBORHOODS
ESTABLISHED AFTER UNIFICATION

From Nebi Samuel

border dividing Jerusalem until 1967

MOUNT
SCOPUS
(Israeli enclave
until 1967)

From Tel Aviv

MANDEL-
BAUM
GATE

NATIONAL
CONVENTION
CENTER

NOTRE
DAME

MUNICIPALITY

OLD
CITY

TEMPLE
MOUNT

MOUNT
OF
OLIVES

JEWISH
AGENCY

JEWISH
QTR.

HEBREW
UNIVERSITY

KNESSET

WESTERN
WALL

To Jericho

ISRAEL
MUSEUM

From Bethlehem

0   500   1000
yards
carta, JERUSALEM

Foreword

AFTER publishing two illustrated books that I wrote jointly with Moshe Pearlman, *Jerusalem* and *Pilgrims to the Holy Land,* George Weidenfeld approached me in 1970 with the idea of writing my autobiography. I was very hesitant about this. Firstly because I have never really been a man of letters. My activity throughout the years consisted basically of initiating projects and seeing that they were carried through, thus always working with a group of people. To write one's story is a more solitary affair. Also, working as I do, sixteen or eighteen hours a day at the job I was elected to do, when would I find the time to write?

Added to this is the feeling of uncertainty a man inevitably experiences when he sits down to tell his own story. Is it really sufficiently interesting? Will it make a book?

In a sense this last hesitation was the easiest to overcome, because whatever uncertainty I may feel about my own story, Jerusalem is of great concern and absorbing interest all over the world. I have experienced it every day for the last decade and more. Jerusalem is in the center of great political conflicts. Its story needs to be told. I made up my mind to write the book, came to an agreement with George – and never did anything more about it. One event followed another, the pressure in the office was too high, the difficulty of getting away from it all, remembering, and relating the memories seemed almost unreal.

In the summer of 1971, my son Amos, then twenty-four, published his first novel, *Don't Ask Me If I Love,* a semi-autobiographical story, comprising, amongst other things, a fair amount of criticism of the country and his parents, particularly his father. The book was translated into various languages and was generally well received. A point that it drove home to me was that throughout the years of my hectic public life, the two of us had never had the chance to get to know each other.

It occurred to me that I could now do something about it. I asked my son for his collaboration as a professional writer, and this provided us with the opportunity to spend many hours in lively discussion. This book grew out of these conversations. Amos's share in it was decisive by asking me provocative questions and helping me to arrange the narrative. Without his perseverance the book would never have been written.

It took a long time to begin writing because grave events intervened unexpectedly, including the Yom Kippur War. I hope that the book conveys, aside from my own personal experiences, something of the story of Israel and particularly the difficult and uniquely exciting story of Jerusalem. At the time the manuscript was completed, our national elections brought about a basic change of government for the first time since the state was founded in 1948. It is too early to say what effect this change will have on the future of Jerusalem. The fundamental concepts of the new government are certainly at great variance with those we had adopted. Yet we hope that Jerusalem will continue to thrive and we shall continue to overcome the difficulties which may arise, external as well as internal.

Of those who assisted Amos and me in our work, foremost I would like to mention my wife, Tamar, who helped me remember many of the events, particularly as she played an active role in them; my assistant Shula Eisner who has borne with me – with good humor – since before I became mayor; and our editor Ina Friedman whose assistance on the book was invaluable. I am also indebted to many other people, regrettably too many to mention individually although a good number are mentioned throughout the story.

Teddy Kollek
Jerusalem
October 1977

FOR JERUSALEM

1 Stoic Indians and Imperturbable Gentlemen

I was born at the dusk of an era. My parents were married in 1910 in Vienna, which was then the capital of the Austro-Hungarian Empire, and shortly afterwards went for a brief period to Hungary, where my father was an employee of a Hungarian timber company owned by the Vienna Rothschilds. He spoke Hungarian fluently, having been brought up in a small Hungarian city where my grandfather taught Jewish religion in the local high school. Of my four grandparents, three had come from the neighborhood of Brünn, then a German-speaking city in Moravia. Brünn was surrounded by dozens of little townships, each with a strong and active Jewish community. (The Jewish cemeteries in those towns went back hundreds of years.) It was the area from which Franz Kafka, Arthur Schnitzler, Sigmund Freud, and other great Jewish minds had come. My paternal grandmother came from Slovakia. The peasantry in Moravia spoke Czech and the Jews were brought up on German; the peasantry in Slovakia spoke Slovak and the Jews were taught Hungarian. But Vienna was the capital for them all.

I was born on May 27, 1911, in Nagyvaszony, a small village not far from Budapest. My earliest memories go back to when I was about two-and-a-half years old. We lived in an apartment overlooking the Danube, and I can recall the lights of the ships passing on the river. A short while later, when I was three, World War One broke out. As my father was a reserve officer (everyone who had been to a university became an officer in the reserves at the end of his training), he was called up by the Austrian Army. My mother and I went to Berlin, where her parents lived. All I can remember from that visit is eating bananas (for the first time). Later that would have been impossible, because the Allied blockade prevented tropical food from reaching Germany or Austria.

Throughout the war years, during the times when my father was back from the eastern front, my mother and I stayed wherever he was billeted. I remember some of those villages and provincial towns, especially a place in lower Austria called Herzogenburg. It was a small village built around a monastery, and I spent my first year of school there. But I didn't get much schooling, because I drifted from one ailment to another, including severe dysentery. It was 1917, and the scarcity of essential products was felt everywhere. My mother thought that chocolate or cocoa would cure me, and she went through great ordeals to acquire a little of one or the other.

I have only two memories from Austria's Imperial days. One is the visit to the crypt of the man whose assassination had brought about the war, the Archduke Franz Ferdinand. The crypt was near Herzogenburg, and once or twice I was taken to the annual memorial ceremony, in which my father participated as an officer. The other memory – an event I likewise attended because my father was an officer – was the funeral of the Emperor Franz Josef in 1916. It was a great state affair, probably the last ostentatious display of the dying Austro-Hungarian Empire. I recall the funeral vividly : a colorful procession, uniforms, horses, flags against the background of the sad faces of the people. Thinking about it now, I suppose they must have realized that a great period was coming to an end. Years later, when I first met Allen Dulles, head of the CIA, he mentioned that he had attended the funeral too. It was shortly before the United States had entered the war, and Dulles was a junior officer in the American legation in Vienna. He also recalled the event in its colorful details. We compared recollections – his as a young man and mine as a five-year-old – and that occasion was the pleasant beginning of what became a close friendship.

After the war, in 1918, my family returned to Vienna and I entered the second year of elementary school. Austria had suddenly changed from an empire to a small republic, but at my age the difference wasn't too noticeable. On the whole, European Jews felt a stronger sense of Jewish identification than national belonging in those days, and were therefore less affected by being on the defeated side in the war.

The first job my father held after being demobilized and returning to Vienna in 1919 was again in Hungary, during the time of the short-lived regime of the Jewish Communist leader Béla Kun. Austria established a section in its Budapest legation to oversee Austrian property under that revolutionary regime. Because of his commercial experience, his know-ledge of Hungarian, and his familiarity with the many Rothschild interests in Hungary, my father was appointed head of the section. He spent a lot of time on trips to Budapest, so that my mother and I, back in Vienna, saw as little of him then as we had during the war. But when this job ended, he returned to the private Rothschild bank in Vienna, where he was in charge of various industries all over Austria.

My father was thirty-seven when I was born. He was a handsome man who cut a rather elegant figure, and he was proud of having been the best athlete in his class. Father was conservative in his general outlook, his politics, demeanor, and his manner of dress. In fact, he was fastidious about his dress, and though very careful not to over-spend, he had a new suit made once or twice a year at one of the best tailors in Vienna. He was also rather pedantic about detailed arrangements in his belongings, in our apartment, and in everyday life. His hobby was collecting glass, small boxes, and miniatures, mainly of the Biedermeier period, 150–200 years earlier. (This eighteenth-century decorative art reached a high level in Austria.)

Father lived by all the old values one would expect: family tradition, honesty, hard work, good records in school, loyalty to his family and to his Jewishness. Since he was the son of a school teacher, it's little wonder that he couldn't bear the fact that I was a poor pupil. He literally suffered from it, and sometimes he really grew angry because of it. Once or twice he even woke me in the middle of the night to talk and ended up smacking me because my poor record and bad behavior had earned me an invitation to leave school. At the same time, he was a generous man and was willing to satisfy practically all my desires. And he was somewhat anxious (a trait I seem to have taken from him when I became a father myself, although I try not to show it). I was not allowed to have a bicycle, for instance, because of the danger of riding in the streets among the trams, buses, and carriages. My relationship with my father was a formal one, but I think I inherited many of his values – his belief that you had to work hard and not try to get something for nothing; his attention to small details; his loyalty to people and to a cause.

My relationship with my mother was a warmer and more open one. She was thirteen years younger than Father and was twenty-three when I was born. Her background was similar to his, although her family had been slightly better off. My mother's father was a merchant, and several members of the family owned small estates in the neighborhood of Brünn in Moravia. But despite the economic difference, my mother had been brought up on the same values as my father: a strong attachment to Jewish tradition, with a fair amount of religiosity and with the family as the most important focus. Mother loved sewing, knitting, and baking. She and Father were both keen on reading, too. They rarely went to the theater or opera, but they regularly attended afternoon tea parties for the local Jewish hospital and other events of that sort. Thrift was of primary importance. In fact, we wore our suits and shoes as many years as we could and had them mended again and again, rather than throwing them away. On the whole, theirs was not a very exciting way of life. But that was the way most people we knew lived at that time.

Every Sunday afternoon the family gathered together, either at our home or at the home of Uncle Emil, my father's brother. For many years my grandmother, a very beautiful woman, presided over these gatherings. I remember her as being much taller than my grandfather, with her white hair parted in the middle and tied in a bun at the back.

She was the real boss of the family. Once a year, at Passover, the whole family traveled by train to Velka Bytca, a small town in Slovakia where my grandmother's older brother, Ignatz, lived. He owned a sawmill and a large rambling farm with cows, horses, chickens, and a most beautiful orchard. The trip took about five or six hours through a picturesque valley studded with ruins of feudal castles. The small town had a large Jewish community, and Saturday mornings found the whole congregation together in the local synagogue.

Ours was a moderately traditional home. We lit candles on Friday evening and went to the synagogue on all the holidays, but we never hesitated to ride the tram on Saturday. As for Zionism, my father supported the idea but was not really active in the movement. He had been a member of the same Jewish students' organization at the University of Vienna as Theodor Herzl, albeit a few years later. When I was born, he named me after Herzl. I don't ever recall being called Theodor at home, though. My parents called me Teddy, and that's how I have been known ever since. Years later, in Israel, when everybody started to take on Hebrew names, I discovered that 'Teddy' actually had roots in ancient Jewish history. According to the Talmud, one of the Temple gates was called the Teddy Gate. So I kept the name I had grown used to from childhood with an easy conscience.

My school was half an hour's walk from home – and I didn't like school anyway, which soon became painfully obvious. Like many Jewish boys, I also learned to play the violin and took private lessons in French and English, but I didn't find any of this particularly exciting. Neither did I feel any strong identification with the models of youth then fashionable in Austrian society: the easy-going, charming Viennese playboy, or the pedantic, serious-minded, scholarly type. But I had always been a keen reader, and my idol as a boy was Winnetou, the stoic Indian chief in Karl May's novels. Later my heroes were imperturbable English gentlemen, the kind who do their duty, try not to make a fuss, and don't show emotion. Those hours spent with my head buried in a book fashioned me to a certain extent. (To this day I am conditioned not to make a great display of my feelings.) And the course I would take in life was also determined pretty early and had a lot to do with the facts of life for a Jew in Austria.

Vienna at that time had changed radically from a renowned cosmopolitan city to the capital of a very small, poor country. But it still was a city of two million people, when very few cities in the world had reached half that size. Vienna also had a glamorous history of emperors, vast treasures, wars won and lost, and the great tradition of the Hapsburgs, who had ruled from Spain to Austria and enlarged their holdings mainly through well-planned marriages – others fought wars; *'Tu felix Austria nube'* ('You, fortunate Austria, marry').

Now Austria was suddenly small and impoverished, and a certain malaise set in. This was long before Hitler and his idea of a Greater Germany, but a substantial number of people felt that the only solution for Austria was to become a part of Germany (though this was banned by the 1918 peace treaties). The idea was not necessarily confined to nationalist circles. It was held by the Social Democrats, a very powerful party with a special ideology in Austria. They were not part of the Second Socialist International or the Third Communist International; they stood somewhere in between and were nicknamed the 'Second-and-a-half International'. The Social Democrats were inspired by great political thinkers – Karl Kautsky, Otto Bauer, Karl Renner, Victor Adler and others – quite a number of them Jewish. The Jews among them believed particularly strongly that the time for nationalism of any kind was over. Certainly they were against any sort of Jewish nationalism.

A Jew in Austria couldn't vote for the Christian Socialist Party, because that was basically a Catholic peasants' party. So the most promising alternative in Vienna was the Social Democrats. They were among the first who tried to solve urban problems and displayed progressive city leadership. The Social Democrats were probably the first in the world to subsidize housing for workers (*'Wohnhausbauten'*) on a large scale and to recognize the importance of recreation – sports fields, swimming pools, parks. Today one would define these things as the quality of life, or perhaps ecology. They put emphasis on cleanliness in the city and the forests and rivers around it. Maybe it was easier to cope with such problems in that age. Anyway, the fact is that most of the Jewish bourgeoisie voted for them. I imagine that even the rich Jewish bankers – the Rothschilds, the Guttenbergs, the Springers, and so on – would have voted for the Social Democrats rather than the Christian Socialists.

There were other political choices for a Jew, of course. Austria already had a small but well-organized Communist movement, and there was also the small but increasingly powerful nationalist movement. (It was split: the larger part was very pro-Austrian, and the smaller section grew more and more pro-German and finally became the nucleus of the Nationalist Socialist movement.) But the nationalists held no promise for the Jews, though some did become Communists. A Jew could also emigrate to Canada, the United States, England, or even to Berlin, and some did. Or he could become a Zionist. But just to stay in Vienna and continue the tradition of the Jewish bourgeoisie, which had produced tremendous talent and ideas in the previous generation – Freud, Adler, Schnitzler, Hoffmanstahl, Karl Kraus, both Zweigs, Mahler, and Schoenberg, to name just a few – was no longer attractive. The atmosphere was no longer there.

Quite a number of youngsters in my generation became Zionists. The

Zionist movements followed the pattern of the established German youth movements, the *Wandervogel*, mixed with the influence of the English scout movement. Their program attracted us mainly as healthful youth activities, though it cannot be denied that we were drawn to the Jewish youth movements partially because of anti-Semitism, which was always latent in Vienna. In fact, for many historic reasons, it was natural that Jews kept together. I had no sense of danger or premonition of an imminent catastrophe for the Jewish people at that time. But I was aware of the indignities suffered by Jews, and it seemed to me that life would be much more fulfilling, and much more interesting, in a country of our own – in Palestine. My grandparents had grown up in an intensively, exclusively Jewish atmosphere. One generation more removed from mine might have been assimilated or indifferent. But to me the feeling of being Jewish and a part of the Jewish people and its history was a natural thing – not aggressive, but deeply rooted.

·I can see now why my joining a Zionist youth movement at the age of eleven wasn't really an arbitrary act. At the time, however, I didn't join because of any major ideological revelation but almost by accident. The fact is, I went to my first meeting because the son of our family doctor, who lived across the street, suggested it, and it turned out to be very entertaining. Our group met two or three times a week and went on weekend outings. We sang Hebrew songs and listened to stories about Palestine. I don't know when I actually became a dedicated Zionist. I think I became so deeply involved partly because I liked the movement activities better than going to school. Eventually I spent more and more time in the movement, and whoever spent time there became important. So I became important, and I suppose that's when I became a Zionist. Once a true Zionist, though, I gave the cause all my time and energy. I couldn't do any differently; it's in my nature.

As teenagers, our main activities consisted of outings on Sundays, when we would pitch tents and go swimming and boating. The great dream of my group, fourteen or fifteen boys, was to have a folding canoe. I remember shocking my parents at my *bar mitzvah* party. The *bar mitzvah* ceremony itself had been celebrated in the most prestigious synagogue in Vienna, the *Seitenstettengasse*. The rabbi was Professor Zvi Peretz Chajes, the Chief Rabbi of Vienna and an outstanding Zionist leader. I don't remember his sermon, but I know I was very moved by it. In the afternoon we had sixty or seventy guests at home, and it was customary for the *bar mitzvah* boy to make a set speech (written for him by a special teacher) expounding on the solemnity of the occasion and thanking his parents. I made my speech, but when it was over I added that I was a member of a youth movement and that a canoe was of major importance, so I would appreciate it if the guests would add a little cash to their presents. It was my first fund-raising venture, and my parents were slightly embarrassed, but a week later another boy from our group had his *bar mitzvah* and followed my example. I think I remember it all so well because when we finally got that canoe, we had to carry it on our backs all the way from the tram station to the Danube, a considerable hike.

Some of our activities in the movement were of a more serious nature – at least in our eyes. During that time (the middle twenties) many Jews came through Austria, particularly from Poland, on their way to Palestine. The last lap of their journey was by boat from Trieste, and Vienna was a station on the way. Tens of thousands of young people passed through the city, and there was a place just outside Vienna where they were put up in a large building owned by the Zionist Organization. We visited that building fairly often and tried to help. I don't think we contributed much to these serious 'grown-ups' on the eve of reaching their final goal, but they received us warmly.

The Jewish community in Vienna numbered over 200,000, about one-tenth of the city's population. Most were Jews who, like my parents and grandparents, had come from various parts of the former empire – Hungary, Poland, Moravia, Yugoslavia, Serbia, and Croatia – and they made up a thriving community. Yet here in the city of Theodor Herzl, the Zionists were a minority in the Jewish Community Council! There were always heated election fights for seats on the council, and the Zionist youth were active in the election campaigns. Our rivals were the assimilationists and those Orthodox groups who were opposed to Zionism. We attended every meeting of the election committees, canvassed homes to get out the vote, and transported people to the voting booths. Since elections were always on Sundays, when there was no school, we would stand a few yards from the voting booths (the legal distance) and distribute leaflets. Finally, the leader of the Zionists was elected president of the community council. It was a tremendous victory for us.

The momentous day of the year was the anniversary of Herzl's death, when all the Zionist groups met and paraded to the cemetery where he was buried. The other highlights of our life were the Zionist Congresses – which I attended, starting in 1923, as an orderly, passing notes between delegates – and the visits of great Zionists from abroad.

All this is not to say that I had no other interests beside the movement. I liked sports and was a good skater and a fairly good skier. And I continued to read a lot. Sometimes, rather than go to school, I sat in a public library and read everything and anything, for days. I particularly remember reading translations of Mark Twain and Poe and books by the great socialists of Austria, Kautsky, Otto Bauer, and Friedrich Adler, who were our heroes. The piece of literature that made the strongest impression on me was the defense of Friedrich Adler, who was put on trial in May 1917 for the murder of Prime Minister Count Karl Sturkgh. He was the first man to be publicly tried for a political crime in Austria after the outbreak of the war. Fritz Adler was a relatively young man, a socialist activist, and the son of a well-known socialist leader, Victor Adler. He chose to dissociate himself from his lawyer and to plead his own defense. Declining the plea of insanity, he accepted full responsibility for the assassination and turned the trial into an attack on the injustices of the political system and the government of Austria. I felt a deep admiration for Adler, not because he had killed a man he considered a symbol of tyranny and a menace to his country, but because of his complete identification with his cause, his ability to state it and stand for it.

I also went to the theater often. In Vienna people of my age and social group – young students and even people from fairly well-to-do homes – used to stand in line for an hour or two outside the theater and get in a standing stall, which had a very good view. This was the fashion at the time, and for a year or two I went either to the Burgtheater or to the opera twice a week. Occasionally I met people in the skating rinks or down by the sailboats. But Vienna was a large city, and I never saw these people again, especially if they were not Jewish. All my friends were Jews. There definitely was segregation – voluntary and instinctive – and I had a very limited social life outside the movement.

When I had a touch of trouble with my lungs (this was before penicillin was discovered), my mother took me to a spa in the Alps for a few months, which was then the prescribed cure. It was a holiday resort and predominantly Gentile. I met a local Austrian poet there, Anton Wildgans, who was well known and, is I think, still highly regarded. It wasn't difficult to sit and talk to him and to the other Gentiles in his circle. But it was a very non-inquisitive communication, because we felt there was no future in such friendships. There were also many Gentile Austrian girls there, and I had one or two light romances, but I had no interest in following them up. I would have had to make a special effort, change my interests, find time, turn things around entirely – and I didn't want to do that. I always had an easy time getting along with Gentiles. I don't think I had any complexes – Jewish or any others. But I wasn't particularly attracted to blondes. In fact, girls, on the whole, did not occupy too much of my time. Of course I had girl friends in the movement, and I even tried to write them poetry, but not often and never seriously. I think I was afraid something might come of it. I was definitely a late starter.

The 1920s went by and I grew from a boy of eleven to a youth of eighteen. The movement split, united, went through crises. There were many Zionist youth movements in Vienna, but our differences were not very important, and as we grew older we all understood what really counted. We became more and more committed to life in Palestine. In previous years members had been lax about achieving this goal, but gradually we saw and accepted that we had to live up to the ideology we preached. Those who did not really intend to emigrate to Palestine dropped out. The rest of us were trained for a life of farming and communal living. Our ideal was not to become merchants or professional men in our new country, but laborers. Zionist socialism demanded a foundation structure of Jewish farmers and workers to rebuild a Jewish country. Agriculture was our goal, and everything led to it – the songs we sang, the stories we were told, the contact with Palestine emissaries from the various kibbutz movements.

In 1929 an economic depression began all over the world, including Palestine. At the same time there were Arab riots in Palestine, and we all signed petitions and volunteered to go there. But stiff barricades had already been erected by the British, who held the League of Nations Mandate over Palestine, and every year only a few immigration certificates were alloted to the Jewish organizations. I passionately wanted to go, but I had to wait. In 1930 I quit high school and went to a movement-run agricultural training farm to prepare myself. The little farm, belonging to the city of Vienna, consisted mainly of vineyards and a cow barn. A group of us lived and worked there. A few times we were employed refilling barrels in the wine cellars – and we drank quite a bit. When you drink in a cellar you don't feel the effect, but the minute you are out in the fresh air you become dead drunk. It was a new experience for me.

I remember having long arguments with my parents that summer. They finally prevailed upon me to come back home and at least finish high school. I don't know whether they really wanted me to go to Palestine or they were just humoring me. But I do remember that, at the very least, they wanted me to go into business, not join a kibbutz. When I finished high school, my father persuaded me to work for a while at a Rothschild enterprise, Witkowitz, one of the largest steel mills in Europe.

The mills of Witkowitz were later part of the drama between Hitler and the head of the Vienna Rothschilds. The story of how the Nazis failed to get a ransom of millions of dollars, learning too late that the mill had been sold just a short time before, is well known. Witkowitz was a tremendous factory built over vast coal mines, and it milled steel imported from Sweden and other countries. I worked there for a week or two before boredom set in and I gravitated to the nearby *Hehalutz* ('The Pioneer') movement. The mill was in a suburb of Mährisch Ostrau, the center of the Zionist Organization in Czechoslovakia. The movement's leading figure there was Dr Franz Kahn, who was to die in the concentration camp of Theresienstadt. He had long been the chief

organizer and secretary of all the Zionist Congresses, and since I had
worked for him as an orderly on such occasions, I knew him well. He
had lost an arm in World War One, but it detracted nothing from his
working ability. I felt tremendous admiration for him, so the minute I
walked into the Zionist office and saw him, my life in the steel mill was
over.

As usual, my parents eventually accepted my decision. They rented a
small room for me at the home of the local cantor and sent me an allowance, since the movement could not afford salaries. A few months later I
moved into a commune and stayed there for the rest of the year. The
communes were groups of people waiting for certificates of entry to
Palestine. Meanwhile they lived together, worked in factories, and
studied Hebrew at night. They rented very modestly furnished houses
where six or eight people lived in one room. These communes also took
care of others who worked for the movement, like myself, so I had
practically no expenses. I slept and ate breakfast at the commune and
then went about my business, which was putting out a Zionist newspaper and preparing winter and summer camps and seminars. In the
afternoon I would meet with my youth group – I was a group leader by
then – and teach them Hebrew songs and dances. Evenings were spent
with the adults, and sometimes we held ideological discussions. I came
to Mährisch Ostrau in the fall of 1931 and stayed there for about a year.

Mährisch Ostrau was also the place where I first fell seriously for a
girl. She was from the local youth movement, came from a good Polish
Jewish family, and had an older sister who had already gone to Palestine.
I remember she was pretty, with dark hair, dark eyes, and a sharp
sarcastic wit. But though I tried very hard to win her over, I had no luck.
She just wasn't interested. She later came to Israel, but we did not keep
in touch, and I haven't seen her since.

Without a salary, I had to live frugally at my parents' expense. Not
only were they generous, but they were very tactful in their efforts to
change the direction I was taking in life. For instance, they pointed out
the advantages of being a merchant in Palestine, or representing
European enterprises there, and insisted that I should at least learn a
trade. Finally I agreed and went to Dortmund, a large German industrial town, where one of my uncles had a garage and spare-parts
business. The experiment ended as before. I worked a few hours a day,
but again I found the local Zionist youth movement, and that's where I
really worked.

Nazism was on the rise, and Dortmund had always been a 'Red' town.
The Nazis were, of course, particularly hard on socialists and communists, although not as rough as they would be years later. At Christmas
time we clashed with the Nazis on our way back from meetings in the
evenings. One time we even ended up first in a police station and then in

a camp. The camp was not like those that horrified the world in the 1940s, but I found it very unpleasant, even for a few days. After my uncle secured my release, I was involved in a few more clashes. But then, because I was not a German citizen, the police warned me that I was outstaying my welcome. So soon after Hitler became chancellor, I started back to Czechoslovakia. On the way, I stopped for a day in Berlin, and what I saw there was enough to put an end to any doubts about my leaving Germany quickly. There were even more storm troopers in the streets there, and the atmosphere was tense. The local Zionists were apprehensive. Perhaps the writing was already on the wall.

In 1931 I again attended the Zionist Congress in Zurich, this time as an orderly to Chaim Arlosoroff, one of the great Labor Zionist leaders. I had picked up a little English by then, and I remember helping him translate from German to English and vice versa. But what I remember best was accompanying him at night on the long walks to his quarters. A leader's life was more frugal in those days, and very few people stayed in hotels. Arlosoroff had rented a room with a family in a distant suburb, and he never took a taxi. After the congress sessions ended at ten or eleven at night, if the tram was no longer running we used to walk the way back together. I made use of these evenings to ask questions about Palestine and the principal issues before the congress. I vividly remember his willingness to talk to a young man and patiently explain things in detail. Once, when it was particularly late, he opened another bed in his room and wouldn't allow me to walk back alone at that hour.

Arlosoroff was murdered two years later on the Tel Aviv beach. His assailants were never caught. As fate would have it, I received a note from him a week after his death. It had been written on the boat that took him back to Palestine after his last trip to Europe, and mail took a long time then. His death was an irreparable loss to the Zionist movement.

Back in Czechoslovakia I ended up in Karlsbad, a small world-renowned spa close to the German border, organizing the Zionist youth movement in the Sudetenland. I stayed there for a few months working as a group leader and teaching Hebrew songs, Zionist history, and so on. Our funds were low, and we leaders lived on practically nothing. We were particularly concerned about keeping in close contact with German Jews, and one way to do so was to ski across the border, bring them underground literature, and then ski back. Crossing the border was still not too difficult during that period. So between 1931 and 1933, I spent much time traveling to visit the youth movements in Czechoslovakia, Rumania, and Germany.

During Christmas 1933 I went to the Maccabee Ski Club on the Keilberg in Czechoslovakia, a beautiful place in the mountains right on the frontier. A large Jewish youth group from Germany used to cross the border and ski there. They were staying on a farm a few miles away from us, and I visited them every evening. One of their leaders was Xiel Federmann, a boy of nineteen with great flair and a tall, dark-haired, very pretty girl friend named Bella. Six weeks after their group had returned to Germany, I was summoned by a local Zionist leader back in Karlsbad. In his office sat a middle-aged couple from Chemnitz, a large German industrial town just across the border. Their accent was clearly foreign, and it turned out that they were Persian Jews who had settled in Germany a few years before, developed some textile factories, and prospered. That morning, on the way to their office, they had been warned that the Gestapo was after them.

In 1934 the Gestapo was not as vicious as it later became. Nevertheless, its threat was very real. People had already been sent to concentration camps, were imprisoned for months without trial, and were beaten. There had been cases where men and women had been shot while supposedly 'trying to escape'. So it was natural that the Persian couple decided to leave immediately, without even going near their home or their factories. There was still some freedom of movement over the borders in the mountain areas, particularly as the slopes were used for sports. The couple found their way through the snow to the Maccabee Ski Club on the Keilberg and then moved on to Karlsbad. They were desperately in need of help because they had left behind their two-year-old son, who was temporarily safe with relatives. They had also left a good sum of money in cash and keys to various safe deposits in other countries. Now they were offering a large contribution to the Zionist cause if somebody would go to Chemnitz and get the child, the money, and the keys.

I had an Austrian passport, which still carried weight with German authorities. More important, on one occasion a few years earlier, I had taken my brother Paul, eleven years younger than I, on a trip to Czechoslovakia, and he was included in my passport as 'brother, born 1922'. All I had to do was turn the 22 into 32 and I had a ready-made document to take the child out. I was worried about going into Germany because of the street fights and my arrest the year before. Not that it made me a major criminal, but there still was some risk. But I decided to go because the situation was tragic, and there was nobody else available. Besides, I had an additional motive. A month earlier we had received worrying news about an unaffiliated Jewish youth movement in Transylvania, the Western Hungarian-speaking part of Rumania, whose members seemed to be drifting ideologically toward one of our competitors. It seemed 'vitally' important that I go there and put them right. But we were so low on funds that we couldn't raise the £20 – a lot of money then – for the return train fare. So I upped the Persian couple's offer by £20. Naturally, they agreed instantly, and that same evening I crossed the border.

My contacts in Chemnitz were Xiel and Bella, and they stayed up with me late that night working out a plan. At first Bella volunteered to travel back with me and take care of the child. But the Gestapo and the frontier guards between Chemnitz and Karlsbad, which was a frequent escape route, were alerted. Xiel and I knew that a Jewish girl with a German passport who went back and forth across the border in a short period of time would be suspect and might even be arrested. So we decided that I would go alone and take my chances with the child.

The next morning the three of us took a cab and inspected the house, which was on the outskirts of town. It was a beautiful villa surrounded by a large garden. The house was locked, and on each of the doors we found the red seal of the Gestapo. Then we located the child with his relatives. His nurse, a German woman who could be trusted, had remained with him. I asked her if she would accompany me across the border, and she agreed. Then we decided that the child, the nurse, and I would each arrive at the station separately. Bella would pick up the child and bring him there, and the nurse was to come to the station with the baggage. Everyone was to show up five minutes before train time.

I spent the night at the house of another member of the movement, who bought the train tickets for me. At dawn Xiel and I went back to the villa and cautiously worked our way through the garden to a side door, which also bore the Gestapo seal. But I had the keys to that door, so we broke the seal and went inside. Then we found the safe-deposit box keys and tens of thousands of marks, far beyond the 200 marks that could be legally taken out of Germany. Fortunately the notes were of high denominations and did not make my wallet bulge. We reached the station, and I felt more than a tinge of discomfort when the child started crying as the nurse and I led him aboard into a third-class compartment. But the train pulled out almost immediately, as Xiel and Bella waved from the platform.

For the ride back I had chosen a route different from the one that had brought me to Chemnitz, because I did not want the same frontier guards to see me coming back with a child. We had to change trains at the frontier and pass through both German and Czech customs. Then came the most incredible instance of sheer good luck that I've ever had. Throughout the ride, which took about an hour, I sat desperately trying to plan what to do about all the money in my wallet, because to be caught with it would mean far more than just losing the cash. I could have thrown it away, of course, but I was young and the challenge fascinated me. I remembered a story by Edgar Allan Poe, 'The Purloined Letter', in which the police are searching for an important document in an apartment. They take the place apart, but they never pay attention to the envelope lying on a desk before their eyes. It struck me that I could use Poe's idea and not even risk breaking the law.

As we walked to the German customs shed, the child was crying again. I think that helped us, because the bawling grated on the guards' nerves no less than on ours. After we passed through passport control without any problem, we came to another guard standing behind a wooden bar. He looked me over carefully. 'Any money with you?' he asked. I wasn't at all secretive. I simply held out my wallet and matter-of-factly said, 'It's all in here,' but I was trembling inside. Then another guard came over, I was searched, and they went systematically through our bags and our clothes. Even the child's teddy bear was pierced with needles. The only article that was left untouched was the wallet, which the guard had tossed aside on the bar. When the guards were finished, I casually picked it up, put it back in my pocket, and we walked through to the Czech side and on to the Karlsbad train.

I delivered the boy, the money, and the keys, and we received the promised contribution and the extra £20. I never saw the Persian family again, but I met Xiel and Bella (who eventually married) when they escaped to England in 1938 and I followed Xiel Federmann's career from the time he arrived in Palestine. Starting as a waiter in Haifa, he worked his way up to become the great industrialist and hotel owner he is today.

I used the £20 to make that trip to Transylvania. Traveling through the eastern part of Czechoslovakia, I saw primitive Jewish *shtetls* for the first time. They were exactly as described by the renowned Yiddish writers, full of robust farmers, teamsters, innkeepers, artisans, blacksmiths, horse traders, dairymen, woodcutters. These people were a far cry from the middle-class Jews familiar to me. I hadn't taken a particular liking to the 'Ostjuden' (Eastern Jews) who had come to Vienna from Poland and Galicia. I must have been influenced by the snobbery of the established Jews toward these more recent arrivals, many of whom came as refugees fleeing the Russian Army in 1915 and 1916. The newcomers spoke Yiddish instead of German and were out of their *milieu* in Vienna. They just didn't fit. Now I saw these same Jews in their own setting, and they didn't seem miserable, apologetic, and scared of every anti-Semite, as did their brothers in Vienna. They were sturdy characters, visibly sure of themselves, comfortable in their surroundings, and they seemed capable of taking on anybody. Unfortunately, as it turned out, they were not able to take on the Germans, and none of them are left.

I finally made contact with the youth movement in Transylvania. It was an important group because it had about a thousand members spread throughout Transylvania, and I had come to save them from the 'worst possible fate' : falling into the hands of one of our rivals. Actually, several rival emissaries had gotten there ahead of me. They were far more experienced, but that turned out to be fortunate for me. They were in no hurry and believed in making their point gradually. They were also lazy and tended to enjoy the pleasant part of camp life while avoiding the hard work. As I had only a few days' time, I joined the training-farm groups, lived with them, worked with them in the fields, and fought for our cause during work breaks, as well as in the evenings. The effort paid off. I persuaded them to accept our line and later that year they joined our world organization. Needless to say I viewed that visit as a triumph for the movement.

That was in the winter of 1934. I returned a few months later to help this group run a summer camp, and in the fall I was back in Vienna working for the movement there. I lived at home and did a lot of reading in my spare time. It was then that I met Tamar, who had recently joined the ranks. She was seventeen and in her last year in high school. While studying for her exams, she was also learning gardening to prepare herself for life in Palestine. She spent more time gardening and in the movement than in school, but she passed with excellent marks, which made a great impression on me. My mother subsequently claimed that I was embarrassed that my girl friend was such a good student, while I had been such a poor one.

Tamar had short brown hair, brown eyes, an attractive face, and a highly developed sense of humor. She came from an Orthodox family, but she herself did not have much regard for religion. I was six years older than she and one of the group leaders in Vienna, so to Tamar and her friends I was a 'big shot'. I came to some of their gatherings and taught them songs or arranged their activities. But my main tasks were to raise the money for the rent on the cellar we used as a meeting place (if I could not get it elsewhere, I asked my parents), keep the cellar in order, and edit the newspaper we issued. Strangely enough, what impressed Tamar the most – at least in the beginning – was my singing. Not that I had an ear for music. I sang completely off tune, but loud.

I think the first time I spoke to Tamar was during a winter camp we held outside Vienna in the beginning of 1935. But we didn't go out then, and were always together with other people. Back in Vienna I had more of a chance to pursue the relationship. Tamar used to come to the club to wash the floor, which gave me the opportunity to talk to her in private. It was not an easy romance because at the time she was in love with another group leader. But gradually she relented. After a while I began to pick her up at school at one o'clock and walk her home. Then at night I walked her home from our gatherings. We used to stand outside her house and talk until long after the trams had stopped running, and night after night I walked for an hour and a half back home again. (I did a lot of walking during that period.) Some of the neighbors complained to Tamar's mother that it was not proper for a distinguished rabbi's daughter to be standing out in the street in the lamplight with a *'goyish'*-looking young man. (I was blond, but since then my hair has darkened.) But her mother said that as long as we were standing under the street-lamp, she had no cause for worry.

Our families met only after I had left for Palestine. I don't think my parents knew much about Tamar and me. With all their understanding, they were reticent people – and so was I – so we rarely discussed personal affairs. After all, I had been away for many years. But even when I was younger, the family gatherings were always on Sundays and holidays, when I was off in the country with our youth groups. I think my parents were happier with my younger brother, Paul, who was always much more attached to the family.

At about the time I met Tamar, anti-Semitism began to reveal itself in various ways in Vienna. For instance, one of the large department stores advertised that they would not sell to Jews. That angered me so that I walked into the store and spent an hour trying on suits, shirts, hats, and other clothing. I finally arrived at the wrapping counter with a load of purchases, and the cashier wrapped each package with great care and gave me the bill. 'Oh, I'm sorry,' I said, 'I forgot you don't serve Jews here.' I saluted him with courtesy and left him holding the packages. On another occasion some of our younger movement members were out playing ball at the Dom Graben, a beautiful spot in the mountains outside the city that served as a meeting place for all the youth movements in Vienna, Christian and Jewish alike. Suddenly some Nazi boys walked over and took the ball away. I was the senior member present, so I walked up to the boy holding the ball, slapped him, and took it back. He stared at me in shock, and when he said, 'What are you doing with those Jews?' I slapped him again. That was enough to drive him and his friends off, but one Saturday afternoon a few weeks later they caught me outside a movie theater in the center of town and beat me up.

The situation was growing steadily worse in Austria. But even without the addition of the Nazi threat, I had long been eager to go to Palestine. Not that you could just get up and go in those days. The problem was not in getting out of Austria, because the restrictions on emigration had not yet come into force. But getting into Palestine was another matter altogether. Under the regulations of the British mandatory authorities, you had to have an immigration certificate before you left your country of departure. These certificates were distributed by the Zionist Organization, so in the end it was the movement that decided who would go when. In my case, each time my turn came to go, the movement decided that I was still needed in Vienna, and there was always someone else who had to leave immediately. But finally, in the spring of 1935, I was handed my certificate to enter Palestine, though I would not go there directly. First Tamar and I went to Switzerland together to attend the Zionist Congress in Lucerne, and from there I went to London on an assignment for the movement.

It was my first time in England, and I had great expectations. Through the many books I had read, I had developed a particular regard and liking for the British and an enormous sense of curiosity. England was exactly as I had imagined it would be, from the case of sea sickness I suffered crossing the Channel to arriving at Victoria Station; from my first fish and chips to walking through Baker Street and remembering Sherlock Holmes, another hero of my youth. The number of his house had been imaginary, but the atmosphere was there. I rented a room with a non-Jewish working-class family in Hackney, and I was absolutely thrilled by London. Imagine coming from a Europe festering with anti-Semitism to find that in Whitechapel the instructions on the fire extinguishers were also given in Yiddish, to accommodate the Jews who had come from Russia and Poland decades earlier. I don't know whether England has become less tolerant than it was then. But when I compare how those strange characters, the Jews from Russia, were received and assimilated around the turn of the century and how difficult it is today for people from parts of the former British Empire – the West Indies, Kenya, Pakistan, and even Cyprus – to find their place and how the tension sometimes explodes, it seems that the British are much more short-tempered today than they were before World War Two.

I stayed in England and worked for a few months in the British branch of our movement under the guidance of a Palestinian (in 1935, the term designated a Jew from Palestine), Lassia Galili, one of the most knowledgeable men I have ever met. I also met Moshe and Ruth Dayan, who were there on their honeymoon. At that time Moshe was studying English. He was, in a sense, the first *sabra* I had ever met. I may have met others before, but Moshe was the son of a famous pioneer settler – one of the founders of the first kibbutz and the first moshav. He was full of life, full of questions, full of curiosity. Ruth was also a *sabra*, and very pretty too, but she spoke English extremely well, since she had spent her childhood in England. It was a surprise to meet such a couple. Then again, with Moshe, surprises of one sort or another continued over the years.

I remained in England for three months. Then I stopped briefly in Berlin and in Mährisch Ostrau and spent a few days in Brünn with Tamar. Like good socialists at the time, we discounted marriage, but back in Vienna we made arrangements for Tamar to follow me to Palestine as soon as possible. At the end of December 1935, I said goodbye to everyone, took the train to Trieste, and finally boarded the boat for Haifa.

2 'Now We Belong to Emir Abdullah'

IN 1935 there were no planes flying to Palestine. In fact, there were few planes flying anywhere. Only a short while before I had left Austria, a great crowd of us had gone down to Vienna's airfield to greet the two pilots who were second to cross the Atlantic, shortly after Lindbergh, and beat Lindbergh's record by making it all the way to Vienna. Flying was still a very unusual business then, so I went to Palestine by boat, the *Gerusaleme*. My fellow passengers were hundreds of pioneers on their first trip to Palestine and a few Zionist leaders returning home. Together we recreated the atmosphere I had heard and read about for years. In the evenings we sat on deck and sang to the accompaniment of a harmonica. I was young and had no burdens or worries. Going to Palestine to settle on a kibbutz was the fulfillment of my dream, and I was elated.

When I arrived in Haifa with £5 in my pocket – a substantial sum in those days – I was met by the man who had brought me into the movement, our family doctor's son, Efra Schallinger. He took me home to Kibbutz Givat Chaim, near the town of Hadera, and the next morning I started working. Some of the kibbutz members earned their living as construction workers hired by the villages and settlements nearby. On my second day in Palestine, we went to a Yemenite moshav and I learned the secret of how to pour a roof. It had to be done in one day without interruption. We worked until late that night and then celebrated by downing a glass of wine and a piece of cake. Everything around me was just as I had pictured it – the landscape, the work, and the pioneer spirit. I was home.

On one of the evenings during the few days I spent in Givat Chaim, I met an old friend from Vienna, Chaim Sheba. He had been a member of our youth movement, one of the few who had gone on to the university, then finished his medical training, and come to Palestine. He had joined a neighboring kibbutz and worked for Kupat Holim, the Histadrut (Labor Federation) Sick Fund. Chaim was in charge of the whole area around Hadera and traveled from settlement to settlement on his horse.

When he came to visit his patients in Givat Chaim, we sat down and reminisced. He was destined to become an outstanding and admired figure not only as a doctor but as a social philosopher, an Israeli Albert Schweitzer.

After a few days I left Givat Chaim and joined a group that was just beginning to trickle in from Austria and Czechoslovakia. It was temporarily spread all over Palestine, but gradually gathered together and established a new kibbutz on the eastern shore of the Sea of Galilee, where there had been no Jewish settlement since ancient times. At first each of us stayed wherever he or she could find work and a place to sleep. Then slowly we converged on Hatzer Kinneret, an old Turkish farm building on the southwest shore of the lake. It had been the cradle of several kibbutzim before us, and we remained there until our eventual settlement in Ein Gev on the eastern shore.

While we were living at Hatzer Kinneret, we worked wherever jobs were available in the surrounding area: for the electric company at Naharayim on the Jordan River, building a seawall for the Public Works Department at Zemach, or paving roads. I acted as the group's treasurer for a while, and it wasn't easy being a treasurer without money. Since we all lived together, like an extended family, we often came up against the kind of problems that newly established families face. For instance, one difficult question we had to face concerned children – whether or not to have them, and, if so, what to do with them. I was against raising families and I argued in the kibbutz assembly that children would be an economic burden. We should wait for more prosperous times. Another problem was where members were to go on their annual summer vacation. Hatzer Kinneret was located in an area of beautiful hills dotted with villages like Yavne'el and Sejera, so I suggested that everyone walk to one of these villages for his vacation. Of course, some of our members wanted to go to far-off Tel Aviv or even Jerusalem. We had long arguments about the problem, though most of them were academic. In that first year, who took a vacation?

The hot climate of the Jordan Valley and the primitive conditions were a harsh initiation. During the first year we were sick most of the time. I had typhus and paratyphoid fever, several bouts of malaria, and sandfly fever. Altogether, I caught various kinds of typhoid five times. The disease was treated by very primitive methods in the British government hospitals, mainly by starving the patients. After my third attack, a friend and I were released together from a British hospital in Safed. Declared cured, we were still weak, as thin as skeletons, and hungrier than I ever can remember. The streets were absolutely deserted because it happened to be the second day of the Palestinian Arab riots of 1936, and the people of Safed – remembering the massacres of 1929, when many Jews were killed – had locked themselves in their homes. There we were in a completely closed town with an Arab attack expected any minute. We could hardly stand on our feet and had no money, so we staggered around knocking on doors until we managed to borrow a few piasters and located a mail truck, which brought us safely home.

The next time I had typhoid I again went to a British hospital, this one in Haifa. But my condition grew so serious that our doctor feared I would not survive a fifth round in a government sick ward, so I was taken to a Jewish hospital in Afula, even though they were not permitted to treat contagious diseases. From there I was sent on to recuperate in Motza, on the outskirts of Jerusalem, and soon I was walking the streets of the city for the first time. Jerusalem was a quiet little town set in the mountains. I remember being impressed by it as pleasant but pretty dull.

By the end of 1936, we were well into our plans for settling in Ein Gev. This was not a simple matter. A group of German Jews had purchased the land in order to produce winter vegetables for Europe, but the project never materialized. The land was close to the border between French-ruled Syria and British-ruled Palestine and was so exposed that it could only be settled by a venturesome kibbutz. Individual farms would be an ideal target for Arab raiders, who could attack and then cross the frontier into relative safety. But we were willing to risk the danger, so a deal was made and the German-owned land was transferred to us.

Tamar arrived early in 1937, and I went to Haifa to meet her. She came as a tourist and had to deposit £100 with the British authorities to guarantee that she would leave before her visa expired a few months later. Meanwhile, we worked and made our preparations for settling in Ein Gev. We were still living in Hatzer Kinneret when Tamar's visa was about to expire. I was a citizen of Palestine, and by marrying me she could become one too. Not only would that solve her legal problem, but she would get her £100 back. That's what convinced us to lay aside our socialist ideals and accept the bourgeois institution of marriage. Otherwise we might not have been married till years later. A marriage certificate was not of much importance in the kibbutz until children were about to be born. In the nearby settlement of Kinneret lived a red-bearded postmaster, Mr Korn, who was also a ritual slaughterer. Every morning he would ride his bicycle to Zemach at the southern end of the lake, where he did his slaughtering, and then returned to Kinneret at noon holding an umbrella over his head to protect him from the sun. Mr Korn also performed marriages. His services cost half a pound and included a bottle of wine and a honeycake; the wedding ring was strictly on loan. Some of us were always at work up the hill in Hatzer Kinneret, where we had a little smithy. So when a couple would come to Mr Korn to be married – very often when they were expecting a child any day – he would step out on the road, put two fingers to his mouth, and give a powerful whistle, and we would come down to provide the necessary *minyan* (quorum required for the ceremony). I don't remember why Tamar and I went off snobbishly to be married in Tiberias and ignored poor Mr Korn. I still have tender memories of the whistling slaughterer-postmaster.

Our treasurer at this time, Benno, happened to be in Tiberias, so we chose him as a witness. For some reason he didn't show up on time, and we had no choice but to sit and wait for him, because you had to have a witness who knew you, and we didn't know anyone else in Tiberias. When Benno finally showed up, it took us all of five minutes to get married. Then and there I decided that I would never spend more time at anyone else's wedding than I had at my own. Tamar sent a postcard to her parents in Vienna saying that we were married and that it had been funny. They were somewhat offended. Incidentally, we never got the £100 back.

When we finally settled in Ein Gev, it was sudden, fast and exciting. The decision to establish our physical presence on our lands was triggered by the arrival in Palestine of the British Royal Commission headed by Lord Peel late in 1936. By June 1937 we were told that the British government was going to accept the commission's recommendation and partition Palestine between the Jews and Arabs. The way things stood in June, our frontier would run down the middle of the Sea of Galilee, with its eastern half becoming part of Arab Palestine. That would mean that the water resources of the country would not be under Jewish control. Water supply has always been of primary concern in our area, and the Sea of Galilee was our main reservoir. So we summoned up our energies and carried out a lightning-quick settlement of the 'tower and stockade' type on the eastern side of the lake. It was completed within one day in June 1937. Hundreds of people came in dozens of trucks and, within a few hours, put up a stockade around the area, a few huts, and a watchtower with a searchlight. By evening we were settled, and a few hours later, when we heard the Peel Commission Report broadcast over the radio, one of our members started chanting, 'Now we belong to Emir Abdullah' (the emir of Transjordan). We all laughed and danced. Spirits were high. We had succeeded. We were right on to the water and ready to fight for it. That was how Ein Gev came to be. I had a definite feeling that I had reached the final stop, that this was the purpose of my life. I had no thoughts of going anywhere else, certainly not of taking any job in public life. The kibbutz fulfilled my needs and expectations more than any other way of life I could conceive of.

There have been many Utopian societies, even in recent history, particularly in England and the United States, and some of them were very similar to the kibbutz movement. But none had shown the vitality and ingenuity of the kibbutz movement, and none had achieved the population – absolute or relative to the population – of the kibbutz movement. The kibbutz succeeded where others had failed not only because it was based upon certain socialist ideals brought by its members from the heyday of socialism in Europe in the 1920s, but because it was fulfilling definite national tasks : guarding the frontiers, making the soil blossom, turning city people into farmers (one of the basic ideals of Zionism). This was a more attractive society than any I knew of elsewhere. Besides, it was a society in which we were never ever bored; there were always new challenges before us.

The terrain immediately around the settlement was desert, but a short distance away were some Arab villages. We actually owned very little land, and over the years we negotiated with our neighbors for a little more. (The problem was really solved only in 1967, after the Six Day War, when Ein Gev was able to expand into what had previously been no-man's land.) A few months after we officially established Ein Gev, we decided to move our camp about a mile to the north, where more land was available. We built a new tower and stockade and immediately started constructing living shacks for the rest of our group, who soon joined us.

In our first year, only about thirty-five of us actually lived in Ein Gev, including only four women. The rest of the 180 members remained in Hatzer Kinneret and other places where there was gainful employment. Our tower-and-stockade camp had only four shacks and a dining hall, and we didn't have a paved road to Ein Gev for a long time. We could drive to and from the kibbutz when the weather was fair, but not after a rain, when the mud was knee deep. The only reliable means of transportation was by boat, and even that was not easy because sudden storms would make crossing the Sea of Galilee difficult and sometimes impossible. It took us a while to get used to crossing in rough weather, and until we did many of us were seasick, I among them. Tamar stayed back in Hatzer Kinneret, and we were separated most of the time. I often went to see her in the evenings or on weekends, sometimes making my way in a small, folding rowboat and returning a few hours later, because there was always a fear that Ein Gev might be attacked and we didn't want to leave it unguarded.

After the rest of the group joined us at Ein Gev, for quite a while there weren't enough shacks for everybody. This problem was solved by a method which we called 'primus', named after a simple, three-legged heater that was common at the time. According to that method, every young couple was joined by a third, 'unattached' person. This naturally created some inconveniences and at times even tension among the couples and their third foot. Tamar and I were joined by a girl from Vienna named Ziva, a very energetic and high-spirited little redhead who is still a very close friend of ours. Our *'primus'*, however, didn't last very long. On one of my visits to Haifa, I bought a giant packing crate for £5 from a couple of new immigrants from Germany. I brought the crate back to Ein Gev, had a door installed, and built a wooden partition that divided the case into two tiny rooms, so we even had a 'living room'. Then Tamar and I moved into our new home – alone.

The most important place in the kibbutz, the center of our social life, was the communal shower (there were no showers in the individual shacks). Each afternoon after work, we all met, marched toward the shower carrying our clean clothes and wearing wooden sandals (without them one couldn't walk), and went on to discuss problems and work out their solutions. The communal shower was in a relatively big shack, with a thin partition dividing the men and the women. That was also the best place for hearing the latest gossip and all sorts of personal stories. Through the wall we could listen to what the girls were saying on the other side, which was sometimes a very educational experience.

Our hardest physical work was loading gravel and sand in Btecha, on the northeast bank of the lake, and taking it over to be sold in Tiberias. We used to set out in our boat at 3 A.M., dragging a pontoon trailer behind. In Btecha we filled our sacks with gravel and sand, a mixture called *'zifzif'*, and loaded the boat by walking from shore on two wooden boards with the 200-pound sacks high on our backs. When the boat was filled, we crossed the lake to Tiberias, a trip that took five hours because of the weight of the *zifzif*. There we again walked on two wooden boards, carrying the sacks to shore, where we poured the *zifzif* on to a big heap.

For a few months we also worked for the Electric Corporation, mending the cement water conduit in Naharayim. We had to dig ten feet into the ground and place iron bars into the cement floor of the carrier. This job provided work for people from the entire area – Jews and Arabs – and we sometimes worked around the clock. That was when I learned to sleep on my feet, and it came in useful in later years.

Every village in Palestine at that time – Arab or Jewish, including the kibbutzim – had a *'mukhtar'* (Arabic for 'head of the village'). I had that title from the start and received £2 a month from the British government for my troubles. The job included obtaining the various licenses to register births and deaths and maintaining official contact with the police. Thus I became the kibbutz's channel of communication with the British. I was chosen for the post mainly because, having been in England, I knew more English than the others and had some experience in dealing with the British. But there was also the fact that I didn't have any complexes about Gentiles. I had gone to a Gentile school and lived next door to a Catholic convent in Vienna, where every morning I saw the Catholic prelate – Prime Minister Ignatz Seipel of Austria – get into

his car and drive to his office. I had no particular respect for Gentiles and
no particular fear of them. Even today, many people in Israel, especially
those from Eastern Europe, are afraid or suspicious of Gentiles. But I
felt equal and did not believe they were either superior or threatening. I
especially liked the British. I thought they were really decent people,
and this feeling was reinforced a few years later, when I spent time in
London during the blitz. But people who had never been to England and
had come into contact with the British only in Palestine had a more
negative attitude toward them.

There was a British police station in Zemach under the command of a
rather difficult man named Townsend, but we had very little to do with
him. Instead we made a point of being on very good terms with
Archibald Pitt, the man under Townsend, who was in charge of the
Jewish Settlement Police. Pitt helped us a great deal and prevented the
Arabs from harassing us when the situation later became tense. Some
Arabs even attacked Pitt's car while he was on his way to Ein Gev, but
he was not hurt. He later was transferred, promoted to major, and
finally drank himself to death. We also maintained good relations with
the Marine Police. In fact, we received a lot of unofficial help from the
British and occasionally even bought weapons from individual policemen
– a pistol or some ammunition that they would later claim they had lost.

Serving as the 'mukhtar' was hardly a full-time job, however, and I
frequently worked on our boat, both as a sailor and fisherman. The
fishing rights in the Sea of Galilee were owned by an Arab family named
Khouri and by their partner, a Jew called Mino (Zalman) Goldzweig
who still lives in Tiberias. They had held the rights from the early days
of the British Mandate and even before. Mino was a big and likeable
fellow who loved to eat and drink. His interests, however, clashed with
ours because he believed we were catching fish that belonged to him.
Even though he was a Jew and basically wanted to help us, we still had
trouble with him at times. When we started fishing near Btecha, which
was in his and his Arab partners' territory, some of the clashes even led
to shooting. Gradually, I became friendly with Mino, and we would
often sit on the Tiberias shore at Muhammed Akawi's restaurant, which
served excellent food. Mino helped me carry out negotiations with
neighboring Arabs for land. In later years, when I traveled more often
to Tel Aviv and Jerusalem and even wore a jacket and pants that
matched, I kept a suit or two at his house for trips after having finished
unloading our zifzif.

For some time I was also the defense commander of Ein Gev. This
was during a very quiet period, and there were no serious attacks on
the settlement. But my position gave me the chance to ride a horse
around the mountains all day, which I enjoyed immensely. One of the
ways in which we guarded our security was to establish good relations

with our neighbors, the Bedouin and the Cherkessians. They visited us regularly, and we, in turn, were invited to their feasts and weddings. As we sat around on carpeted mattresses, with a large bowl of rice in the middle of the circle, the host would tear off pieces of meat, and each guest would take some in his hand, shape it into a ball with rice, and place it in his mouth. First served were the village notables and important guests, then the common people, and finally the women. If a wedding was being celebrated, the men danced the *debka*, a high-spirited dance, and we sometimes joined them.

We also became friendly with the rich and powerful Kurdish family that owned Btecha, where the Jordan River runs into the Sea of Galilee, about 100,000 acres of mostly fertile land that had been swept down from the mountains over the millennia by the rains. Great cities had existed in that valley in the early Christian era. The ancestor of the family that owned Btecha, Yousef Bek, had been a vizier in the Turkish sultan's court. He had been appointed the 'Emir el-Hadj', the man who organized the annual pilgrimage (*Hadj*) to Mecca bearing the sultan's gifts. The pilgrimage would start from Damascus, pause in Kuneitra on the Golan Heights, and then continue down to Mecca. (This was at the turn of the century, before the Germans built the Hejaz Railway.) In the late nineteenth century, the 'Emir el-Hadj' made use of the pilgrimage to acquire vast stretches of land from Btecha on the Sea of Galilee all the way up to the Golan Heights. It was a simple process. The Turkish authorities had begun registering land ownership, which frightened the sheikhs and the *mukhtars*. Registration could mean only one of two things: either you had to pay taxes or you had to join the army. For those who joined the army in Ottoman times, service was officially seven or eight years, but most never returned Turkey was constantly involved in wars in the Balkans and elsewhere, and very few soldiers survived. So when the Emir el-Hadj offered to do these landowners a favor and register their lands in his name, they were only too happy to agree. He became the owner and they remained tenants.

In the late 1930s, we developed a close friendship with the descendants of Yousef Bek. I grew very attached to two of the Bek's sons (Bek is a courtesy title similar to 'the Honorable'). The oldest, Mohammed, had been a page in the sultan's court and then went to school in Vienna. He spoke excellent German with a Viennese accent, which drew us together. My friendship with the Bek's youngest son, Fouad, developed much later, during World War Two, when I was doing undercover work in Istanbul and passed through Beirut on the way. The family owned a lot of property in Lebanon and Syria, as well as in Palestine. Fuad entertained me in a Beirut nightclub and astonished me by lighting the cigarettes of a dancer with thousand-franc notes.

The Bek's descendants now live in Geneva, having been thrown out of

Syria by the nationalist-socialist Ba'ath Party, which does not particularly favor capitalists (especially Kurdish capitalists). I still correspond
with Fouad. Not so young now, he writes me and other Israeli friends
sad letters, hoping we will compensate him for the land the Syrians
confiscated and part of which we have been occupying since the Six Day
War.

The Bek's house in Btecha was a two- or three-hour ride on horseback from Ein Gev, and we visited there from time to time. One time
Ein Gev arranged to grow rice together with the Bek in Btecha and,
since the distance was after all considerable, several of our members
actually lived in the grandeur of the Bek's house. Compared to the
shacks we were living in, or any accommodation we were likely to have
in the future, it was a palace. Set right on the lake front, the house was a
two-story structure built of black volcanic rock with a tile roof and an
outdoor wooden staircase up to the second floor. The kitchen, servants
quarters, and storerooms were down below, while the upper story had a
large central room with doors leading to the bedrooms. All considered,
I wasn't surprised at how quickly our members agreed to the joint
rice-growing project.

I happened to be visiting the house when the family experienced the
first strike in its history. There had been a long-standing arrangement
that tenant farmers who lived on the land would receive seeds and draft
animals from the Bek in return for a certain percentage of the crop.
Apparently, a quarrel had broken out about how much the farmers could
afford to give, and they refused to plow until the dispute was settled.
When we arrived Fuad told us that the tenant farmers were on strike
and things might be a little unpleasant, but lunch was being prepared
and we should stay. Before the meal was served, the heads of the twelve
or fifteen striking villages were ushered in and seated at one side of the
table. Opposite them was a group of uniformed gendarmes from
Kuneitra, the closest large police station. The officer of the gendarmes
snapped his whip down on the table a few times, the strike was over, and
everyone left but us. The Bek had a marvelous Cherkessian cook, and
the food was delicious.

In all, the first fourteen months I spent on Ein Gev, from June 1937
to September 1938, were exhilarating for me. I was doing what I had
come to Palestine to do, and though it was hard work, it was very
satisfying. But there were also personal difficulties. Tamar and I were
separated for most of that first year. She stayed back with the group in
Hatzer Kinneret, and our time spent together was mostly limited to
'visits'. Then, with the political situation in Europe growing worse, the
geographical gap between us widened from a small lake to a large
continent, as I went off to England for a year. Tamar had a hard time
getting used to the separations. She was lonely, and for the first years of

our marriage we both sometimes sought intimacy elsewhere. Those early years were often a little shaky, but this changed later and we have lived a happy life together. But at that time, when I got the call, I left both my wife and my kibbutz behind to take on a mission abroad – the first of many.

3 Two Tours in London

AFTER the *Anschluss* in March 1938, when Austria was overrun by the Nazis, I had no idea about the fate of my family. The newspapers in Palestine, and all over the world, carried stories about battalions of storm troopers marching through the streets of Vienna. We were all very worried about our families, and we read the papers and listened to the radio constantly. But there was no mail coming through from Austria, no personal news. It was a distressing period. The growing power of the Nazis left people with a feeling that the world was coming to an end. When I finally received a letter from my family postmarked Prague, it was a great relief.

In September of 1938, I was sent to England to work with the Habonim youth movement there. On my way, I decided to spend a day in Prague with my family. They had escaped from Vienna in such haste that almost all their belongings were sacrificed – house, furniture, bank accounts. My father left behind a fine collection of antiques, managing to save no more than a dozen pieces of fine glassware and enough money for subsistence. He assured me that the family would not stay long in Prague. The Sudetenland had been occupied by Hitler, and although the rest of Czechoslovakia was still free, everyone could see the end coming. So my father at last agreed to make Palestine their destination.

My brother, Paul, went first, joining a group of Youth Aliyah, then a newly established organization that brought youngsters to Palestine for two years of schooling and often saved children whose parents failed to escape Europe in time. Paul and his group happened to be placed in Kibbutz Givat Chaim, where I had spent my first days in Palestine. My parents were finally able to leave Czechoslovakia before the end of 1938. They crossed the mountains at the Czech border on foot, my sixty-four-year-old father carrying his precious glassware through it all, and they finally arrived safely in Haifa.

Meanwhile, I had continued on to England to take up my assignment. I started my work by training young people for kibbutz life in Palestine on the David Eder Farm in Kent. The farm was named after one of the early English Zionists, who also happened to be Sigmund Freud's first disciple in England. (His wife, Edith Eder, a great lady full of gentle wisdom, was one of the founders of WIZO, the Women's International Zionist Organization.) Soon, however, I became involved in bringing Jewish youth from Germany, Austria, and Czechoslovakia over to England. In November 1938 events in Germany became even more terrifying, starting with the infamous *Kristallnacht*, which is a somewhat euphemistic description for what was actually a pogrom. Thousands of young people on our training farms in Nazi territory were arrested and placed in concentration camps. Similar persecutions followed in Austria and later in Czechoslovakia. We were involved in frenzied activity, using every possible resource – political and otherwise – to get these endangered young people to England, Holland, and Denmark.

Jews were still permitted to leave German-occupied countries, but we had to provide a destination and visas for them. The difficulty was in securing these visas. We were helped mainly by women's committees – headed by the late Rebecca Sieff and Blanche ('Buffy') Dugdale, Lord Balfour's niece – and by other English friends, such as the Labour leader Michael Foot and one of the outstanding journalists of that period, Frank Owen. We had to approach the Home Office, which was empowered to issue entry permits, as well as the various labor unions. Vast unemployment had created a crisis in Britain. We were not allowed to bring in competing labor or in any way add to the burden of the economy. But in agriculture there was a shortage of manpower, so we negotiated with the two existing farm unions and finally received permission to bring Jews into England if we could guarantee work for them on farms.

This brought about additional problems. If we could find work only for boys, the girls would have to stay behind in Germany. Fortunately, most of these youngsters, in the Zionist spirit, had taken on Hebrew names. Since the British authorities were not familiar with modern Hebrew, we managed to bring in as many girls as boys. A visa would be issued in the belief that it was for a boy, but when a girl appeared she was not turned back. Eventually we found work for about three thousand young people.

One enjoyable experience I had was in the Cotswolds, an area near Bristol, where I was scouting for farm jobs. I visited a monastery of German monks who had left Germany and bought a farm in England because, as believing Christians, they faced great difficulties from the Nazis. I had written them beforehand that I was a Jew from the Holy Land and wanted to call on them. When I arrived the monk who received me said : '*Bruder, Kommst Du von Nazaret?*' ('Brother, do you come from Nazareth?'). They had never heard of Ein Gev, of course, and had only a dim idea of the Galilee. But Nazareth was glorified as the setting of Jesus' childhood, and when they learned that I actually lived nearby, they opened their hearts like true Christians. Dozens of our young men and women found work on their farm.

In the spring of 1939, I left London with a two-fold mission. First I went to Czechoslovakia, where I was to get Czech government receipts for a few hundred thousand English pounds, part of a complicated deal between our organizations and several Western powers. The plan simplified the financial problems of Czech Jews emigrating from the Central European cauldron. Whoever wanted to emigrate from Czechoslovakia for political reasons – and this applied to any Czech citizen, but concerned mainly Jews – would deposit money in a special Czech bank account and be issued a receipt. Once he arrived in England, he would receive English money against his receipt. My job was to get these individual receipts as well as receipts for general Zionist funds out of Czechoslovakia, which had just been overrun by the German Army. Then I was to go on to Vienna. There was some danger attached to this itinerary, but I had good luck. I also had a Palestinian passport, which was backed by the might of the British Empire.

After completing my mission in Czechoslovakia without a hitch, I calmly went on to Vienna, where I had an appointment with Adolf Eichmann. Eichmann had been 'in charge' of the Jewish problem in Germany, and immediately after the *Anschluss* his authority was extended over the Jews of Austria. He had opened an office in Vienna, and I was to go there in order to extend to Austrian Jews the agreement we had with Germany for letting Jews out. In England my job had been to obtain entry visas and send them across to Germany, where they meant freedom for our young people. Now I came to Vienna with a large supply of British entry permits made out to Austrian Jews. My task was to present them to Eichmann and convince him to let them go.

I arrived in Vienna by train and took a taxi to the Zionist office. On the way I passed the house where I had lived from 1918 to 1935. Our little upstairs balcony was draped with a large flag bearing a swastika. Once at the Zionist headquarters, it was not difficult to get an appointment to meet Eichmann. The Jewish authorities dealt regularly with Eichmann, who maintained contact with Jewish representatives even in the concentration camps. I was told to go to the Palais Rothschild, a beautiful house in the Prince Eugen Strasse where the Rothschilds had lived since before the Napoleonic wars. The story of the Rothschilds in the Nazi period is well known. All of them had left Vienna except Louis, who was confined in the Metropole Hotel until a large ransom was paid for him. But he never lost his composure or failed to put the Nazis in their place when he chose to. There is a story that when the Gestapo came to take Baron Louis von Rothschild to the Metropole, he ordered them to wait until he had had his lunch. Several months later,

when they came late at night to release him, he left a message saying :
'Do not disturb me until morning.'

My appointment with Eichmann was the first time I had ever visited
the private home of the Rothschilds. I walked through a large, elegant,
wood-paneled room up to a desk, and there he was – a neatly dressed,
clean-shaven young man in a brown uniform with the swastika on his
arm. He gave the impression of being a minor clerk – not aggressive,
not loud, and not impolite. But he kept me standing throughout the
interview. When asked what I wanted, I explained that I had entry
permits to take Jewish youngsters living on Austrian training farms to
England and eventually get them to Palestine. He was very businesslike
and asked me a few technical questions. How many English entry
permits could I provide? How soon could the people leave? Would the
permits include boys and girls? After ten or fifteen minutes, he agreed
to the scheme and I left. Eichmann did not make any special impression
on me. I began to hear more about him in 1943, when I was doing rescue
work in Istanbul. But at the time all I saw was a Nazi official who handled
Jewish affairs, and while we hated the Nazis, none of us foresaw the
horrors to come. The next time I saw Eichmann was in Israel in 1961,
when I was in charge of making the technical preparations for his trial.

I returned to England and remained there until the summer of 1939.
Then I went back to Ein Gev, and a few weeks after my return World
War Two broke out. The kibbutz faced a dilemma. We were right on
the Syrian border, which became a very active smuggling area during
the war. The route went from Jaffa up through Palestine and Syria to
Turkey and from there across to Germany. All the Arab villages around
us were deeply involved in the operation, and we were approached to
enter the business. Our real interest was not in smuggling goods and
making profits but in smuggling weapons and Jews in from Syria. Yet it
was all intertwined : the same illegal band dealt with everything – be it
people or goods – and we vitally needed to maintain good relations with
the Arabs. I was for participation on the grounds that it would enable us
to receive weapons and strengthen our defenses. But the majority at Ein
Gev, supported by members of nearby kibbutzim with whom we consulted, opposed it on moral grounds. Looking back, I think the majority
was right; there must be a careful limit to expediency. So instead of
joining with the Arabs, we worked out a *modus vivendi* with them. We
turned a blind eye to their operations, and the Arabs, in return, ignored
the illegal Jewish immigration and the transfer of weapons from Syria.
Neither activity was reported to the British officers at the border.

In December 1940 I was on the move again. I was asked to return to
England on a mission for the Keren Hayesod, the central Zionist fund-
raising agency. Our purpose was to prove that even during the blitz in
England, Jews were interested in Palestine and willing to contribute to

constructive development there. As it turned out, we had well-attended
meetings in England while bombs fell around us. This time Tamar came
with me to London. We started out from Tiberias, where seaplanes
took off from the water. Landing on the Nile, we spent the night in
Cairo, flew on and made stops in Luxor, Khartoum, and on Lake
Victoria, and eventually reached Durban. (We could not fly the shorter
route over the Mediterranean because of the enemy presence, so we had
to go via South Africa.) The seaplane always started early in the
morning, when it was still pitch-dark, and finished its day's travels by
noon. It was heavy and slow, but it had a comfortable cabin large enough
for twenty passengers and was designed like a pleasure cruiser. Elegant
stewards in white jackets served drinks and meals, and the pilot made a
special detour for us low over the Nile to show us the wild animals.
After a five-day flight, we boarded a boat to Capetown and then to
Freetown, where we joined a convoy of forty ships. We finally reached
Glasgow in February after a voyage of nearly fifty days.

Tamar and I stayed in England for a year, which was longer than
planned. During that period I had my first close working relationship
with David Ben-Gurion, who was in the country until the end of 1941,
when he left for the United States. I also spent a good deal of time with
Chaim Weizmann. I remembered Ben-Gurion from my boyhood, when
I had seen him at the Zionist Congresses. Now he was in England to
persuade the British to establish a Jewish fighting unit. Later he was to
become bitterly disillusioned with British Middle Eastern policy, though
he was never to lose his admiration of the British for their stubborn
wartime courage. But even then he was convinced that the only power
that might eventually help us was the United States, and he was making
every effort to get there. He finally reached New York and stayed for a
considerable period, preparing the famous 1942 Biltmore Resolution, in
which six hundred Jewish leaders demanded that a Jewish commonwealth be established in Palestine forthwith. But meanwhile we were
both in England, and Ben-Gurion had time on his hands. He even began
studying Latin and Greek then, and became quite proficient. I took him
on several visits to training farms where the youth we had brought out
of Germany in 1938 continued to work. We did a lot of talking on
those trips, and I grew to know him.

My tremendous admiration for Ben-Gurion developed gradually over
the years; it was not there at the start. My first impressions of him had
been neither particularly strong nor particularly favorable. My affinity
at the various congresses, and when I first came to England, was for the
much more refined people who had grown up in Central Europe and had
acquired a more Western demeanor – first and foremost, Weizmann
himself. I had little taste for Ben-Gurion's fiery phrases. Even the salt-
and-pepper politicians in Austria, who were rather revolutionary, had

used milder forms of speech than he did. But my respect for Ben-Gurion grew as I learned the power of his political analysis, his great foresight, and his understanding of historical forces.

I clearly remember one incident in England that illustrates this aspect of his character. It was at a Sunday morning meeting in an Anglo-Jewish club where, speaking in Yiddish, Ben-Gurion unleashed a violence I had never observed in him before. He shocked Tamar. It was the first time she had ever heard him speak, and she was unhappy with what she saw and heard. He called the British 'pigs'. I was shocked, too, not only by his language but by the startling viewpoint he had adopted, one with which I firmly disagreed. At that time everyone from Weizmann down believed first and foremost in Churchill and then, to a lesser degree, in Roosevelt. The accepted Zionist strategy was directed primarily at influencing Churchill to support the partition of Palestine or the establishment of a Jewish State. The target in America was to influence important American Jews, like Morgenthau, Brandeis, and Frankfurter, in the hope that they would persuade Roosevelt to follow suit. Influence and persuasion – what else was there? We all believed that policy would be decided by high-ranking individuals in England and the United States. But on that day Ben-Gurion declared that only power would decide our fate – the military power of the Jewish population in Palestine and the massed weight of the great body of American Jews. American Jewry did not yet wield the influence it would later assume, neither in the Democratic Party nor in the economy. Nobody foresaw that American Jews could have an organized, formidable impact on American policy; that they would be roused, united, and willing to make sacrifices for the creation of a Jewish State. Nobody but Ben-Gurion. He foresaw it in 1941 and kept repeating it from then on, despite the fact that most people believed, as did I, that he was on a visionary course that would lead us into chaos. Ben-Gurion was proved right. All the others – Weizmann, Stephen Wise, Nahum Goldmann, Abba Hillel Silver – hadn't the least inkling of the historic development that Ben-Gurion saw so clearly in 1941 and 1942.

As time went on, I learned more and more to appreciate Ben-Gurion's political intuition. Again and again everyone around him was absolutely convinced of a policy other than the one he chose. I also came to appreciate his single-mindedness, the ability to concentrate on one matter alone. This was true of Ben-Gurion even in little things : he guarded his own personal timetable and was unwilling to meet people we thought important or attend meetings we deemed essential because it was more important for him to concentrate on the central problem and not be diverted by minor matters.

Ben-Gurion was only one of the Zionist leaders I got to know during that period in England. At the Jewish Agency offices in 77 Great Russell

Street, I met an extraordinary group of people when I arrived. Among them was Lewis Namier, a baptized Jew and probably the greatest British historian of our time. The foremost expert on the Georgian period in England, he taught at Manchester University, where he had met Weizmann and become intensely interested in Zionism. He was also constantly consulted by the British government on foreign affairs. Namier was an odd personality. He had a Polish background (his original name was Namierovski) and seemed a snob, in the sense that he was well versed in the history of the British aristocracy, hobnobbed with the blue-blooded, and loved style. But he was no snob about Palestine and Zionism. His friend Blanche Dugdale, whom I mentioned earlier, was a member of the Cecil family, one of the great political families of England, which goes back to the Earl of Salisbury (minister to Elizabeth I). The group also included Harry Sacher, who had been a lawyer and an editorial writer for the *Manchester Guardian* right after World War One, when it was the best newspaper in England; and Leonard Stein, who had been an outstanding English barrister and left his practice in order to join Weizmann and the Jewish Agency in the early 1920s.

I think that from a purely intellectual point of view, never before had such a group been available to Zionism. There was Leon Simon, a literary man and a great Hebraist, who ran the Postal Savings Bank in England and later came to Israel and started our postal bank. And finally there was Selig Brodetski, one of the brightest mathematicians at Leeds University, who gave up his academic career to become a Zionist official. Then came a slightly younger generation, including Israel Sieff, a man of the world, a great connoisseur of wine, women, and art (he had been a dynamic Zionist for decades and was still eloquently rallying British Jewry after the Six Day War); and Simon Marks, the brains behind the most imaginative chain store in the world, Marks and Spencer. And I mustn't forget a secretary who worked with them all, though mainly with Weizmann (whom she called 'Charlie'). Her name was Doris May, and she was a Catholic. She had a first-class university education and was extremely capable, a fitting member of the team. It was she who taught Ben-Gurion Latin and Greek, and her great ambition was to climb Masada, which she eventually did years later.

It is interesting that with the exception of Weizmann's children – one of whom was lost with his fighter plane over the Channel in the Battle of Britain and the other drifted away – the offspring of these people remained Zionists and are today among the leaders of English Jewry. It is likewise remarkable how many Gentiles were in that group.

It was also during that stay in England that I became friendly with the Wingates, though I had met Orde back in my first year at Ein Gev. Early one Saturday afternoon, a civilian car had driven into the kibbutz and a sloppily dressed officer stepped out. We had heard stories about Orde Wingate, a strange British officer who was organizing people to fight the Arab terrorists with their own tactics, and we knew some people who had joined Wingate's Special Night Squads. He was already a legend, and we welcomed him enthusiastically. Wingate wanted to see Ein Gev, so I accompanied him on a 'tour' of the settlement and then drove back with him to a kibbutz in the Jordan Valley where he had some recruits. He spoke comparatively little. What impressed me more than anything else were his burning eyes. I was also taken by his wife, Lorna. She was the prettiest girl I had ever seen.

We met again in London about two years after he had been thrown out of Palestine by the British and right after his great success in Ethiopia, from where he had also been withdrawn. He was in London for a while before being assigned to Burma, where his amazing success in irregular warfare was one of the turning points in the war in the Far East. I saw him often during this period, and we frequently lunched together in a Jermyn Street restaurant that he liked. He felt lost and extremely dejected. His ideas, which had proven themselves in the field and later changed military history, were consistently rejected by his superiors. He even tried to commit suicide.

Tamar and I used to visit the Wingates' small apartment at 49 Hill Street, where Orde told us great stories about fighting the Italians in Ethiopia. He had a very strong, interesting face – not handsome, but lively. Lorna told us the story of how they met. She and her mother were traveling by boat from Australia, and Wingate, then thirty, was also a passenger. Lorna was only sixteen, and her mother was still young and very attractive. The two women competed for Orde, and Lorna won. They were married the following year. Lorna was a wonderful girl – idealistic, enthusiastic, straightforward. When Wingate was away, he seldom wrote, but he cabled her from time to time. She worshipped him as a child worships a hero, though he was not an easy man.

One of the stories Lorna told about him was about his first assignment in Palestine. He was on the High Commissioner's staff and, as such, was officially invited to various formal affairs. At one party the door opened and the German consul walked in. This was in 1937, before the war, but at a time when Hitler's power was soaring. Though Wingate had been invited as a British Army officer, he said, 'Lorna, this is no place for us,' and they walked out as the German walked in. Such behavior was highly unacceptable in official society, but Wingate was a man who never failed to stand up for his convictions. I remember his intimate knowledge of Palestine and his desire to return and fight our war.

Wingate was deeply religious and belonged to the Plymouth Brothers, a sect fanatically attached to the Bible. The last time I saw him, he took me to the village in Kent where he had been born and brought up. We went to a pub there and I sat and listened to him quoting from the Bible. That was not unusual for him, but on that day he seemed like an Old Testament prophet. He left soon after for Burma and the air crash that killed him.

During that year I was based in London while engaged mainly in raising funds for the Keren Hayesod and recruiting people to our cause. Watching the British in their everyday life was a tremendous experience. I can't imagine any people under duress behaving better than the British did during the blitz. They never lost their nerve. Sitting through the bombing at night and then going out the next morning to tread on the shattered glass that covered the sidewalks was an unnerving experience. I can still hear the crinkling noise and recall how unpleasant it was. But the British walked on as though it were nothing, taking their blankets and pillows down to the underground every night and staying there till morning without fuss or complaint.

After a year Tamar and I finally secured passage out of England. I must have had a premonition that my trip to England would be prolonged, and it was important to me that Tamar be with me during this period. It was a strenuous year. I had encountered a dazzling variety of personalities, from Ben-Gurion to Wingate, and I had made contact with one of the British Intelligence units, which was to influence my activities in the coming years.

Our traveling companion on the way back typified some of the fascinating personalities that era produced. Manya Shochat had been an anarchist in Russia and then joined the fighting Jewish guards, Hashomer, in Palestine. At the beginning of the war, she was sent on a mission to the United States, which she found too tame. So when the blitz began in England, she came right over; Manya wanted to be where the danger was. Nobody knew quite what to do with her, as she had a poor command of English. So she returned home together with Tamar and me. We left from Liverpool, where we experienced another heavy air raid on the last night in England. It was late in 1941, a few days before Pearl Harbor, when we began our forty-five-day trip in a convoy to South Africa. From Durban, in a series of hops, we flew home. It was the most difficult time of the war.

Just before leaving Liverpool, I learned that Manya had received a large sum of money to pass on to someone in Palestine. She intended hiding it in her stocking so she could smuggle it out of England in violation of the existing currency regulations. With great difficulty, Tamar and I convinced her to remain a law-abiding guest. Then, ten days out of port, we were told to sleep in our life jackets because an enemy submarine had been sighted. Manya's first reaction was how lucky it was she had left the money behind. Imagine, it would have been lost if the ship went down!

4 Interlude in Istanbul

Bᴀᴄᴋ in Palestine, I found myself increasingly involved in intelligence work, partly as a result of my contact in London with the
British department known as the Subversive Operation Executive
(SOE). Moshe Shertok (Sharett), who ran the Political Department of
the Jewish Agency (our sort of government on the way to independence), and Reuven Shiloach, who ran the division that dealt with
foreign intelligence organizations, especially the British, asked me to
join them. I was appointed as Shiloach's assistant, thus beginning my
career in public life.

That was the summer of 1942, three months after my return to Ein
Gev. My headquarters were in the Jewish Agency building in Jerusalem,
and after roaming around for apartments, I finally settled in with the
Rumenik family right across the street from the Jewish Agency building.
Rumenik's wife decided to join the British Auxiliary Women's Corps
about then, so for some of the time he and I lived alone in the apartment
in a bachelor's set-up, which was not particularly orderly but certainly
served my purpose.

Since Tamar remained in the kibbutz, I drove to Ein Gev every weekend and on holidays in an old Oldsmobile that belonged to the Jewish
Agency. Cars were a pretty rare item at the time – so rare that when
you were on the road and saw a car in the distance, you could almost
always recognize it and knew to whom it belonged. No cars were
manufactured in Palestine, and on the whole it was almost impossible to
get a permit to import them. They couldn't be transported by sea
because there was a blockade and the Mediterranean was sealed, except
for military convoys. So in order to get a permit to buy a car, even a
second-hand one, you had to convince the British of the usefulness of
your occupation in connection with the war effort. As I worked in daily
contact with British Intelligence, I had no difficulties getting the permit.
I drove quite a lot around the country, visiting our various units and
recruiting people for new jobs.

My boss, Reuven Shiloach, in charge of undercover affairs for the

Political Department of the Jewish Agency, maintained contact with the Intelligence Department of the British police (the CID), British Military Intelligence branches, and to a lesser extent with American and French Intelligence. I worked closely with Shiloach and therefore saw a lot of the British. I also found it easier to communicate with them than he did. He wasn't particularly easygoing on the social level, but Jerusalem was a small city in those days, and socializing was important. For example, the Friday night gatherings at the home of Gershon Agron, the editor of the *Palestine Post* (who a few years later became mayor of Jerusalem), were the highlight of the week. They were always attended by 100 to 150 people, mostly Jews but quite a few British, including foreign journalists and the staff of the Government Press Office. Sometimes officers came as well – the ones who preferred intelligent conversation to playing cards and drinking. I also met the British almost every day at lunch at Hesse's Restaurant. Hesse's was then a kind of officers' club for both the army and the police, but anyone could sit down and have a drink or coffee with them. Like these officers, I was, after all, alone in the city, and I ate in restaurants all the time. And wherever I ate there were always Englishmen, and we always talked.

The British in Palestine were bored. They rarely had their families with them, and they didn't know what to do with themselves. Entertaining them now and then was an act of mercy as well as good policy. We invited them for a drink out of decency and hospitality. Our 'policy' was to be simple and human; there really was no need to spy on the British. We did not want them to be suspicious of us either, so that we could work together with them, even though there was a difference in emphasis between our respective aims : they mainly wanted to defeat the Germans; we wanted to save Jews. It was not an easy relationship to cultivate.

I had several good friends among the Englishmen in Jerusalem during the war. One of them was the head of the Criminal Investigation Department, which dealt more with Jewish and Arab underground movements than with common criminals. His name was Giles, and he was an extremely thin man, with hollow cheeks, sparse hair, and glasses. He came from a long-established English colonial family in the Middle East, and he and his brother, both born in the area, had made careers of police work. One brother served in Egypt, where he reached the top of police intelligence, and the other in Palestine. I knew them both because I traveled a lot between Jerusalem and Cairo. Their inclination was toward the Arabs, mainly because they understood them better – a traditional British colonial attitude. But the Giles brothers were certainly not anti-Semites. When it came to vital war needs, they welcomed every bit of cooperation from us. Their basic intention was to help preserve British power in the area. I was able to confirm this strictly objective attitude when I met Giles in England in the early 1950s. We sat in his London club and reminisced, and I was impressed by his sincerity when he expressed both his political detachment and his personal friendship.

Another friend was Rymer Jones, Giles' boss, the inspector general of police. He was a literate man and slightly more in sympathy with us. He stayed in Palestine almost until the end of the British Mandate in 1948, returned to London, and eventually became one of the big five of Scotland Yard.

The man I liked best among the British, though, was Lieutenant-Colonel Henry Hunloke, chief of Military Intelligence. The son of the Captain of the Royal Yacht Squadron, Henry had married the daughter of the Duke of Devonshire and became a member of Parliament, from which he resigned to join the army. He was a very pleasant man and a wonderful raconteur. His best tale was about the crowning of George VI. It was discovered that Hunloke had exactly the same size head, so he was asked for the full-dress rehearsals and was crowned several times with full pomp and regalia in Westminster Abbey.

Hunloke was not particularly in sympathy with the Jewish community in Palestine. None of the British were, for Palestine was, for all practical purposes, a British colony. In theory, all Britain had was a Mandate over Palestine, and the League of Nations had some theoretical authority. There were even annual meetings in Geneva at which the British Mandate authority was required to deliver its report. But this was all academic. In reality the situation was becoming very complicated, with Arab riots on the one hand and Jewish aspirations and pressure for more and more immigration – particularly after Hitler's rise to power – on the other. In that atmosphere of British colonial rule, we were trying to create the foundations for an independent Jewish existence. Some believed we would have a state; a few believed it should be an independent dominion as part of the British Commonwealth, which looked as if it would last for eternity. I did not care very much at that time whether we would remain part of the British Empire or not, as long as Jews would have free entry into the country.

This was not yet the time of our serious struggle against the British. In fact, a close relationship developed between us when the war started. We were in it together against Hitler. Sometimes the British in Palestine joined us in opposing political decisions made in London. The various intelligence services with which we worked were torn. On the one hand, they wanted to exploit our war potential, and during certain critical periods of the war our value was very high and constituted a good portion of their overall capacity in terms of both knowledge and manpower. On the other hand, the British were constantly instructed from London not to make too much use of our potentials so that they would not be obligated to us at the end of the war.

In spite of the cautious attitude in London, however, a working relationship was created. Traveling with a British officer along the frontier in Galilee to determine where to blow up a bridge in case of possible enemy penetration created a natural sense of camaraderie, and differences seemed to disappear. One way we cooperated was in devising post-occupational schemes – special plans in case enemy forces should enter Palestine. (That was when the German Army still seemed invincible.) Moshe Dayan was in charge of one, a program to establish radio-transmitting stations throughout the country in order to interfere with the German radio and to report news of what was happening behind enemy lines. Dayan had about fifty operators trained and hidden everywhere, including his wife, Ruth.

When this work on post-occupational schemes came to an end with the British victory at El Alamein late in 1942, new ideas were developed. The Haganah had a plan to drop young people from Palestine behind the enemy lines in occupied countries. These young volunteers were immigrants who had come from occupied countries in Europe comparatively recently, and we trained them for their dangerous assignment. The severe persecution of the Jews had not yet begun in countries such as Hungary, Rumania and Bulgaria, and a young Jew could still melt back into his old community rather easily. Once settled in, he could provide valuable information to the British and at the same time keep us informed on matters concerning the Jews. Our plan was to send hundreds of these young people as parachutists. The problem was to train them and get them behind enemy lines, and for this we needed the British.

Trying to make the right connection, we finally came upon Lieutenant-Colonel Tony Simonds of MI 11 in Cairo, the department in charge of getting British pilots and other POWs out of enemy-occupied countries and bringing them back to active service. Tony was about my age, slim, blond, and every inch a British officer whether he was in uniform or not. We became close friends and have kept up this friendship until today. After the war, he left the army and retired to Cyprus where he bought a farm and produced flowers in a very picturesque spot on the road from Nicosia to Kyrenia, near the beautiful Crusader's abbey of Belapaese. He enjoyed the role of a retired English gentleman who made a little extra money from growing his own beautiful flowers. The tragedy was that Belapaese was right on the border between the Turkish and Greek areas in Cyprus, and during the fighting in 1974 the farm was burned to the ground.

MI 11 was enthusiastic about our plan to send parachutists into Eastern Europe. In the end, it materialized not for hundreds of paratroopers but only for thirty-six, some of whom never returned. The scale was limited because of anti-Zionist pressure in London. For instance, in 1944 we had 250 paratroopers ready to be dropped in Hungary. They were fully trained and waiting impatiently. Reuven Shiloach happened to go to Bari, the Italian seaport and then a British Forward Headquarters. There he received word that the whole plan, which had been worked out in great detail, was to be cancelled. Sitting opposite the British officer who informed him of this decision, he was able to read a cable upside down – an art he had developed in long years of intelligence work. It plainly stated that the political disadvantages of creating obligations to the Jews of Palestine far outweighed the tactical advantages of such an enterprise. Therefore it was finally decided, at a very high level in London, not to go ahead with the project. Still, the few paratroopers who did get through – including Hannah Senesz and Enzo Sereni, who never returned – had the important psychological effect of giving hope to great numbers of Jews, for word of their presence soon spread. They also raised the morale of Jews in Palestine, who were frustrated because of their inability to help the Jews in Europe.

Another important wartime contribution was an office we established in Haifa to interrogate every recent arrival and record what he knew about his country of origin. The British were interested in even the most trivial facts. For instance, if the bakers in a certain town in Bulgaria were given an increased order for bread, it might mean the German Army was getting reinforcements.

In December 1942, Eliahu Epstein (Elath), who dealt with Arabists and Middle East experts in the Western world on behalf of the Political Department, returned from a trip to Istanbul and Tehran, where he had met with many British and American experts. He came up with the idea that by working with the Americans and British outside of Palestine, we could gain political advantages in various ways, while boosting our efforts to save Jews in Europe. After a few meetings with Moshe Sharett, it was decided that I should go to Istanbul and establish permanent contact with the British and American services there. Nothing similar had been tried before. I was not really asked if I wanted the assignment. In those days your readiness to do a job was taken for granted; you were just told what to do. Anyway, going to Istanbul sounded rather exciting, and I left almost immediately and was there by the beginning of 1943. I traveled by car from Haifa via Beirut to Tripoli and from there to Aleppo, where I boarded the Taurus Express. The whole trip took no more than two days.

Danny Shind met me at the train station when I arrived. I had known him many years, as he had been a member of Ayelet Hashachar, a kibbutz not far from Ein Gev, and we had met on various occasions.

Shind had been in one of the groups that had organized 'illegal' immigration' to Palestine from Latvia and Lithuania even before the war began.
As the undercover representative of the Jewish Agency in Istanbul, he
was the most inventive of our little group. Whenever one of us blew up
or became depressed, he was always able to calm us down or cheer us up
with one of his good stories.

From the train station at Haidar Pasha in Asia, we crossed the
Bosporus to Europe by ferry. It was a queer feeling that few people have
today, because since then a bridge has been built to link the two con-
tinents. But at the time it was an adventure to cross from Asia to
Europe, certainly when you did it the first time. This was the Hellespont,
where Leander had tried to swim across and never made it. The trip left
me with a longing to see much more of the city than we were able to
manage. But soon details of Hitler's death camps started reaching us and
killed our appetite for beauty and sightseeing.

I joined a group of three men who worked closely together. Aside
from Shind, it included Venya Pomerantz, who worked for the 'illegal'
immigration effort (known as Aliyah Bet), and Menachem Bader, the
oldest among us and the most experienced in financial matters. I held
him in high regard from the days of my short visit to Prague in 1939,
when he had been involved in the operation to transfer Jewish property
to Palestine. My job was to stay in contact with the British and
American services and also, to some extent, with the press, so that we
could bring important facts to the world's attention. It was a task that
required someone who spoke English well and who had experience in
communicating with Westerners, which is why I was chosen. Venya's
job was writing letters to the camps and ghettos in Eastern Europe and
deciphering the replies. He also interrogated the few Jews we were able
to smuggle out of Europe and get to Turkey. Shind's task was to purchase the boats that were sent to Rumania and Greece and brought the
refugees. Bader was the treasurer of the whole operation. There were
also others who came for longer and shorter periods. We all had some
'false cover'. I went to Istanbul as a journalist for the *Ein Gev Diary*.
Venya, who had done carpentry back in his kibbutz, was ostensibly
buying timber.

Our ability to stay in Istanbul and to operate at all depended largely
on the British and somewhat on the Americans. Since Turkey was
neutral, Istanbul was filled with agents and spies from every country.
It was impossible to do anything there without having the cover of
either the Axis nations or the Allies. Both sides had their share of
agents, and they were all being watched by the Turks and by each other
without let-up. When you arrived at a hotel, you handed over your
passport. It was returned a day later after the concierge had shown it to
the Russians, the Americans, the Germans, the British, the Italians, the

Turks, and probably the bartender in his favorite café. All the concierges and receptionists were on the payroll of each of the embassies and consulates. In every apartment house, the moment a tenant moved in, the janitor reported it to the Turkish police, and the information spread because each policeman was also in somebody's service.

You had the feeling of being surrounded by the enemy all the time, and as we could not fully rely on our allies, the British, it wasn't a pleasant feeling. Though we went out comparatively rarely, sometimes we had to meet a contact or entertain someone at a restaurant. The best restaurant was Abdullah's, which served excellent Turkish food. Every time we went there, we heard German, Hungarian or Rumanian being spoken. The place was full of embassy officials or devious characters of one sort or another, and there was the smell of the enemy around. I remember seeing German Ambassador von Papen entertaining some people at Abdullah's. On another occasion a German agent approached me in a hotel lobby. Someone apparently told him that I had just arrived from Germany. At any rate, he came over to talk to me and quickly left very red faced. The only explanation I had for that incident was that someone had seen in my passport, or on a railway ticket, or heard me mention the name Beirut and mistook it for Bayreuth, Germany.

With all these secret enemies wandering about, it was remarkable there was not more violence. But Istanbul was as safe, in a way, as Switzerland. The enemy countries needed common neutral ground for many necessary arrangements and exchanges, and we were invariably involved in some of these deals. Anyway I don't think that there was much real danger involved in our stay in Istanbul. After all, we were interested in something that in terms of the war effort was only a sideshow: the Jews of Europe. It wasn't worth anybody's while to try to eliminate us.

Because of the Byzantine arrangements that were in effect, the atmosphere in Istanbul was sometimes absurd. Once a friend and I were approached on the street by a man who said: 'I heard you speaking Hebrew. I am in trouble. Can you help me?' He told us he was in Istanbul to buy dried fruit for a company in Palestine. After two weeks, according to law, he reported to the police for a renewal of his permit to stay in the country. The officer asked, 'Who are you working for?' The man said, 'The fruit company.' The officer, annoyed, snapped, 'Don't give me that! I want to know who you're *really* working for.' He was probably the only man in Istanbul who was truly interested in dried fruit. The police captain, outraged, refused to renew the man's permit, and the poor fellow was ordered to leave on the next weekly train. I took my honest fellow-Jew to one of my British contacts, who called the police captain and said the man was a British agent. Then the man was free to stay as long as he liked and buy dried fruit to his heart's content!

Though most of us were undercover, there were two Palestinians in Istanbul who openly and officially represented the Jewish Agency – Chaim Barlas and Yosef Goldin. We found ourselves in a tense relationship with Barlas. He was in an admittedly uncomfortable position, as he was not supposed to do anything illegal. But we regarded him as hopelessly inflexible about the most trivial details. For instance, on Passover eve 1943, three illegal boatloads of Jewish refugees arrived in Istanbul, and we did not want to be found in our rooms in case of an investigation. We had to have a place to stay for a few hours, but when we showed up at his hotel, he turned us away so as not to compromise the Agency. With no time to go elsewhere, however, we insisted on staying. He had a tough assignment, and we didn't make it any easier.

During my first few days in Istanbul, I persuaded Shind of the advantages of moving out of the Pera Palace hotel to an apartment of our own. The Pera Palace was a large hotel that had once been luxurious. Herzl stayed there in 1901 when he came to call on the sultan and try to persuade him to give the Jews a charter to develop Palestine. Since then the place had become dilapidated; only the high ceilings and large rooms remained as clues of its former glory.

We soon moved into apartments in the center of town. Menachem Bader and Venya lived on one of the main streets, just across from the German embassy. Shind and I took another apartment around the corner. Ours was a five-room apartment: two bedrooms, a dining room, a sitting room, and another room where we put up people who came from Palestine and stayed for short periods of time. Mrs Hornstein, our elderly Turkish-Jewish housekeeper, ran both households and cooked for us all. We rarely went to restaurants because we did not want to be seen too often.

We restricted our contact with the local Jewish community to only four or five leaders. This was during the period when the *varlik* (a special Turkish tax imposed on Jewish, Greek, and Armenian merchants) was making life difficult for the minorities, especially the Jews. But the Jewish community had some influential connections, and their leaders were of great help to us. When boats with refugees arrived from Greece or Bulgaria, the Turkish Jews helped us provide food and water for them. They also served as our contact with the Turkish authorities, and they knew how to bribe when necessary. The leading figures were an Austrian Jew and a German Jew, Brod and Goldenberg.

Simon Brod was a good, sweet man with a freckled face, a sense of humor, and a cigarette forever hanging out of the corner of his mouth. His father had come to Turkey as a tailor from somewhere in the Austro-Hungarian Empire. Brod, in turn, had become a clothes merchant and apparently acquired quite a fortune (part of which he lost through the *varlik* tax, but he still seemed well off). Brod was about fifty-five and not in the best of health, but he left his business to devote himself fully and wholeheartedly to rescue activities. At 3 A.M. he would be at some distant railway station if someone was expected to cross the border from Bulgaria, Greece, or Rumania; or he was at a distant jetty of the Istanbul harbor when a boat was scheduled to arrive. He knew all the Turkish and British officials and happened to have an apartment in the same elegant building where the British passport-control officer in Istanbul lived. They had known each other for many years and had a good relationship, which reinforced our own contact with the British official. Whenever we were in financial difficulties, he advanced us money. He knew where to buy gold sovereigns (when this was the currency particularly needed) and where to get dollar bills. In short, Brod was invaluable, and I cannot imagine our operation going on without his help. Many years later, I returned to visit Istanbul mainly to see him again. He also visited us once or twice in Jerusalem before his death some years ago.

Goldenberg had run the Deutsche Bank in Istanbul until the Nazis came to power. He was not as active as Brod, but he had some very important connections – used only on rare occasions, but then extremely valuable. His beautiful wife, also Jewish, was rumored to have been Kemal Ataturk's mistress.

It was in Istanbul that we started hearing about the mass extermination of Jews. I don't know if I could ever convey the impact that those days had on me and on the other members of our group. As time went by, the picture looked grimmer and grimmer. Every day we received news of the Nazi extermination campaign. It was hard to believe or grasp the meaning of it all. Very often we were the first and, for a time, the only people outside the Nazi-occupied world to know. It was an intolerable burden and the most shocking experience of my life. I think it changed my outlook on the world entirely. We lived with the knowledge that an incredible disaster was overtaking our people and we were completely helpless to do anything about it: the world remained indifferent. Then rare trickles of Jews – sometimes just two or three individuals who had somehow escaped from the camps and whom we got out of Rumania, Bulgaria, or Greece – started arriving in Istanbul. I shall never forget the way they looked and the stories they told. It made me see the utmost urgency of our historic mission to create a Jewish state in Palestine.

I particularly remember one young man whom I took back to our apartment for the night. (The next day we arranged for his journey to Palestine.) I no longer remember which camp he had escaped from, but his face, frail figure, and shabby clothes have remained with me ever since. He was about twenty years old, just skin and bones, with a shaven head and very dark eyes. He remained very quiet and didn't want to eat anything I offered him. The only thing he would take was a few cups of soup. Looking at him I remembered myself at his age, leading a very comfortable, pleasant life in Vienna. He didn't tell me very much about the camp. I heard detailed accounts of the horrors of the Holocaust before and after that night, but all I have heard and read since has left less of a mark on me than that one brief encounter.

We were in a permanently frenzied state of mind because of the news of the exterminations. We sent letters to every address we had – thousands of letters all over the world – in the hope of getting people out of the endangered areas and the death camps and making the world realize what was happening. In the end, we saved only a small number of people, microscopic in comparison to the number killed. But we did all we could with our very limited means and tried to console ourselves that at least our efforts gave the Jews of Europe the feeling that someone, somewhere, was trying to help them. Considering the circumstances under which we were working, even small achievements were great victories. For example, Hungary fell entirely under German rule only in December 1944, but before then we were satisfied if we got people out of Poland and brought them into Hungary through Slovakia. After all, there was hope that we might get them from Hungary to Rumania and then to Turkey by boat.

We knew by then that incredible numbers of Jews were being executed every day, but the world refused to believe. So we tried every means to make the world understand, pounding away at the British and the Americans by making innumerable copies of every letter that came from the occupied countries, and distributing and broadcasting them through all available media. Istanbul sent forth the first shock to the world's conscience. We were the first to get the authenticated facts. The few boats of Aliyah Bet brought to Istanbul the first people who had been in the death camps, had witnessed the mass killings, and had escaped.

At first we truly believed that this would start a worldwide drive to save the Jews of Europe. But our frustration grew when we realized that we were powerless to trigger any of the Allied Powers into action against the now-undeniable existence and growth of the extermination camps. Franklin Roosevelt's White House did not respond to the pleas from American Jewry. America had other priorities. Not one of the Allied countries could be persuaded to take even token action – to recognize the existence of the camps by making a single bombing run over the railway line leading to one camp. To this day I do not know why. The White House and the State Department offered excuses that did not make sense. Henry Morgenthau, Jr, secretary of the treasury, became convinced by our information but he, too, was ineffective to bring about action. The only thing we could do was to send messages to Weizmann in London and to Abba Hillel Silver and Stephen Wise in the United States in the hope that they could arouse the world. We did so through every possible means – mail, cables, and traveling to Jerusalem and telling the story there, so that someone else would make the journey (very few people could get passage to the United States at that time) and tell the facts.

Years later I met an American journalist, Arthur Morse, who was possessed by the need to find out why none of the Allies acted to prevent or stop the Holocaust. I encouraged him to continue his research and try and get it published. The resulting book, *While Six Million Died*, gives a much more detailed and gruesome description of the inertia, particularly of the Americans, despite the persistent warnings about what was happening. Still, he never came closer to an explanation for the lack of Allied action than I did.

It became quite clear that the search for a homeland was not only an exercise in order to preserve the dignity of the Jewish people; and not only an objective whose value could have been challenged by the viewpoint supporting the dispersal of the Jews as the salt of the earth among all the nations, as some Jews and Gentiles continue to maintain. It became obvious that a country of our own was an absolute necessity to save the Jewish people from extermination. That, of course, conditioned our activities then and later. We felt that the Great Powers had deserted us. Whatever excuses the Americans and British presented to justify their total indifference to what was happening to the Jews in Europe, we felt we were justified in disregarding the regulations of these countries directed against us as laws without any moral weight. It was therefore our absolute right to flout these laws : to save Jews and bring them into Palestine despite the British White Papers and regulations; to acquire arms for our self-defense despite various laws and embargoes imposed by the British and other nations. We were strengthened in this feeling by the support of a great number of outstanding personalities who were universally regarded as men of integrity and ideals in Western society. They supported our activities not only in speech and writing, but often by putting their lives on the line for our cause.

Despite our sense of urgency and indignation, it was difficult to move even our closest contacts in Istanbul itself. But they helped us in our day-to-day affairs, and considering the odds against our operation, I suppose we should have been grateful even for that. Immediately after my arrival in Istanbul, I called on Major Arthur Whitall, the British passport-control officer, at the British Embassy. The passport-control office was the cover for Intelligence, and Whitall was the one with whom I was to establish contact and work closely. He was a tall, lean man in his fifties, always polite, always even-tempered, very human, and even compassionate to the extent his official position permitted. He supported our 'cover' and was helpful in every way that was not blocked by the Foreign Office. I went on to meet him about once a week in our apartment or his, or, more rarely, in his office, and he kept us in touch with the various Intelligence units. He also let us use his diplomatic pouch. Sundays at 10 A.M. our letters were brought to his office, and we knew they would be delivered in Palestine. We used a crude semi-code, which I am sure the British could have deciphered easily, but there was no sign of distrust. Whitall's entire staff was straightforward and cooperative.

Besides Whitall, we had many other contacts, including Lieutenant-Commander Wolfson in Naval Intelligence with MI 11. Though he was of Jewish parentage, I believe his parents had him baptized as a child. He helped us get Jews out of Greece in special kayak boats. MI 11's basic interest in that operation was the RAF's prisoners of war; the Jewish refugees were certainly secondary. Many pilots had been captured in the bombing of the Ploesti oil wells, and these airmen, as well as those downed during the battle over Crete, were badly needed by the RAF. So we established a joint operation to rescue both Jews and British pilots and bring them by boat from Greece to Izmir. Years later Wolfson became a director of BOAC and died in a crash on a Trans-Atlantic inaugural flight.

I also established contact with Captain Cedrick Seager, the American military attaché in Istanbul. He came from a British family that had lived in Turkey for generations, similar to the Whitalls. His brother, still a British citizen, worked for British Intelligence in Aleppo. Seager had a pleasant smile and was eager to listen. He was more open in his attitude, manner of speech, and relationships with people than the British officials, with whom we had more dealings. I always remember him in a dark blue, but not particularly elegant suit. He later joined the State Department and for a while was in charge of Technical Assistance for the Middle East – Point Four. I met him again in Washington in the early 1950s, when I worked in the Prime Minister's Office.

Seager was a wonderful man full of human sympathy. But the Americans could not do much for us. They were not yet a power in Turkey and wielded much less influence than the highly experienced and long-established British, who still had an empire and great prestige in the Middle East. The cluster of American military attachés, diplomats, and agents of the newly established OSS were involved in comparatively primitive operations. Seager did let us send cables in his code to the American consul in Jerusalem, who transferred them to the Jewish Agency. This was useful, because despite the friendship of the British, we had business they might have felt compelled to oppose.

The great days for us were when couriers arrived from behind enemy territory. We always met them in our apartment. Some couriers were Jews, some Gentiles, but most of them were double agents who worked more or less openly for both the Gestapo and us. There was much profit to be made in the shrewd transfer of currency in exchange for gold or the trade in optical instruments for cash. A man who could travel freely from Budapest through Rumania to Istanbul under Nazi protection could make a fortune merely by transferring money, diamonds, optical instruments, gold, even tea and coffee.

Our most important courier was Bondi Gross, a Hungarian Jew who had connections with both the Nazis and the Jews. The high-echelon Nazis used him mainly to amass money for themselves, and perhaps also to get information, and we always took that into account. He made regular trips to transfer goods to them, and that guaranteed his survival. We also dealt directly with Gestapo agents who visited Istanbul. We paid them for their services, but they had more important reasons for coming. They could already sense a disastrous ending to the war, and they wanted to buy insurance in case the Allies won. Oddly enough, their connection with us made them more important because they were people who actually had contact with the enemy. Through them we sent all sorts of things back to Hungary, Slovakia, and Poland – medicines, letters, money. We once sent money into the ghettos of Poland with a Gestapo man. He entered one of the ghettos, got into the bunker, delivered the money, and actually brought us back a letter and a photograph – the only letter that ever came out of that particular city.

While we generally did not establish contact with official enemy representatives in Istanbul, Bondi Gross once brought us an Hungarian general – in fact, Hungary's deputy chief of staff. He sat in my room all night with Seager and an American general, and we talked about military cooperation with the Allies. By then it was clear that the Allies would emerge on top, and all these people wanted a clean bill of health with the victors. The Hungarian gave me a pair of binoculars as a gift for establishing contact with the Americans.

From Pressburg, Slovakia, we received word from an extraordinary woman, Gisi Fleischer, that much could be achieved by bribing important Gestapo people in Slovakia. She had already made contact with a certain Count Wislizeni, a high-ranking Gestapo officer who was later sentenced to death in Nuremberg. We sent money to Gisi and her group, who passed it on to the count. He then split the bribe with other Gestapo officers in return for delaying the transports of Slovakian Jews to the extermination camps. A surprisingly high percentage of enemy agents worked with us in good faith. The only important exception I can recall was in August of 1944, long after I had left Istanbul, when $150,000 was sent to Gisi Fleischer with one of the double agents. A few weeks later we heard she had been executed. We never heard from the agent and we never learned what happened to the money, but it's possible that he was caught and killed as well.

During my stay in Istanbul, I went to Palestine five or six times, about once every month. Traveling was our only means of proper communication, because we felt that letters could not possibly convey the story, and we certainly couldn't send money, gold, and diamonds through the British diplomatic pouch. And we had to get money to the occupied territories, even to the concentration camps, because we were convinced that the Jews there could not only bribe people but also buy arms, medicine, food, and even freedom. Complicated moral questions constantly arose. We often traded money and diamonds that went into Germany and might help their war effort, and this hardly left us with a pleasant feeling. But our first priority was to save Jewish lives, and we had no time for fine distinctions.

The money, supplied by the Jewish Agency, was raised from Jews in Palestine and throughout the world for rescue activities. Most of the time we had to send either gold or diamonds into Europe (dollar or Sterling bills were sometimes accepted but at other times rejected), and we had to bring the currency or diamonds from Palestine. At the beginning of the war, Jewish refugees from Antwerp had established a diamond industry for industrial and war purposes. It was therefore relatively easy for us to acquire diamonds. But the British did not allow us to take either diamonds or currency out of Palestine into a neutral or enemy country, so we had to smuggle them out. Some risk was involved, but we were never caught. We placed the diamonds in all the usual hiding places, the soles of our shoes, in shaving-lotion bottles, and so on. The real checkpoint was in Aleppo, where you crossed from Allied to neutral territory. Our clothes and belongings were checked, and on various occasions we were even told to strip, but we managed.

From Aleppo to Istanbul I traveled on the Taurus Express. It was a train of international renown, almost as well known as the Orient Express of Agatha Christie fame. High-ranking Turkish officials, as well as Englishmen and Americans, were always fellow-passengers on the trip. The most outstanding personality I met on the Taurus Express was Cardinal Spellman. One day I found myself sitting opposite him in a dining car (I recognized him from photographs). He was visiting small American military contingents all over the globe, as he continued to do until the end of his life. We talked about Palestine and about Zionism, and I had the impression that in spite of his close relationship with some New York Jewish leaders, he was relatively uninformed. Many years later, when I was in New York in the early 1950s, I met him again through Bartley Crum, an American lawyer who had served on the Anglo-American Commission. Cardinal Spellman was a stamp collector, and I presented him with sets of the recently issued Israeli stamps. His attitude toward us was generally positive, but his influence on Vatican policy was very limited in matters concerning Israel and Jerusalem.

One day an American Jew, Dr Joseph Schwartz, arrived in Istanbul in the uniform of an American Army colonel. For the first time, American Jewry had made a small dent and was permitted to help in rescue activities beyond enemy lines. Their work was facilitated by putting their representatives in American uniform. Schwartz had begun his career in social work as an official in the Joint Distribution Committee, which had been founded at the beginning of World War One to alleviate the misery of Jews in Eastern Europe, and he came to Istanbul representing the JDC. He was one of the most intelligent, decent, and devoted people that I was ever fortunate enough to meet. A marvelous speaker who never had to resort to bombastic rhetoric, Joe Schwartz was a Hebrew scholar, a very convivial human being with wide interests, and always ready to help. I came to know him much better over the years through his leadership in the United Jewish Appeal, the Israel Bond effort, and American Jewry in general.

At about the same time, we established a branch of our Haifa interrogation office in Istanbul. This was done for two reasons. First, it seemed wasteful to wait until the refugees reached Palestine in order to get fresh news. Second, we wanted a good working relationship with the British outside their mandatory area. The British in Palestine were supervised by Cairo headquarters, which had strict orders from London regarding all political matters. Istanbul was a neutral city, and although the British headquarters there were much more provincial, they were also, in a sense, more independent. We could make more headway in Istanbul, so we shared with the British the valuable information gleaned in our interrogations. We also had strong contacts with Jews still in Hungary, Rumania, and Bulgaria, mainly through Zionist organizations and youth movements. The leaders in Hungary were Rezo Kastner, whom I had met in Transylvania in 1934, and Yoel Brand. They worked together with Gisi Fleischer in Slovakia and others on the Rescue Committee that had been set up in Palestine, as well as abroad, to save Jews from the Nazis. Like us, they had no choice but to work with Gestapo officials and double-agent couriers.

The famous Yoel Brand story unfolded almost a year after I had left Istanbul and returned to Palestine, but in a way I was still involved. On May 15, 1944, Bondi Gross and Yoel Brand arrived in Istanbul airport carrying German passports. They brought the Allies an offer from the Gestapo to trade the lives of a few hundred thousand Hungarian Jews for trucks, coffee, tea, and other non-combat goods. The Germans gave Brand and Gross ten days to return with an answer, and the Turks permitted Brand and Gross to stay in Turkey for twelve days (Gross decided not to return to Budapest but to cross to Allied territory and seek refuge there). The offer, of course, had to be passed on immediately to our leaders, so Venya carried the proposition to Palestine. He arrived late at night and I was waiting for him in his kibbutz, having arranged for him to meet Ben-Gurion and Sharett the next morning.

We all listened to the details of the offer and opened consultations with the British High Commissioner. It was decided that Sharett should go to Istanbul to see Brand, but the British were unwilling to recommend that Sharett be granted a Turkish visa. We did, however, obtain permission for a meeting in Aleppo, Syria. So Ehud Avriel, who had replaced me in Istanbul, brought Brand to Aleppo on the Taurus Express. As soon as the train arrived, however, Brand was arrested by British agents. The next day, under British supervision, he met with Sharett and Reuven Shiloach. A meeting under such circumstances could not bring us any additional insight, so Sharett returned to Jerusalem, and Brand – despite British promises to let him return to Budapest as he had obligated himself – was taken to Cairo, where he was held by the British until the end of the war.

We could not persuade the British to accept any part of the Nazi proposition. 'Even if you won't do it,' we argued, 'at least create the impression that you will!' Sharett carried the matter to London, where he was asked by Lord Halifax: 'What will I do with a million Jews?' As for the transport equipment, which the Germans claimed would be used only against the Russians, the British said: 'The war is our first concern. By winning we will also save Jews. We will save the world. The Russians already suspect we want to make a separate peace with the Germans and turn against them. We cannot endanger the alliance.'

I finally managed to see Brand while he was held in Cairo. I think I was the first of our people permitted to meet with him. He was brought to my hotel room and we talked for a few hours. Brand was a redhead with a round, red face. I saw this small, stout man deeply incensed. Here he was entrusted with a vital mission to save Jews, and he felt we were not making a proper effort. If we truly understood the gravity of the situation, he suggested, we would be tearing the world apart to awaken it to the fact that here was a way to save Jews, and nothing was being done! I agreed; I was desolate. But it was impossible to make him see how helpless we were. After the war, we spent many, many hours with Brand, helping him to set himself up and find work for himself and his wife, Hansi, who had miraculously survived in Budapest. But Brand never forgave us. He always felt that the Jewish Agency had betrayed the Jews of Hungary.

Then there was the tragic affair of Hungary's other Jewish leader, Rezo Kastner, who had made a deal with the Nazis. He raised or received enough money to secure the release of about 1,600 Jews from the death camps and got permission to help them leave the country. But then he had the impossible task of choosing who would be saved from among hundreds of thousands. He named those he thought most needed, including members of his family. Years later, in the famous Kastner trial in Israel – actually a libel action brought by Kastner against a man named Malkiel Greenwald – Kastner was morally destroyed. He was branded by the judge as having dealt with the devil, and shortly after he was assassinated by zealots.

I believe the Kastner trial was such a central issue at the time because it was the first time that a large number of Israelis lost confidence in the establishment – in this case certainly for unjustified reasons. This was the first major blow to the leadership of Mapai, the country's largest political party. Kastner represented the establishment. The same Jewish Agency leaders who had tried to save Jews from the Holocaust (and obviously did not succeed) were now running the government, and many asked to what extent they were capable of fulfilling such a task. As with the Dreyfus trial, whose importance stemmed from its anti-Semitic repercussions, the Kastner trial had a deep significance far beyond the incident itself.

Looking back on those agonizing years for us in Istanbul, and even more difficult for those who assumed leadership in Europe and had to make snap decisions and incalculable choices, I am still bewildered when I hear judgments passed by people who were far from that time and place. In my opinion, the judgment in the Kastner trial was one of great arrogance and injustice. Is there any way of knowing how the judge or any one of us would have acted in Kastner's place? For anyone who was not in Europe or deeply involved in the rescue efforts, it is impossible to even imagine what it was like at the time.

5 Odd Attachments

A T the end of the summer of 1943, I was replaced in Istanbul. I returned to Ein Gev for a short period and then joined the Jewish Agency in Jerusalem again. Besides my work with various Allied Intelligence departments, which now spread and brought me fairly often to Cairo, I continued to take an interest in happenings in Istanbul and Europe. During the time I spent in Ein Gev, however, I also helped with 'illegal' immigration of Jews from Syria.

Taking advantage of the war confusion, an Arab came down from the mountains above Ein Gev bringing Jews from Damascus and Aleppo. He did not ask an exorbitant price for his services, and he brought in a considerable number of Jews. One of the members of Ein Gev even remarked how much more efficient it would be if this Arab were running the Immigration Department of the Jewish Agency, instead of those who were producing such negligible results.

We had to be careful about these operations. The British were keeping an eye on our Arab friend, and police cars checked on Ein Gev frequently. Early one morning, a few minutes after the arrival of a group of Jews, we saw a cloud of dust in the distance and hastily packed the 'illegal' immigrants into a hut. Sure enough, along came the police. We happened to know the sergeant and his two constables, so we welcomed them, took them to the dining hut next door, and treated them to a hearty breakfast, while the refugees slipped out and were put on a boat to Tiberias. Hundreds of Syrian Jews arrived across that border during 1943. Then it came to an abrupt end. One day the Arab disappeared, and we never found out what had happened to him.

Glad to be home again, I set out on horseback to tour the hills overhanging Ein Gev, going deep into the Golan Heights. The border was still open then, and we often traveled to Fiq, in Syria, where there was a Syrian district office. At Ein Gev we also built a little guesthouse specially for the Arabs from Syria, so that they could stay overnight on their way to and from Tiberias, where they did their shopping. We already had a doctor stationed permanently at the kibbutz, and he treated

Arab patients from the area. This casual, neighborly relationship went on until the frontier was sealed during the War of Independence.

Ein Gev was interested in acquiring lands in Btecha, the great valley in Syria owned by our friend the Bek. We had a youth group training in the kibbutz and the youngsters wanted to found a new settlement of their own. I suggested that it should be in Btecha. This in itself is evidence of the peaceful rapport we had with our Arab neighbors. Otherwise, who would have dreamed it would be possible to settle the other side of the frontier?

In 1943, when Ben-Gurion was in Tiberias, where he came every winter for a rest, I urged him to visit Btecha. I thought that if he saw the valley he might be inspired to help us, and in any case it was a beautiful area. So I took Ben-Gurion by boat to the northeastern bank of the Sea of Galilee, where we had some horses waiting. It didn't occur to me to notify anyone. Crossing the border into Syria during wartime was a bit risky, but Ben-Gurion enjoyed the idea. We rode up from the lake and met with a friendly Bedouin sheikh. I introduced Ben-Gurion as a professor of archaeology, and the sheikh gave a large feast. We then set forth to Btecha, and on the way we passed the ruins of ancient synagogues – proof of the dense Jewish population that had lived there in the first and second centuries A.D. Ben-Gurion looked down at the valley and recalled that at the beginning of this century Jews had settled there briefly. 'How could they leave such a beautiful place!' he exclaimed. He was absolutely indignant and insisted that everything be done to acquire the land again. We returned to Tiberias in the evening, and soon all of Jewish Palestine was furious : 'How could you risk Ben-Gurion's life like that? What if someone had recognized him?' There was a great uproar, but Ben-Gurion had enjoyed the day.

Our efforts to buy land in Btecha dragged on until the expulsion of the French from Syria. Although Arab nationalism had not yet become acute, the Syrians became less friendly. Despite our official border passes, they made it increasingly difficult for us to move to Btecha and back, and the negotiations came to a halt. But by that time I was already back at my Jewish Agency post in Jerusalem.

When I returned to work for the Jewish Agency in 1944, there was a definite feeling in the air that the tide of war was changing. The Allied armies were marching up the Italian boot; the Russians had pushed the Germans across the pre-war Polish frontier; and an Allied victory was clearly on the cards – sooner or later. Alongside the optimism, however, was the grim knowledge that although the Allies were on the advance, the plight of European Jewry was not getting any better. Both these factors – the good and the bad – helped to bring about a change of mood among Palestine's Jews. We began looking more to the future, our political future in this country, and preparing to return to the struggle that had begun in 1939, when the British severely limited Jewish immigration to Palestine.

One clear-cut change that had taken place in Zionist policy during the war was the call for the establishment of a Jewish state in Palestine. There was no longer a question about what a 'homeland' for the Jews meant. In May 1942, at the Biltmore Hotel in New York, Ben-Gurion had addressed a sort of mini-Zionist Congress (a full-fledged congress couldn't be held because of wartime conditions) and clearly stated that since the British mandatory administration could not be depended upon to advance the cause of Jewish interests in Palestine, the only answer was to turn the British out and establish a sovereign Jewish state.

There is no doubt that the Holocaust was a major influence on this revision in Zionist policy. Here we were desperately trying to get Jews out of Europe, and the few we did succeed in finding boats for were still subject to the rules of entry certificates and quotas established by the British White Paper of 1939. When the war first broke out, the Jewish Agency adopted the policy summed up by Ben-Gurion's famous epigram: 'We shall fight the war as if there were no White Paper, and fight the White Paper as if there were no war.' And it's true that during the early war years we continued to build and strengthen the Haganah, the Jewish Agency's underground self-defense organization. But we really didn't go very much out of our way to make life difficult for the British. We were, after all, allied with them in our fight against the Nazis, and there could be no doubt about the fact that between the two, the British were certainly the far lesser evil. So we sought ways to cooperate with them in the war effort. But the British had always been wary of our eagerness to help – not because they thought we were insincere, but because they worried about the price they would have to pay for our services once the war was over. Nonetheless, we continued to work with the British until the end of the war.

Back at the Jewish Agency in Jerusalem, I often went to Cairo to see Levi Avrahami, the head of the Haganah mission there, and to keep in touch with our men and women serving in the British Army. At the same time, we brought to Cairo young Jewish refugees trained to penetrate the German and Italian POW camps in North Africa, a service the British valued very highly. We also used our connections and freedom of movement to bring back to Palestine considerable quantities of arms, which greatly contributed to our survival in 1948.

Thousands of Palestinian Jews who served as soldiers in the British Army had access to rifles, grenades, and boxes of ammunition, all of which we transferred regularly to the Haganah stores in Palestine. One of these soldiers, Shalom Levin, was once caught while returning to Palestine in a ten-ton truck loaded with arms and ammunition, all taken from British Army stores. He was traveling on a pass I had obtained for him from Colonel Hunloke. (The colonel, of course, believed it was intended for some activity connected with our joint efforts.) Despite that episode, however, the British did not really tighten their check on us. I am sure they were aware of what we were doing, but they had a vital interest in our cooperation and were willing to pay a price.

We also maintained close ties with some Egyptian police officers, especially a few Coptic officers who were my contacts. The Copts were aware that the Jews and Christians shared a similar fate in the Middle East, and they cooperated with us warmly – usually on small matters, but every little bit helped. For example, one of them obtained a permanent visa for me to enter Egypt, whereas before I had had to get a new British permit for each trip. They also kept us informed on the constantly shifting political situation in Egypt, information that was greatly valued by the Jewish Agency's Arab Division.

During one of my trips to Cairo shortly after the British victory in El Alamein, I went to visit Maurice Oldfield, an officer in Security Intelligence. He had been a student of Namier in Manchester and was to rise to a central position in British Intelligence. As I waited for him in his office, I noticed a document on the shelf. It was a report to the British government written by Aaron Aaronsohn, a Palestinian Jewish scientist who spied for the British during World War One, when Palestine was still part of the Ottoman Empire. On the typed report were hand-written comments by T. E. Lawrence (Lawrence of Arabia). I leafed through the report and left it in its place, a fact that I deeply regretted later. We were in thick with British Intelligence in this war, but the Aaronsohn story was a tale of unusual bravery in World War One. In fact it was a legend in Israel, and that historic collector's item is now lost to us.

One of the more colorful figures who worked very effectively for our department in Cairo was Yolande Harmer, the closest we ever got to a Mata Hari of our own. Yolande was petite, blonde, fragile, and always elegantly dressed. She came from a French-Jewish family that had lived in Cairo for decades. Yolande was intimate with Egyptian high society and counted among her friends people like Azam Pasha, the first secretary of the Arab League. Whenever I came to Cairo, I took her out to lunch or dinner, and very soon I had a better sense of the mood in Egyptian political circles than I could have learned from a detailed report by the brightest political journalist. She often came to Jerusalem as well, not only to report to us but also to visit a wide circle of acquaintances, mainly British officers who had served in Egypt and moved on to Jerusalem. Yolande's official occupation was journalism, although her writing was very limited in scope. She was a socialite. The upper class of Cairo then consisted in large measure of European descendants, people with Spanish, French, Belgian, Italian, British, or Greek passports. Many of them were Jews whose parents or grandparents had come to Alexandria or Cairo as merchants or developers of transport systems, electricity concessions, and industries. It was a glittering society of what we today would call 'beautiful people'. Now none of it is left.

Another person who figured in my Cairo days was Yehuda Arazi, a Palestinian who had come from Poland in the 1920s. His fabulous career as an arms smuggler and organizer of illegal immigration was just beginning, but there was already a price on his head, and he was hiding from the British in a Tel Aviv apartment. I visited him there a few times, and we finally managed to smuggle him out to Cairo. He was so pale from the months of confinement in that apartment and so nervous in the presence of strangers that we had to find him another hiding place in which to recuperate. At first we kept him in a little houseboat on the Nile, until he regained a normal appearance and manner. Then, with the help of Freddie Fredkens, a Belgian Jew who was serving as an RAF pilot, Arazi was dressed as a Polish Air Force officer and given appropriate documents. (This was when General Anders' Free Polish units were still in existence.) Freddie flew Arazi to Bari. Arazi's English was not good enough to pass him off as a British soldier, but his Polish was good enough to get him past the British. His only trouble came toward the end of the trip, when he suddenly encountered a real Polish officer. But he got by somehow, and pretty soon he was active in Italy organizing boats and saving Jews.

Towards the end of the war, the rise in incidents of Jewish 'terrorism' (a word whose meaning changed entirely in the 1970s) created problems for us with the British. The Jewish Agency and the Haganah were openly opposed to the violent methods of the Irgun Zvai Leumi and the Stern Gang, the two dissident Jewish underground military organizations in Palestine. We were against terrorism both in principle and because we were also sincerely convinced that our best friends were alienated by such actions. We knew, for instance, that Lord Moyne, the British minister of state in the Middle East, was a close friend of Churchill's, and we believed that the views of Churchill and his circle concerning the fate of Palestine would be decisive after the war. Why turn them into enemies? After the murder of Lord Moyne by Jewish terrorists in 1944, the Jewish Agency worked in close cooperation with the British to demonstrate our disavowal of terrorism and prevent further incidents of that nature. In matters like that, we kept faith with the British.

I have always believed that in national affairs a single central authority must be responsible. While I personally had engaged in countless illegal enterprises – from transporting a Persian-Jewish child across the border to stealing British guns and ammunition, smuggling Jewish immigrants across frontiers and into Palestine, and bribing freely to ease the plight of Jews trapped in Europe – I had always opposed anarchy within our own community. The plea that one must act according to one's conscience cannot be a justification for independent decisions by every group or individual. I also believe that a government is obligated to see that its orders are carried out, that its decisions are implemented, not flaunted. It was imperative that the Jewish Agency, our 'government' at the time, act against the terrorist groups, who claimed the right to make decisions on their own and endangered the policy adopted by the majority. When it was decided at the highest level of the Jewish Agency and the Haganah to move against these groups, and I was assigned a role in the so-called 'season', I accepted this task as a necessary step on our road to statehood. I was opposed to the Irgun and Stern group then just as, after the Yom Kippur War, I was against those who established settlements in occupied territory with total disregard for government policy.

This period of a growing conflict of interest with the British led to some odd attachments. Official policy notwithstanding, we all felt a sympathy for our own rebels, since we were all Jews and shared the same basic aims. Moreover, even though our official attitude was one of law-abiding cooperation with the British, we knew in our hearts that they would eventually favor the Arabs. They had a romantic attitude toward the nomads of the desert. Despite all their knowledge of the *souks* in Cairo, Baghdad, Aleppo, and Damascus and their dealings with Arab merchants and politicians, these attitudes had not changed. Nurtured by romantic travelers, by the stories of the Battle of Omdurman, and by the great British watercolorists of the nineteenth century, their romanticism was a very deep-rooted feeling. In spite of their knowledge of the Bible, the figures of the Old Testament lacked the same element of reality.

Yet the British often faced situations where they turned to us for help. For example, late in 1943, Churchill, Roosevelt, and de Gaulle were due to pass through Baghdad en route to the Tehran Conference, and the British had received letters carrying threats that Jewish terrorists would act against them upon landing in Habania Airport near Baghdad. Iraq was then under British control, and there was a deep sense of uneasiness among the British, so they turned to the Jewish Agency for help. I suggested the perfect man for them – Ezra Danin. Ezra was in charge of the Arab Department of our Intelligence. His family had come from Iraq three generations back. In fact, Jews had lived in Iraq a thousand years before the Arabs arrived there, and they felt very much at home. (Today, as a result of Arab persecutions, this Jewish community has almost totally disappeared.) Ezra was a brilliant man with important contacts in the Arab world and a deep understanding of the Arab way of thinking. He was a farmer by profession and lived in Hadera, half way between Tel Aviv and Haifa, where he owned land.

When we were approached about the assassination threats, I suggested that Ezra and his friend Josh Palmon go to Baghdad. Ezra could establish connection with Iraqi dignitaries and with Iraqi Jews of high standing, while Josh would mix with the people. We had no real proof that the threats had come from the Irgun or the Stern Gang. But the British were so worried that they wanted to fly these two emissaries by special plane. Josh immediately said, 'God forbid! They'll know right away we're agents.' So I took Ezra and Josh to Lod Airport for their flight in an ordinary military transport plane. Back in those days they used to weigh the people boarding a plane, and Josh and Ezra were both so hefty that four soldiers were taken off to make room for them. Ezra could eat almost as much or more than I did!

The two of them stayed in Iraq for three or four weeks. Ezra, under cover as an agricultural expert checking why eucalyptus trees were dying, met with members of the government and prominent Jews and Arabs, while Josh mingled in less respectable circles. They returned after they had found the authors of the threatening letters – some Jewish high school boys who had done it as a hoax.

Meanwhile, I continued to drive the old Oldsmobile between Jerusalem and Ein Gev almost every weekend, and I always filled the car with guests, particularly British officers and journalists. I felt it was important for them to enjoy the beauty of the country and see a kibbutz. Most important, I wanted them to see Jewish farmers, fishermen, boat builders – to correct the image some still had of the Jew as a city-dweller and a middleman. On one of these trips in 1944, I took along Kermit and Archibald Roosevelt, whom I had met on a trip to Egypt. They were both Arabists, so I took them riding up the Golan Heights to the Arab townlet of Fiq. At that time, Franklin Roosevelt was president of the United States, and the two young Roosevelts created a small sensation. They were actually Teddy Roosevelt's grandsons and therefore closer to Mrs Roosevelt's side of the family, but the Arabs didn't differentiate between one branch of the Roosevelts and another.

We had a grand meal with the *mukhtar* and other notables, and when we came back to the horses, Kermit's jacket had disappeared. This was a terrible reflection upon Arab honor and hospitality, and we searched for that jacket for hours, as they would not let us go without it. Meanwhile, it was getting late, and the descent back to Ein Gev was difficult even in daylight, so I suddenly had an inspiration. I announced that one of the horses must have eaten the jacket. Everybody agreed instantly. No doubt about it! Obviously some stupid but innocent horse ate the jacket. Amid happy goodbyes, we left for Ein Gev before dark. I wish we could solve other Arab problems so easily.

Despite the loss of his jacket, by the way, Kermit Roosevelt later became the brains behind Egypt's Nasser. He was in charge of the CIA's

Middle Eastern desk, and it was he who maintained contact with the Egyptians during the Naguib period and the Nasserite revolution. Roosevelt must have been convinced that he could preserve American influence in Egypt and the Middle East by supporting revolutionary movements. Kermit retired from the CIA long before Nasser died, but because of his special knowledge he remained influential in Middle Eastern affairs, particularly in connection with oil matters and economic development.

In 1945 the weekend trips to Ein Gev became less frequent, since Tamar left the kibbutz and joined me in Jerusalem for a few months. Reuven Shiloach had gone to the United States with his wife, and Tamar and I moved into their flat when I took over the Intelligence Department of the Jewish Agency. With the war winding down, it was a comparatively quiet period, and we had become so used to excitement that this quiet sometimes became boring. It was then, I think, that I learned how you could put a pin all the way through the muscle of your arm without feeling any pain or spilling any blood. There was always a good audience for that trick (this was before television, of course). But the quiet didn't last long for me.

In June 1945, a few weeks after the end of the war, I was off to Europe again. My assignment this time was to aid in the Jewish Agency's political work in England. On the way I stepped on the soil of Germany for the first time since 1939, passing through ravaged Munich and Frankfurt on my way to Paris. Immediately after arriving in Munich I went to visit Dachau. By this time all the inmates had been evacuated, but the camp had not yet been redesigned as a memorial. Not even the greatest artist could have captured the sense of immediacy of that moment, when you felt that the ovens had barely cooled.

In Paris I tried to get a visa for England, which was not easy at the time. So I spent a few weeks there at the Royal Monceau Hotel. Right under the roof were rooms that had once been used to accommodate the servants of the hotel's distinguished guests, who stayed on the lower floors. By taking one of these rooms, I had the advantage of living in a high-class hotel while paying very little. Most of the other floors were still occupied by American and British Army personnel.

I was one of the first Jewish Agency people to reach Paris after the war. The offices for immigration – still 'illegal' immigration – had not yet been set up properly, and at least for a few weeks I was very much on my own with a lot of free time. This was when I really came to know Paris. Life in the city quickly returned to normal. I had no particular interest in the regular Paris nightclubs, but I shall never forget the evenings at the various *chansonniers*, places like 'Lapin Agille', which were frequented mainly by the French and here or there a French-speaking Allied soldier. And there was always the beauty of Paris. I had no urgent assignment and my only obligation was to go to the British consulate every day and ask whether my visa had arrived. Other than that, I could do as I pleased. I hardly knew anybody in Paris, but I called a few times on Baron Guy de Rothschild, whom I had met in Palestine. In fact, I became quite friendly with Guy and his wife, Alix, who later assisted us greatly with the Israel Museum. I also went to Port de Buc a few times to visit Davidka Nameri, a kibbutznik preparing boats to take illegal immigrants to Palestine. Making those old craft – the only kind we could afford – seaworthy and building bunkers for hundreds of immigrants was quite an art.

After a few weeks, my visa came through and I went on to London, which was to be my headquarters for about a year. In 1945 the Labour Party in England was campaigning against the ruling Conservatives and had promised the Jews of Palestine far beyond what even the Zionist Congress had proposed. I was very skeptical about these promises. I couldn't help feeling that if the Labour Party won it would default its undertaking, and the Conservatives under Churchill would be better for us in the end. I knew a variety of people in the Labour Party. I had met Clement Attlee back in 1941, had known Michael Foot, and had met Herbert Morrison, the future home secretary, several times (he was indeed a friend). I had also come to know Nye Bevan, the party's most charismatic leader, and many people on the fringes, so that I was able to get an overall impression of Labour's mood. And even though I had met Ernest Bevin himself only once – hardly enough to judge his personality from my own impression – the people he worked with caused me to have strong forebodings.

For instance, I knew Creech-Jones, the Labour Party's 'shadow' colonial minister. The Colonial Office was very important in the days of the empire, and Palestine fell under its administration. I met Creech-Jones a few times at the home of Berl Locker, who headed the Jewish Agency office in London. Creech-Jones was a sweet, soft, pleasant man who struck me as being very much like Locker himself, and I had no more faith in his strength than I had in Locker's. Creech-Jones was well meaning, but when it came to a real fight, particularly with Bevin and Attlee, he was hardly my candidate. My doubts about Berl Locker, whom I liked personally, were precisely because he pinned his hopes on Creech-Jones and Labour. It was obvious who the real leaders were – strong and stubborn people. Bevin may have been a great foreign secretary for England. He had demonstrated his courage as a union leader in many industrial fights, and he understood and dared to stand up to the Russians. But he was not our friend, and he did not pretend to be. Locker's source of hope, the nice colonial secretary, had no chance against Bevin when it came to making good on the pro-Zionist pre-election promises. Throughout that year in London, I found myself in sharp conflict with all the naive Jewish supporters of the Labour Party.

When the Labour Party did come into power, we used every means to remind them that it would be decent and intelligent to fulfill their campaign promises for a Jewish state. Once I approached a high Cabinet official with facts and figures on our position in America. Britain and the Sterling bloc, to which we belonged, were facing serious foreign-exchange problems, and I spelled out the vast potential in business investments – even gifts – that could be drawn from the Jews in the United States. I demonstrated the comparative strength of our military resources, should we have to defend ourselves. And I even showed him how uniquely useful an independent Jewish state could be by infiltrating people into Russia and Eastern Europe and providing reliable information so vital in the Cold War, then at its height. My point was that the British had more to gain by going along with us and supporting statehood than by placating the Arabs – and this was at the time when even the Anglo-American Inquiry Commission had recommended that 100,000 survivors of concentration camps be allowed to enter Palestine immediately. But the Labour Party did not pay the slightest attention to the commission or even to their own promises.

Tamar joined me in London in 1946, and we lived for a while in the Wingate apartment on Hill Street. Orde was dead, and Lorna, on an extended visit to Scotland, had offered us the place. When the war had ended, Arthur Koestler had come to Palestine to write a novel and stayed with us in Ein Gev and in Jerusalem. (His novel *Thieves in the Night* is dedicated, among others, to Tamar and myself.) Now I looked him up in London. Among his friends were some Labour people, like Michael Foot, whom I had met in 1938 but now grew to know much better, and Nye Bevan and his wife, Jenny Lee. Harold Macmillan, Koestler's publisher, had just returned from his wartime post as British minister of state in North Africa. Back in publishing, he became a Conservative member of Parliament. Koestler took me to see him, and we talked about Palestine. Then Macmillan helped me arrange a meeting in the House of Commons with members from the Conservative, Labour, and Liberal parties. I was to talk to them informally in my capacity as an officer in the Haganah. We felt it was essential to keep British public opinion on our side and against the British government's policy, and were trying to obtain the support of as many members of Parliament as possible.

Such meetings ordinarily do not attract more than a dozen people. This one, however, just happened to take place hours after the news reached London that the Irgun Zvai Leumi had blown up part of the King David Hotel in Jerusalem, with heavy loss of British lives, so the room was overflowing. Hundreds of members came, and they subjected me to a very tough grilling. But since the Haganah and all the Jewish

Agency officials firmly opposed the Irgun and the Stern Gang and had fought against terrorism from the beginning, I was able to hold my ground.

Koestler and I also spent many evenings together pub crawling. One evening we went to the 'Gargoyle' – a nightclub later famous as the hangout of two British Intelligence defectors, Burgess and McLean – and we were joined by Dylan Thomas. We all drank a lot and ended up in Michael Foot's apartment on Park Street, where Dylan Thomas picked up the *Oxford Book of Verse* and read poetry aloud until daylight. We were all slightly drunk and sentimental, and his voice was beautiful. It was an unforgettable experience. Thirty years later Richard Burton, another Welshman, brought this episode vividly back to me by reading poems by Dylan Thomas at the Jerusalem Theater.

Despite all our efforts in London, the political situation in Palestine continued to deteriorate. Then on Saturday, June 29, 1946, news reached us that the entire Jewish leadership in Palestine had been arrested by the British and was being held in a detention camp at Latrun. The only ones not caught were Moshe Sneh, then commander of the Haganah; Ben-Gurion, who was in Paris just then and was planning to come to London a day or two later; and Golda Meir, who took over Sharett's duties as head of the Agency's Political Department. It immediately occurred to us that the British might arrest Ben-Gurion if he came to London. Since we didn't dare to discuss matters by phone, and there were no more flights that day, I rented a plane – a Piper – for the first time in my life. It was not very expensive, and it made the trip to Paris in an hour and a half. I went straight to see Ben-Gurion at Claridges, on the Champs Elysées, and we conferred on the Latrun arrests. On the spot, he laid the groundwork for a conference that brought American and British Zionists to Paris, and I spent the next few days meeting with members of the 'illegal' immigration staff in their little office.

I was again staying at my favorite hotel, the Royal Monceau, where Ho Chi Minh had his headquarters at the time. A day or two after my arrival, an Indo-Chinese holiday was celebrated. There were quite a few Indo-Chinese in France then, since the French had ruled the area for many decades, and crowds of students and families, all in native dress, descended on the gardens of the Royal Monceau to honor Ho Chi Minh. It was very colorful, and I walked over to Claridges and asked Ben-Gurion to come and see the festivities. He came. He looked. The ceremony didn't interest him very much, but he found the Royal Monceau more attractive than Claridges and moved in the next day. Soon after, Ben-Gurion and Ho Chi Minh met and took to each other. They had several long talks, with the result that Ho Chi Minh offered hospitality in Indo-China to a Jewish government in exile. The two men had much in common, as both foresaw an approaching struggle for liberation in their different parts of Asia. I sat in on one of their meetings. Ho Chi Minh spoke French and a little broken English; Ben-Gurion knew some French, and I helped some with translations. Obviously Ben-Gurion did not accept Ho's offer.

I often saw Ho Chi Minh as he walked out of the hotel and the six *Gardes Républicaines* raised their sabers and stood at attention. But soon their number was cut, first from six to four, then to two, and one day there were none. Ho Chi Minh left for home, and the Indo-Chinese war started. Ben-Gurion, however, stayed at the Royal Monceau for a while, and that hotel has become a center for visiting Zionists ever since.

In mid-1946 Tamar and I returned home. These were the months when we had intensified our efforts to bring survivors of the Holocaust to Palestine, and the British had stiffened their blockade of the country's coasts. I particularly remember Christmas Eve of 1946, when I took the journalist Jon Kimche to Haifa, where a boatload of 'illegal' immigrants was due. On the way we had to pass several British police roadblocks, but the pass from my old friend Giles saw us through easily. We witnessed how the immigrants were brought in under cover of darkness and dispersed among the nearby kibbutzim. Kimche wrote for the *Evening Standard* and other English papers, and the title he chose for his article about that night was 'Operation Christmas'. It contrasted the world's prayer for peace on Christmas Eve with the ordeal of these refugees, cold and half starved, clambering through the dark to reach the peace denied them by the Christian masters of Palestine.

At about the same time, our 'illegal' immigration office in Paris devised a plan to bring Jews from Rumania to Palestine. The Rumanians, who bore no love for the British, were happy to be rid of some Jews on condition that the transfer would be a one-time operation and not originate in a Rumanian port. Eventually two large ships, the *Pan York* and the *Pan Crescent*, were prepared to carry over 15,000 people between them. The passengers and the boats were divided up between the Bulgarian ports of Varna and Burgas and were waiting there when the Americans discovered the plan. This complicated matters even more, because the United States regarded the immigration of Rumanian Jews as Communist infiltration of the Middle East. Everything came to a complete halt, and the decision on how to proceed had to be made by the Jewish Agency members in Paris who had started it all – Shaul Avigur and Venya.

Meanwhile, Moshe Sharett, who was in the United States at the time, cabled that the boats must not be allowed to leave. The leaders in Paris did not know what to do, and they called me in Jerusalem. After consultations, I told Venya to disregard everything and let the ships go. Still they hesitated, but a few days later Sharett flew to Switzerland, where Venya and Avigur met him, and instructed them to start the ships off at once. At first they were bewildered about his turnabout. But it was easy enough to understand. Being a very cautious man, Sharett had hesitated to send that message from the United States. The boats left Bulgaria and arrived in Haifa, where the immigrants were stopped by the British and sent to detention camps in Cyprus – a temporary fate and at least more hopeful than wandering homeless in Rumania.

Between the steady struggle to bring into Palestine as many refugees of the Holocaust as possible, worldwide sympathy for the survivors, international disgust at the British for beating and deporting them when they arrived on the shores of Palestine in their ramshackle boats, and the opening of armed resistance activities by the Haganah and the two dissident organizations, we were finally impressing the British that their Mandate over Palestine was more of a burden than it was worth. The postwar economic situation in England was very serious, and internal pressures were growing to abandon Palestine and withdraw the large troop contingent stationed there. In addition to our own struggle, Arab nationalism was growing, and the Mandates of the French were being abolished in Lebanon and Syria, leaving the British alone in the area. One inquiry commission after another had recommended the partition of Palestine and the creation of two sovereign states – one Jewish and one Arab – but each time the British had disregarded their findings.

Then, in February 1947, with the task of keeping order in Palestine growing steadily more difficult, the British government suddenly decided that it had had enough, and it dropped the whole problem into the lap of the United Nations. It was a great victory for us, but rather than being the beginning of the end, we all knew that it was only the end of the beginning. The British were only half of the problem we faced. Now we had to deal with the fact that although the countries surrounding Palestine had achieved their independence from the colonial powers, they were determined that we would not have a state of our own.

In 1947 I spent a few months in Ein Gev but was soon drawn back to the Jewish Agency in Jerusalem as the tension in the country was steadily escalating. Tamar came and joined me for a few months, and she was expecting. On the night of September 14 I paced up and down the street in front of Sha'arei Zedek Hospital with my old friend Yossi Hamburger (Har'el), who had begun his career as Weizmann's body-guard and had gone on to command several illegal ships, among them *Pan York* and *Pan Crescent*. It was the eve of Rosh Hashanah, the Jewish New Year, and the streets were deserted. Midnight passed and I finally gave up the vigil and went to sleep. Early the next morning, when I walked into the hospital, I learned of Amos's birth. But my first acquaintance with my son was short. A month later Tamar returned to Ein Gev with Amos and I left the country on a new assignment.

6 The Top of the Copacabana

IN October 1947 Ben-Gurion assigned me to join the Haganah mission in the United States, which had been established soon after World War Two. Two years earlier, at Ben-Gurion's request, Henry Montor, director of the United Jewish Appeal, had brought together an extraordinary group of about forty Americans utterly devoted to the Jewish cause. Ben-Gurion went to New York, and they all met at the apartment of Rudolf Sonneborn, an American businessman and a Zionist from his early youth. Every man there represented wealth and potential. Ben-Gurion laid it on the line. He told them the destiny of Palestinian Jews would depend on the outcome of the armed struggle, and he asked their help in brainpower, energy, and skills, as well as money. From that moment these dedicated men, and many others who joined them later, began to prepare everything necessary not only for survival but for our victory in 1948.

Ya'akov Dori, subsequently the first chief of staff of the Israel Defense Forces, had already set up the mission in New York and returned to Palestine. He was followed by Shlomo Shamir, a former major in the British Army, who was head of the mission when I arrived. Yehuda Arazi was constantly in and out of New York initiating the acquisition of all types of arms. I believe Ben-Gurion intended from the start to make me head of the New York mission, but he wanted to test me first. When Shamir was recalled to Palestine soon afterward to assume field command, I was given his complicated and unpredictable job.

It was my first time in New York, and since no one could be sure what would happen and how long my stay would last, I went without Tamar and Amos. Shamir met me at La Guardia Airport and took me to the Empire Hotel on Broadway and 63rd Street, then a respectable middle-class neighborhood. My room was a modest $5 per night.

I had, of course, met a good number of Americans before coming to the United States: Intelligence men in Istanbul and Cairo, the various consuls in Jerusalem (who had all been very pro-Arab), and some writers and journalists who had been to the Middle East. But although

I knew a few Americans, I had no defined attitude toward the United States. I was much less informed about the country than I had been about England when I first went there, and I hadn't had an opportunity to be impressed by Americans in the same way I had by the British, particularly their behavior during the blitz. In short, I went to America rather unprepared, and on the whole it was a rather pleasant surprise. The openness of the society; the basic decency of people; the willingness to talk, explain, guide, share information with strangers; and the efficiency and politeness of service all seemed much more natural and casual than in England. It was similar to the informal behavior of Jews in Palestine, but in many ways superior to it – certainly in efficiency and consideration of others, which are still sporadic in our hard-pressed society.

On the whole, I came to like the Americans much better than the British, as far as traits of character are concerned. I still admire the stoicism and reticence of the British (which, to my regret, seem to be disappearing). If we Israelis could put a rein on our superfluous talk and learn how to hold back a bit, I believe it could do us a lot of good. But in America I admired the fact that there is little secrecy and mystification. Americans clearly state their case; with the British you always had to guess what they were *really* getting at. That straightforward and open approach is a tremendous advantage and often makes life much easier.

From my first days in America, I was drawn into a whirlwind of activity, some of it risky. My work touched on experiments in weapon production, chemistry, and physics; speculations on ship purchases; dealings with factories and junkyards; liaison with spies, mobsters, movie moguls, statesmen, bankers, professors, industrialists, and newspaper men; and no lack of illegalities, from petty to international. And every second the dream of a Jewish state was in jeopardy. I gradually found my own way to cope. It seemed like an impossible job for one man, but it soon became obvious that a single center was necessary to bring the various experts and specialists into contact with their potential co-workers, advisors, and suppliers. I was, so to say, the traffic cop, a job I later assumed again in the Prime Minister's Office and in the Jerusalem Municipality.

Among our activities was a special unit that dealt with the purchase of ships and equipment and the recruitment of personnel to take the ships to Europe, pick up immigrants (mainly in the south of France and Italy), and transport them to Palestine. My old friends Davidka Nameri and Danny Shind were in charge, and local Americans like Joe Boxenbaum, an ex-major in the American Army whom I had met in Paris after he had been demobilized a year before, helped them. The work had legal and illegal sides, for there was an American embargo against exporting war material or even recruiting people to serve as soldiers in any foreign country. And British Intelligence was after us as well. Hank Greenspun, from Los Angeles, masterminded the operation of loading boats with war material from California and sending them via Mexico, Hawaii, and the Philippines. Deals were made with South American governments to buy tanks and innumerable other things and ship them on to Palestine. Other goods – blankets, tents, canteens, and so on – were often bought from army surplus through dealers in the United States. This last activity was the legal side of our operation. The unit in charge of it was called 'Friends of the Haganah', and it published a news sheet called *Haganah Calling* under Rusty Jarcho, a red-haired American with garment trade-paper experience. But even this unit, sooner or later, became a cover for illegal dealings.

Still another unit, Land and Labor for Palestine, handled the recruitment of American volunteers. The basic idea was perfectly legal; people would go to Palestine to work on the land; they would not become soldiers themselves, but replace others who had joined the Army. Land and Labor had a special office on Broadway that was run by Wellesley Aron, a former major who had commanded a Jewish unit of the British Army in the war.

The day after I arrived in New York, I went to Lake Success, where Moshe Sharett and Rabbi Abba Hillel Silver were working to round up votes for the roll call on the Palestine partition resolution, scheduled for November 29. At the same time, we engaged in secret activity conducted by two Americans. A U.S. Army veteran was in charge of our Intelligence, aided by a lawyer who had been in the OSS (the forerunner of the CIA) during the war. The information their operations obtained for us was not vital, but it was sometimes useful. We also had a good contact at the British consulate in the Empire State Building. Shortly before Israel became a state, we learned that the British were going to abandon their military camp at Sarafand, near Tel Aviv. The Jewish Agency was ready to pay hundreds of thousands of pounds for that camp and had been on the verge of negotiating the deal when we sent them the information. Thus they secured the camp for nothing (although in the end, as a result of protracted negotiations in order to secure British recognition after the establishment of Israel, we paid compensation for every bit of British property that we took over).

On the fateful day, November 29, 1947, I went back to Lake Success to watch the U.N. vote. I remember the tension and then the thrill. We kept a score card of the countries and the way we expected them to vote. In most cases our projections were right, and when the necessary number of 'pro'-votes had been cast, we were elated. The U.N. had decided on the partition of Palestine into two states, one Jewish, one Arab. The British Mandate would end on May 14. We finally had the official basis for the declaration of our state. That night great crowds of people danced in the streets of New York.

After the vote, Sharett stayed in New York for a while, and I reported to him fairly regularly. After all, some of our operations could have been very embarrassing to the Jewish Agency and to him personally. When he left, I continued reporting to Abba Hillel Silver, chairman of the American section of the Jewish Agency, who came in to New York from Cleveland every week. I usually saw him early in the morning at breakfast in his hotel, the Sulgrave, on Park Avenue and 64th Street. Silver always opened his newspaper to the stock exchange page. Over the years I became accustomed to the fact that for many Americans the Wall Street news took first place. It did not detract from their devotion to Israel that they did not look at the world news first. After all, a great deal of the wealth that is so important to them is given generously to Israel. Still, it was a bit of a surprise to see a rabbi open the paper to the financial page.

The Jewish Agency used those considerable financial contributions made by Jews and other friends all over the world to finance the purchase of arms in France and Switzerland. The problem was how to transport them to Palestine. The British had ensured that we could not purchase arms legally, like other nations, because we were not yet officially a sovereign state. Our most important objective was to be thoroughly armed on our first day of independence; otherwise the new state would be destroyed by the Arab countries, with their comparatively well-organized armies, on the day of its birth. There was only one way we could manage it: we had to find a country that would purchase arms for us in its own name but with our money. That same country should appear to take delivery, but then we would take over, run the British blockade, and hand the arms to the Haganah in Palestine. We were looking for a Latin American country, and one of the Zionist leaders in New York knew a man in Nicaragua who knew another man who was a close friend of the Nicaraguan dictator, General 'Taco' Somoza. So early in my stay in New York, I was elected to fly to Nicaragua.

I arrived in Managua, the capital, on my first trip to Latin America. Managua was a small town then. My host was Lazlo Weiss, a Hungarian Jew, who was a newcomer to the country. But his friend Pataky, another Hungarian Jew, was a business partner of Somoza's. Weiss was a Zionist; Pataky was not, but he was generally in sympathy with our aims. He also had an ulterior motive – a young nephew who was footloose and fancy free and popular with women. Pataky was so eager to get the young man straightened out that he agreed to promote our deal with Somoza if we would take his nephew to Palestine and keep him there.

Our list of needs was clear : letters to the Nicaraguan ambassador in Paris and the consul-general in Zurich authorizing us to purchase machinery and arms in France and Switzerland; instructions to the ambassador and the consul to facilitate the shipment of this materiel to the ports of Marseilles, Trieste, and Genoa; and two Nicaraguan diplomatic passports, one for Yehuda Arazi, who would be doing the actual purchasing, and one for me. None of this came easily. I was asking a small country to take enormous political risks, even though it would not be financially involved in our operation. I heard endless arguments for and against my request, but I was finally given the letters covering $3 million worth of machinery and arms, a large amount at that time.

Somoza, as well as the foreign minister and the president, had to sign the letters. It was a perfectly honorable deal, perfectly proper. They couldn't imagine anyone doing otherwise, and they cooperated because of their strong basic sympathy with our cause. Our agreement included the understanding that Nicaragua would vote for Israel in the U.N. whenever the occasion arose, a point to which they pledged themselves out of genuine conviction (and indeed, Nicaragua has remained a true friend of Israel over the years). In the two days I was there, we had long talks about the Jewish problem, and all the Nicaraguan officials showed real interest and sympathy. I even received the indispensable Nicaraguan diplomatic passports.

I had my best times with Somoza in his palace residence while his barber was tending him in the morning. Those two mornings, while he was being shaved, manicured, trimmed, combed, and brushed, I tried to condense for him the meaning of Zionism. He became a political and personal friend, and before leaving the palace I was honored with a military ceremony.

Pataky's nephew later arrived in New York and immediately took to my secretary, a very attractive woman who, aside from helping me with reports, letters, and phone calls, was hostess to many people when I was busy. When young Pataky showed up, we had to keep him happy. He was about thirty, a very big fellow, and he took one look at her and insisted on taking her to the Copacabana. She was a bit afraid of him, so my deputy went along. My secretary and Pataky danced all night, while the fifth wheel sat at a table writing to his wife in Kibbutz Afikim. Pataky went on to Palestine and stayed a while, walking around with two large revolvers on his hips. He spoke English with a marked Hungarian accent and was accepted with humor. Later he joined the Israeli Army and took part in several battles. Eventually, when the fighting died down, he became bored, left Israel, and settled down somewhere along the line. Today he is an important official in Nicaragua who keeps his contacts with Israel ever fresh.

Back in New York, I found myself involved with Yehuda Arazi again. I had been friendly with him since 1945, but I remember him from even before the war, when he was already engaged in purchasing arms in Europe. In Italy he launched a daring and imaginative scheme for illegal immigration. His most famous exploit, the hunger strike on the immigrant ship *Fede* in La Spezia harbor, became the basis for the memorable scene in Leon Uris' *Exodus*. When he arrived in New York, the British still had a price on his head. The stories of Yehuda's inventive and successful services are legion, so one can tell of some of his unsuccessful ventures without detracting from his achievements.

Yehuda Arazi never belonged to any organized framework. In New York he operated out of his apartment on the West Side. He received money and instructions from Ben-Gurion and Eliezer Kaplan, the treasurer of the Jewish Agency, and he had a habit of going over everyone's head. No one could *ever* tell him what to do. Yehuda had always been a loner, an individualist, and a very strong personality, and that was why he had succeeded in Europe before World War Two and again in Italy at the end of the war. But by the time I took over in New York, his plans were all more imagination than reality. Early in my stay, there was a mishap on a pier, and a cargo of disguised explosives was discovered when a crate broke. Mayor O'Dwyer, who was friendly to our cause, saved us from massive investigations. But Arazi could not afford to take chances and, together with several others, he had to leave the country immediately. He returned to Rome, leaving me with two headaches. One was nothing less than an aircraft carrier!

Yehuda had had an idea that on May 16, 1948, he would arrive in Israel on an aircraft carrier loaded with planes, tanks, and a whole division of trained Jewish soldiers. He actually bought an obsolete U.S. carrier from a scrap dealer – a bargain for I forget how many thousands of dollars – but he refused to tell us where it was. He simply would not believe he could never get such a monster out of the United States, despite the embargo laws. We finally located the carrier near Baltimore, but it was impossible to do anything with it, even though our people were outstandingly resourceful at circumventing the embargo. We could smuggle out planes or guns or immigrant ships, but there was no way of disguising that huge ship; nor was there any purpose in doing so. The trouble we had trying to dispose of it without being identified and investigated was incredible. We finally sold it for scrap, just as it had been bought as scrap, and got our money back.

Yehuda also left me with a group of people who had already received an advance payment from him to prepare a guided missile. The idea was that the missile could be aimed to fly directly, for example, into King Farouk's bedroom! I soon learned that America had been allocating hundreds of millions of dollars yearly to develop guided missiles, and it would take years before they would be operational. We may be very clever people and can do things other people won't even consider trying, but this idea seemed a bit too much even for the optimists. Then the cash demands came, so that dream was liquidated too. Actually, I was taken to a field and shown the guided missile. It was the size of a toy plane and took off and landed by remote control. But when I consulted our scientific committee, they gave the 'invention' a brief screening and discarded it.

The Haganah center for the United States was my suite at the Hotel Fourteen, an old-fashioned, respectable residential hotel at 14 East 60th Street, off Fifth Avenue. The Hotel Fourteen was owned by Ruby Barnet and his wife, Fannie. Fannie was a great Zionist who had worked with all our leaders, and she was the dominant power in the family. She was a typical American career woman who had been secretary of Hadassah and led her own professional life. A secretary of Hadassah then was a manager, and she had run Hadassah efficiently for a few years. She had also served as Weizmann's secretary, and when Ya'akov Dori arrived in 1945 to establish the Haganah operation, he settled at the hotel and Fannie volunteered to do his secretarial work. She was a slim, cockeyed blonde, and very quick in her repartee. Barnie was more of a regular businessman, a hotel operator, and very polite to the clients. He was always well dressed in a bow tie, wore rimless glasses (which then were the great fashion), and parted his hair on the side. But he had much less flair than Fannie. While Barnie was a good Jew, he was really more interested in his business affairs and investing in the Virgin Islands than in our day-to-day operations. This was all to the good, because we really didn't want the hotel owner involved in our nefarious activities. He would come in from time to time and say: 'You're not eating enough,' or 'Why don't you rest a little more?' Barnie was a kind of big brother to us. We also paid a reduced rate.

It was a great problem to get into hotels then. This was before many of the present hotels in New York were built, and with people coming back from the war, rooms were in great demand. And if it was very difficult to get a room, it was almost impossible to keep one for a long period. So we were lucky to find Fannie and Barnie. Living at the Hotel Fourteen had one other great advantage. It was close to impossible to get your hands on a white shirt. This had been true throughout the war, and everyone wanted one. In fact, there was almost a black market for white shirts! Barnie knew where to get them, and it was an important plus for me.

Our people soon gravitated to the hotel, and before long we were all living there, against every rule of conspiracy. We had offices on the ground floor as well as the top. My quarters consisted of a large living room, office, and a small bedroom. I must add that the basement of this hotel had been rented out to the famous 'Copacabana' nightclub – a separate enterprise locked off from the rest of the building, and a sharp contrast to our upstairs lives. We called it the Copahaganah. During these years I only went there once. It was my first visit to an American nightclub, and I remember listening to Lena Horne.

We had working contacts with other offices, of course. Aliyah Bet, for instance, was downtown in a shipping office near Wall Street, which handled our secret arrangements with the waterfront and dock people to facilitate our many illegal shipments. Davidka Nameri, who was in charge of that operation, was an old friend and neighbor from the Jordan Valley. He had helped us set up Ein Gev on its first day. In fact, all differences disappeared because of our close personal relationship, and our two offices became one cooperative until Aliyah Bet operations gradually diminished and closed down after May 1948, since immigration was no longer illegal.

This was the first time that I was responsible not only for what I did myself, but for a large group of people and tremendous amounts of money. It was not easy. It was also not easy to assert my authority over the ten or fifteen people who, though directly and indirectly under my command, were certainly all my equals or had qualifications superior to mine. To coordinate this operation demanded a great deal of patience, as well as luck and sheer physical stamina.

We worked seven days a week – long days. At 3 A.M. we would often go for combined supper and breakfast to a nearby Longchamps restaurant. In fact, my office staff worked so hard and for so little pay that sometimes, at the office's expense, I would take them out for an evening's relaxation. This happened very rarely and usually after periods or incidents that created much tension : an F.B.I. chase we had successfully avoided, a boat that had left safely, or a purchase of planes or arms that had been completed. On one or two occasions we went to the Savoy Ballroom in Harlem. It was a very relaxing experience to listen to good jazz and watch good dancing. We also went once or twice to Greenwich Village, where Shoshana Damari was appearing. One night we went to a club where they had Russian food and music, and Eliyahu Sacharov, the man who took over some of Arazi's work, and I stood up and sang, with the balalaika accompanying us. Eliyahu was from Russia, and he knew the Russian songs. I couldn't understand or speak a word, but I sang just the same.

The office was crowded all the time. In came a scientist with a new invention or some people who swore they could get planes – and how could you tell they couldn't ? In fact, some of the strange ideas people brought us were on the mark. For example, we learned that you could get arms out of an armory on a Saturday night, but you needed a few gangsters. 'After all, you don't pick up arms in the supermarket.' That turned out to be true. The American authorities who kept tabs on us came, as did many Jews whom I couldn't avoid seeing. Among the visitors were Jews from Latin America who had raised large amounts of money and were anxious that it go directly into the war effort. They were not very enthusiastic about sending monies raised specifically for defense through the normal channels, so they came to our office with suitcases full of cash or checks. The outstanding personality of them all was Menashe, a Polish Jew with the unpronounceable surname of Krzepicki. He had arrived in Brazil as a youngster, gone into the jungles, and finally worked his way up to become the head of one of the country's great export-import companies. He kept his faith with Israel, and particularly with Jerusalem, and until today he and his wife, Hilda, are regular visitors and help the city in many ways.

After the U.N. partition vote which meant we now had official sanction to establish a Jewish state, we formed a new organization, Materials for Palestine (which later became Materials for Israel). Its function was no longer illegal. We needed blankets and tents and boots. Every Thursday we had a Materials for Palestine lunch, and people from all over the country stood up and announced their donations: so-and-so many thousands of blankets, so many thousand pairs of boots, and so on. Most of these supplies were bought from army surplus in the United States for a few cents on the dollar. The people who helped us were often the surplus dealers themselves or people connected with them. We also encountered a great deal of sympathy from unexpected sources, like the Irish along the waterfront. They saw us as comrades-in-arms against the British, and Irish sentiment is strong (even today, Irish Americans are financing the IRA). We had Jewish gangsters with us, too. They often came from religious backgrounds, and some of their neighborhood fights as youngsters had been drawn on ethnic lines. So when Israel was gaining, they felt that they as Jews were gaining.

Sometimes the general sympathy we had in the harbors and on the waterfront was not enough. For instance, we were shipping many obsolete planes – obsolete for the United States, that is, but very useful for us – that we had bought cheaply: AT 6s, PF 40s, and some Pipers. The United States regarded these as military hardware forbidden by the embargo laws, so we had to disguise them. We packed the wings, body, and so on separately, and entire planes were shipped out as dismantled, prefabricated houses. To accomplish this, we needed more than the few Jews and even the many Irishmen on those docks. We needed the Italians, too, and the hidden underworld power. This was before the establishment of the Waterfront Commission in the 1950s. The docks of New York were a jungle then, but there were definite boundaries in that jungle. Certain gangsters controlled specific piers, and you could get on and off any pier if you made the right connections. We even established contact with the Mafia and once with the famous organization, Murder Inc., headed by Albert Anastasia. No one ever committed a murder for us, but they made certain that our shipments went through.

I never had dealings with any of their figures personally, but I knew some by sight (Anastasia was pointed out to me once). We had to be extremely careful, because the F.B.I. never let up its watch on us. In the winter of 1948, I felt we were being watched too closely at Hotel Fourteen and moved the office to the Fisk Building on West 57th. For a while I lived at the Park Plaza, now the Sheraton, a few blocks from there. The Park Plaza had a very pleasant barbershop, with the special advantage that it was open from seven in the morning until eleven at night. One morning I walked through the lobby to the barbershop and there was a great ruckus. Shots were heard, people were scattering, and on the barbershop floor lay Anastasia, who had just been shot. That was unnerving.

Of all the operations we ran, I think the one we put the most effort into was getting planes. Al Schwimmer, who was in charge of that, was a man with tremendous qualifications – imagination, and wide experience both as a pilot and in general aircraft affairs, and a great personality. I learned to trust him implicitly, and Al more than justified my complete faith in him. Through Al, we bought four Constellations from army surplus, paying $15,000 for each. One was cannibalized for parts; the other three were put back into flying condition. Only one of them reached Israel in time for the 1948 war. It was flown from the States through Panama and Dakar to Zatec, Czechoslovakia, and then on to Israel filled to the brim with arms. The other two were impounded by the Treasury Department and the F.B.I. They reached Israel when the war was over, however, and were the beginning of El Al, our national airline.

Al Schwimmer also bought ten C 46s that flew via Panama and Dutch Guiana to Czechoslovakia, our main supplier in early 1948. All planes were taken out of the country as aircraft of a Panamanian airline, which we owned. Panama actually designated us as its national carrier, and we flew them there through Mexico or another Central American country. The nephew of the Panamanian president was a good friend and acted as our lawyer, obtaining all necessary permits from the government. The fact is that the Panamanian government did not know our real motives. It was simply interested in some kind of an airline for the country, but we never reached the point of functioning as such.

Al's outfit, with more than a dozen people, also had various companies that served as covers for our operations. One company was presumed to be flying vegetables and meat between Miami and San Juan. Its planes flew to San Juan, where they were refueled as if to go to

St Thomas, but instead they flew to the Azores and from there to Czechoslovakia.

We also bought four B 17s, the 'Flying Fortresses'. Three of them were flown out through Florida to Zatec via San Juan and the Azores. But after they had passed through the Azores, a great hue and cry was raised, and the fourth plane was impounded in Tulsa, Oklahoma. One side of the Tulsa airport was under the jurisdiction of the National Guard. The plane was seized on the civilian side and moved over to the military area. When our people in Tulsa informed us about it, I met with Al and a few others and we decided to take the plane out secretly. Al and Leo Gardner, another of our pilots, arrived in Tulsa on a Saturday evening and took a taxi to the airfield. It happened that there was a dance for the base personnel that night, and many guests were coming from the city. It was also raining hard, so when they came up to the gate and the Marine guard asked if they were guests, they said yes, and he just let them in. They left the cab outside the recreation hall and walked to the plane on the other side of the field. Prepared by our people in advance, it was ready to fly. They climbed in, started the engines, and moved across the airfield without lights. Then the tower noticed and tried to stop them, but they took off just ahead of the airport police cars.

The following morning they arrived at Westchester Country Airport, where a few of us were waiting for them. A crew under Irwin 'Swifty' Schindler, another Jewish U.S. Air Force pilot, was all set to take the plane through Nova Scotia and the Azores to Czechoslovakia. The plane was quickly refueled, and Swifty and his crew took off. By then, of course, the whole U.S. air-control system was alerted that a 'Flying Fortress' had left Tulsa for unknown parts. The big question on the airwaves was 'Where the hell is it?' We had a fighting chance, however, because our people at the Westchester Airport had seen to it that the plane's arrival had not been reported. So the plane took off again, we returned to New York. But two hours later the F.B.I. was on to it. That enormous plane, flying in daylight, could not go unnoticed. It did safely get to Nova Scotia, but in Halifax the plane and crew were seized by Canadian authorities and held for a week. We were in touch with Swifty all the time. Finally, the Canadians, under U.S. pressure, agreed to give the plane only enough fuel for the flight back to the States, certainly not enough to reach the Azores. We told Swifty to accept the Canadian offer and meanwhile arranged for a full load of fuel to be put into the aircraft. Swifty did reach the Azores, and there, waiting, was a Portuguese friend who had helped us on previous flights. He had arranged with the authorities for this plane to go through, but by the time it landed the U.S. had put so much pressure on the Portuguese that it was grounded there after all. The crew returned to the States and then went on to Israel, in time for the war. The plane remained in the Azores and is probably still there.

In addition to the Flying Fortresses and the AT 6s, we flew out thirteen C 46s and three BC 4 Constellations and dismantled and shipped more than fifty Pipers, from which Molotov cocktails were thrown during the War of Independence. We also bought four A 20s, but they never got past Fort Lauderdale, Florida. At one point, one of our pilots went to the Munitions Control Division in Washington and tried to obtain export licenses for the C 46s and the Constellations. This was while we were discussing secret arrangements in Czechoslovakia, and he was questioned about whether the planes would be flying there. Apparently the State Department knew.

We were still looking for countries through which we could get the planes to Israel. The C 46s had to leave the States by April 15, because at that time a new provision of the Export Control and Arms Limitation Law went into effect and would have prohibited taking out aircraft of the C 46 class without a license. A license was needed for everything going to Europe, because the American government was afraid war material would fall into the hands of the Communists, but they weren't needed for Latin America. So a few hours before April 15, the C 46s were flown out of the United States southward. It was hard for the F.B.I. to check on surplus planes because hundreds were sold after the war. They did try to stop us from taking the C 46s to Panama but were unable to do so because registration, export licenses, and everything else were in order.

At least once I used Al Schwimmer for something other than procuring planes. That was when the *Kefalus* was being loaded with arms in Tampico, Mexico, and we had to carry out a financial transaction there. A Palestinian passport would have caused immediate problems, and there was no one else around with an American passport, so I asked Al to take $250,000 in cash to Mexico City and give it to a certain Cabinet minister. Before Al left, I got in touch with our Mexican contact, an exceptional fellow who was supervising the boat loading, and arranged for him to meet Al at the Mexico City airport and take him where he had to go. Before leaving, however, Al decided he was not going to carry all that cash in a suitcase without a gun. He was advised against it, but decided to take the gun anyway, carrying it in his belt under his coat.

In Mexico our contact met Al at the airport, but as they walked into the street, a plainclothesman stopped him. He demanded Al's gun, having spotted it when he had taken something from his pocket. Al handed over the gun, and then the policeman stopped a cab and ordered the two of them in. All the way to the police station, the officer and our man Tido were talking in Spanish. Tido was trying to pay him off. He later explained to Al that if he had been a Mexican, the policeman would have taken a bribe. But it was unusual for an American to carry a gun, and the officer felt there was something fishy here – something international. Tido kept talking and talking and finally managed to convince the policeman just before they reached the police station. The driver pulled over to the curb. Tido asked Al, 'Do you have twenty dollars ?' Al did, and the policeman took it, returned the pistol, and left. Then Tido told Al how lucky they had been. If you went into a Mexican police station with $250,000, naturally they would want a share. And afterward, naturally they would have to kill you. They couldn't let you live to tell the tale. Al delivered the money and Israel received the arms. When he came back to New York, though, he told me, 'These missions are not for me. I feel safer in an airplane.'

Al had another company in Burbank, California – a legitimate one with about 200 mechanics who serviced other aircraft besides working for us. He also ran the Panamanian Airline and Service Airways, Inc., a dormant company in New York registered in Swifty Schindler's name. We used all of them at our convenience. The money needed to operate them came through me. Most of it was supplied by the Jewish Agency, but a few times I raised considerable sums from friends.

Sometimes disorganization was so widespread that it seemed almost a necessity – and in fact things worked well for quite a while. Besides Schwimmer's operation, there was Ralph Goldman's group, purely an intelligence unit. We also had a group in Los Angeles trying to get arms out via Hawaii and the Philippines. This operation had been started before I came to New York, and all I had to do was provide the money and encourage Hank Greenspun when his wife tried to persuade him to come home and not waste his time on hopeless adventures. He could not even tell his wife he was involved with the Haganah.

Hank lived in Las Vegas then. He was tall, husky, and handsome with light blue eyes and a flattened nose that made him look like a boxer. A man of tremendous courage and charisma, he was, in fact, a great fighter by nature, but his profession was law. The qualities he showed while working with us were later proved again when as publisher of the *Las Vegas Sun* he fought corruption and the state's senator, McCarran. But he is best known for his campaign against Senator McCarthy. When McCarthy was at the height of his power, Hank was the first to consistently discredit him and put him on the defensive. Starting the fight as a lone voice in the desert, he eventually got the press all over the country behind him and brought McCarthy down. As Frank Sinatra, certainly a fighter himself, put it on one of the occasions when we discussed mutual friends and Hank's name came up : 'I wouldn't like to run up against him in a dark alley.' Over the years, Hank has remained as deeply involved with Israel as ever.

Besides being organizationally dispersed and complex, we were also disorganized in our bookkeeping. As I have said, money came from two sources: the Jewish Agency and groups of Jews to whom I turned directly. The greatest disorder existed, of course, in our illegal trans-actions. They had to be in cash, and there were no receipts or written records. I remember asking Joe Boxenbaum to get some kind of accounting from Yehuda Arazi before he left. Joe went and was given a suitcase filled with scraps of paper, but he couldn't make anything of it. Then we had an accountant come in and try to put some order into Yehuda's accounts – if you can call them that – and he spent months examining the 'data'. The man we finally put in charge of accounts for all our legal and illegal operations was Abe Cohen, who now manages the Israel Philharmonic Orchestra, but these accounts could never really be properly kept. Not that there was ever a question of misusing funds. In those days everybody lived so frugally and was so utterly devoted, without thinking of himself, that we had complete confidence in one another. Still, we had to keep records.

We spent many nights in the Hotel Fourteen stacking money, some-times in small denominations, to give to Al Schwimmer for the planes. I once said to Joe Boxenbaum, 'Look, Al is getting a lot of money. Someday I will have to account for it. But I can't get an accounting from him.' So Joe went to Schwimmer and said, 'You received $100,000 from Teddy last week. What did you do with it?' Al sat down and wrote everything he could remember on a piece of paper, but neither he nor we could figure out where each and every dollar went. All we were sure of were the results, which under Al were remarkable.

The legitimate, or legal, side of our mission – a very large part of our work – was also disorderly until the arrival of a man who deserves the country's everlasting gratitude. It was sheer accident that we got his services, and we almost missed out on him. Hundreds of letters poured into our office from people who wanted to volunteer, and so many were crank letters that we became somewhat nonchalant about them. One day Sharett, who was staying in New York for a while, gave me a letter from a Dr Sherman in Tel Aviv saying that his son would like to help and asking if somebody would see him. Sharett had not made much of a point about it, so it was days before I took the letter out of my pocket and invited Meir Sherman to come see me at Hotel Fourteen.

I had expected an Israeli student, but in came a man of my own age who had a degree in economics from an American university. Coming from a kibbutz and having lived in Jerusalem, I was not familiar with the leading citizens of Tel Aviv, so I did not know of Meir's father, one of Tel Aviv's first doctors. Palestine-born Meir combined his *sabra* ruggedness with American efficiency and great business acumen. He was an executive in a large import-export house, the Anglo-African Com-pany, owned by a wealthy Jew from South Africa who had settled in the

United States. Meir already commanded a high salary and began by helping us part time. He finally left his prosperous job and worked exclusively for us as a volunteer. Meir brought orderly administration and economic wisdom into our widespread and varied legitimate businesses.

All in all, there was often a cloak-and-dagger atmosphere about those days. All of us were constantly followed by the F.B.I., and two of our secretaries sometimes took home folders at night in case the offices were searched. I myself was never questioned by the F.B.I., but all the people around me were. They shielded me as much as possible from those of our people who were 'hot', like Hank Greenspun or Al Schwimmer. I tried to be the image of respectability. There was a time when we could not allow Al and Hank in our office. I would sometimes talk to them on the phone, and if necessary, my assistant would meet them in a restaurant. Sometimes, despite standing instructions, I would visit them in their hotel, which they changed daily. We tried to keep our many affairs separate and not even let people in the mission know what did not concern them. One day I was sitting in the office dictating cables that ordered Cadillacs to be sent to Israel. Of course, it was only a code name for some illegal equipment, but Rachel Mizrachi, my secretary, who wasn't in on the code, was disturbed by this. 'Don't you think we are being a bit *nouveau riche*? We hardly have a state and we're ordering Cadillacs?' I told her that, after all, a prime minister needs a Cadillac!

At the end of April 1948, I returned home for my first visit. From then on I went back to Israel practically every two months to keep things running smoothly. But that first trip was not easy. Although flying to Paris was simple, getting a flight out of Paris was a problem, because regular airlines had suspended their services to Palestine. The Palestinians – that was us at the time – who had gathered in Paris finally found a South African plane to fly to a makeshift strip near Tel Aviv. (Lod Airport was then in the fighting area and, I think, still occupied by Arabs.) Our plane was a small, two-engine, unheated craft, and we nearly froze to death.

I was fortunate, on May 14, 1948, to be in the hall of the Dizengoff Museum in Tel Aviv when Ben-Gurion proclaimed the State of Israel. I was one of the few there who had also been at Lake Success on November 29, 1947, but the 14th of May was by far more exciting. There was no seat for me in the little hall of the museum. Every chair had been appropriated by those chosen from among the hundreds who had seniority rights – men of Ben-Gurion's generation, pioneers old enough to be my father or grandfather. Besides, I had arrived only a few days before and had not notified the proper officials. Anyway, when I came to the door of the packed hall, even though I knew everybody, I don't think I would have had a chance of getting in if I had not just arrived from the United States. At that particular time, America had a glamor and grandeur for us, and some of it had rubbed off on me. The hall was so crowded that I could barely stand up against one of the columns.

In addition to the invited guests, people by the thousands were standing outside. The number who had received invitations was by necessity very small. How everybody came to know about the ceremony is still an enigma to me. I believe it was purposely not announced in advance to avoid international complications or even an attack by the Arabs. Inside there was tremendous excitement. But what I remember best was the enthusiasm of the people when, after a relatively short ceremony, we walked out on to the street and the people started singing and dancing and greeting Ben-Gurion. It was an unforgettable moment.

That same evening, I accompanied Moshe Sharett and Reuven Shiloach to the 'Red House', actually a brownish-looking building, which was the headquarters of Ben-Gurion and of the Defense Ministry. We sent out cables appointing ambassadors. They must have been sent with Ben-Gurion's knowledge and consent, but all I can remember is that we did it. Ehud Avriel was sent a cable in Prague appointing him ambassador to Czechoslovakia, and Maurice Fischer, in Paris, was made ambassador to France. We also appointed Mordecai Eliash to represent us at the U.N. and Eliahu Epstein (Elath) to be ambassador in Washington. We finally found somebody to send out the cables and went home. At dawn on May 15 came the first bombing of Tel Aviv by the Egyptians.

Tamar had come to Tel Aviv from Ein Gev to spend a few days with me. She had a slight fever but recovered quickly. The tension of that week of independence was very high. Everybody knew that war would officially be declared at any moment. Ben-Gurion was sure that the Arab armies would invade. When Tamar realized this, she tried to get back to Ein Gev. When she reached the Sea of Galilee, she was told to try and go straight on to kibbutz Alonim, just southeast of Haifa, where the older children had been evacuated. She had been working with these children and was expected there. Our eight-month-old son, Amos, had been evacuated to Haifa. Tamar tried to stop a truck. There was almost no traffic on the road around the lake, and the cars that did come along were going so quickly, because of the fighting, that one of them grazed her and she fell. Fortunately, she was not hurt and only her dress was torn. Somehow she reached Alonim. After some time the children in Alonim were also transferred to Haifa, and Tamar stayed there with Amos throughout the war. I went to Haifa twice to visit them, but I did not get to Ein Gev at all.

Since I was needed urgently back in the United States, I tried desperately to reach New York. Passenger traffic was as erratic from Israel

Above Teddy (left) with his parents and brother, Paul, vacationing in Karlsbad in 1925.

Right Teddy (left) in a youth movement summer camp in 1933.

Left Tamar at the age of seventeen, when Teddy first met her.

Below Teddy (second from right) with some of the founders of Ein Gev in 1937 (courtesy The Matson Photo Service).

Opposite, below Kibbutz Ein Gev, wedged in between the Sea of Galilee and the Golan Heights, in its early years.

Opposite, above Teddy and Tamar (in background) just before boarding the flying boat on their trip to London in 1940.

Above Teddy (right) with
Golda Meir and Gideon Rafael
next to the three-seater
Beechcraft that took them out
of Israel on their way to the
US immediately after the
establishment of the
State of Israel.

Right Tamar and Amos in
Washington in 1951.

Teddy and Osnat.

Above With Prime Minister David Ben-Gurion and Chief of Staff Moshe Dayan.

Opposite, above Unmoved by an intense Kirk Douglas and 'Memi' de Shalit in the cabin of an El Al plane (courtesy Zinn Arthur).

Opposite, below Danny Kaye relaxing in Teddy's office as Teddy chats with Chaim Topol (courtesy Y. Barzilay).

Below Ben-Gurion and Teddy on the Sea of Galilee, 1945

Above Congratulating
Prime Minister Eshkol
on his marriage
to Miriam
(in background).

Left Posters for the
municipal elections on a
public bulletin board.
The captions on the
posters for Teddy read
'For the sake of our city,
give Teddy a hand.'

as it was to the country. Somebody finally located a little Beechcraft with three seats. Even Tel Aviv had become hazardous by then, because of the Egyptian bombardments, so we used the small Haifa airstrip. There were three passengers on that plane : Golda Meir, on her first United Jewish Appeal mission; Gideon Rufer (Rafael), who represented Sharett on some Foreign Ministry business; and myself. The plane stopped in Cyprus, Athens, and Italy to refuel and finally reached Nice. It took a whole day – from 4 A.M. until late at night – to get to Nice. We were the first people to arrive with makeshift Israeli passports and were received by the French customs as great heroes, although (or because) nobody believed Israel had a chance of surviving through the year. From Nice we took a regular flight to Paris and from there we flew on to the United States.

A few days after the Declaration of Independence, the Israel Defense Forces were established, and now, instead of representing the Haganah, the underground military arm of an unborn state, we represented the Ministry of Defense of the State of Israel. Zvi Brenner soon joined us. We were almost neighbors – he came from a kibbutz in the Jordan Valley, not far from Ein Gev – and almost 'relatives', as he had married a girl who was a member of the youth movement with me back in Vienna. Zvi had come to Palestine from Illinois while still a teenager. He had a rich military background, having started out in one of Wingate's Special Night Squads and served in the Jewish Brigade in Italy during World War Two, when he was wounded in the knee. He and I ran the still unavoidable irregular side, since the U.S. arms embargo was still in force. Meir Sherman was joined by Aryeh Manor, who became his deputy on the purchasing, shipping, and financial side.

From the day I returned to New York, the immediate pressure on us was to find planes, arms, money, and men. Our country was in hourly peril, and the urgency was great. We trained the first twelve pilots in California and were lucky to enlist two young American Jewish aircraft engineers. Both men were classified by the United States government and could not leave the country without special permission, so they took unpaid leave and served in Israel under assumed names. They helped advance the fledgling Israeli Air Force tremendously.

There were many other American recruits. Most of the pilots, Jew or Gentile, volunteered because they believed in Israel. In general we refused to take soldiers of fortune. One young American who had applied to join the air force was a shady character from the West Coast, and our people were probably not very cordial. At any rate, he returned to the States and showed up at Materials for Israel office, together with his father, demanding money. We could not get rid of them, so we told them to come again later in the afternoon. One of the men who had worked for us was a policeman named Leibel, and he looked like a true

Irishman. When father and son showed up and repeated their demands and threats, we told them we were calling the police. Leibel appeared, they disappeared, and we never heard from them again.

Our most famous 'recruit' was Col. David (Mickey) Marcus, and I had great affection for him. Mickey was a West Point graduate, had been a colonel in the Rangers, and ended up in the U.S. Military Government in Germany. He was just ready to settle down with his wife in their lovely house in Brooklyn when we came along early in 1948. Many conversations took place, and Mickey was not very enthusiastic. He had just had five years of the army. Before the war he had been in the office of the district attorney, Tom Dewey, 'crime busting' in New York. Now he wanted to open his own law office. Still, under the influence of Sharett and his former commanding officer, Gen. John Hildring (who played an important role in our affairs at the time), Mickey was persuaded to visit Israel.

I met Mickey a short time before his first visit to Israel. He returned to the States in March or April 1948 with no real intention of going back again, and painted a gloomy picture of the situation. But he was extremely important for us then. Our army had to be organized. A few of our own men had been officers in the British Army, but none of them had the kind of authority that came with Mickey's training, experience, and personality. The attitude of many of our ex-underground soldiers was 'These spit-and-polish brigade officers, what do they really know?' and it took some time before our own 'British' soldiers could make their influence felt. The irregulars of the Haganah and the Palmach made up the bulk of the army. On his first visit, Mickey found a common language with them more quickly than our former British Army soldiers had.

Mickey did go back, and I became better acquainted with him when I was in Tel Aviv in May. We spent many evenings together talking and drinking Israeli brandy (the only kind available) in one bar or another along the seashore, and of course I did all in my power to encourage him to stay. In spite of it all, he went back to the States without a definite promise to return. We met several times again in New York, and finally he was persuaded. He returned to Israel and took formal and official command of the Jerusalem front.

Early one morning not too long after, a few hours before the first truce was to go into effect, the telephone rang. It was a call from Tel Aviv informing me that Mickey had been killed. I was badly shaken. In a way I felt personally responsible, because I had been decisive in influencing him to return to Israel. I could not bring myself to talk about it to anyone in our group. But without doubt I was the one who had to tell Mickey's wife, Emma. At that time I did not know he had been killed in a tragic accident. A Jewish sentry mistook Mickey for an Arab when he approached in the dark wrapped in a bed sheet and couldn't remember the password. I don't think this was general knowledge even in Israel at first, and I certainly assumed he had been killed in action.

To this day I can remember the ride in the taxi to Brooklyn. It was a very long and difficult hour. I couldn't think of what to say. My mind kept on going back to how much Emma had been against Mickey's involvement with Israel; how after years of Mickey's absence in World War Two, she had been looking forward to finally settling down with him. She was very much in love with him, and now this had happened.

Emma was a schoolteacher. She was a tall, good-looking woman with an exceptionally strong character. I went to her school and saw the principal, who sent for her. It was in his office that I broke the news. She behaved very courageously, almost as if she had expected it. She did not learn the details about her husband's death until many months later, but it made no difference to the fine image of Mickey Marcus' life. He had been a brave and outstanding military man in the United States, and his contribution to Israel's morale and fighting capacity is an important part of our history.

I had seen Emma Marcus often after Mickey's final departure to Israel. I would go to their house every few days bringing her messages from Mickey or letters that could not come through the ordinary mail. They had no children, and after his death she was very much alone. She still lives in the same house, and in recent years she has gradually lost her eyesight. We invited her to Israel in 1973 for the Twenty-fifth Anniversary of the state, and I think the trip meant a great deal to her, notwithstanding her failing eyesight. Emma had been left without means, except for her earnings as a teacher, and we worked out an insurance plan in the United States and paid the premiums in order to get her a pension. I visited her not too long ago at a hospital. She had undergone an eye operation, but unfortunately it did not help her very much.

Mickey's body was flown back to the States during the first truce in the War of Independence, accompanied by Moshe Dayan and Yossi Har'el, both colonels. They arrived on July 2 in a DC 4 that we had acquired a few months earlier. Ruth Dayan came along as well. Since they did not have properly ranked uniforms, Ruth took a sample from a British uniform along and during the flight, which was more than twenty-four hours, she embroidered all the insignia. I met them at the airport with Emma. Later we went to West Point, where Mickey was buried. The service was attended by a small group of friends and the commander of the academy.

Dayan was anxious to return home immediately because fighting was about to resume any day, and the papers reported new clashes. Getting him back to Israel was not simple, though, since there were still no regular flights. I finally found a solution. Our nation's first money was being flown over (it had been printed in the States), and international law specified that only a military guard could be on a plane with money. So I arranged for Colonel Dayan to fly as a guard. Moshe went, but under no circumstances would they let Ruth on board. A few days later, however, I had to transfer some documents to Yehuda Arazi in Rome, so I gave Ruth the papers to take to him, hoping Yehuda would find a way to get her from Rome to Israel (which he did). Besides the documents, I gave Ruth a bag of glass prisms for army communication instruments and rolls of paper for map making, both of which were very important for the army at that time. When Ruth landed in Haifa, a customs bureau had already been set up, and the brand-new officials would not let her bring in the prisms and the map paper without paying duty. Her argument that it was urgent material sent from the Defense Mission to the army made no impression. Later she told me that she was almost hysterical. Not having the money, she had to leave the package behind for the army to pick up later.

I emphathized with Ruth's frustration, for we were constantly under great pressure to obtain things for which we did not have enough cash. During the first truce, when Dayan was in New York, he told us that simple Piper planes could be of great tactical value, since bombs could be tossed from them by hand on the advancing Egyptian columns. Our purchasing policy was still very haphazard, but this purchase could be made legally; only shipping them out – which we managed to do – was irregular. So we secured $80,000 from a supporter in Philadelphia and bought the planes. Meanwhile, Pinhas Sapir, then in charge of the Defense Mission for Europe, called me from Geneva. 'How is it that you waste the state's money on this?' I simply told him it was not the state's money. Those personal contacts with American Jews were often lifesavers.

In late May 1948, we needed $1 million for the purchase of airplanes within a day. We knew we could get the money in a month, but we had to have it then and there. It looked as if we had used up all our benefactors. I ran into an old acquaintance, Joseph Shulman, who said, 'You know, I have a rich friend whom I have never approached. I don't think he's interested in Israel, but let's try.' That same morning we went to Manhasset, Long Island, and called on Bill Levitt, who had just built his first Levittown. He was expecting us, so I simply explained, 'I am the head of the Haganah Mission and I would like to borrow a million dollars. We'll pay it back in two months.' He asked a few questions, including 'What do I get as security?' I replied, 'Nothing more than a promissory note from the State of Israel.' We met again the following morning after a lengthy consultation during the night with our ambassador, Eliahu Epstein, and Oscar Gass, our economic adviser. I brought

Levitt a note from the 'Provisional Government of Israel. Note Number One. One Million Dollars. Signed, Eliahu Epstein.' We received the million dollars and repaid it on time – without interest, of course.

State or no state, the manner in which we conducted our activities didn't change much after May 15, 1948. At the Hotel Fourteen we assumed that our telephones were bugged and we tried not to talk about sensitive matters from our rooms. One simple precaution was to make our calls from pay phones, and for long distance calls we took a bag of quarters with us. One summer evening in 1948, I went to call our man in Mexico City. We had a boat leaving Mexico with high octane gas for our fledgling Air Force, and we had been unable to obtain gas anywhere in the world until a Mexican banker got it for us. I called our man from a booth in a drugstore on 58th and Madison, and the conversation went on and on. When I finished, it was midnight. I was alone, and the drugstore had closed. It was an uncomfortable situation. I didn't want to ring the police for help and bring them into it, and I didn't know who else could let me out. The first thing I did was to eat some ice cream, which was delicious. Then I found a door that opened from the inside into the building. I ran into a night watchman, told him my story, and gave him a couple of dollars to let me out.

When the Mexican banker had told us he could get the high octane gas, we had two problems: getting a boat that could slip through the embargo and reach Israel, and making sure the boat owners would not cheat us. This was a typical headache. In New York we found a Greek company of dubious nature, and the captain demanded $70,000 in cash. But we had a sympathizer, a prominent figure in the underworld, who was nicknamed 'The King' (I never learned his real name). Zvi Brenner, who kept in contact with him, decided to tell him our problem. They drove to the waterfront in Brooklyn and went to the office of the Greek company. 'The King' introduced himself, and that was apparently enough. The boat went to Mexico, took on the octane, and sailed to Israel. There was no monkey business.

But we had to pay a price for our own monkey business. Altogether ten Americans who worked for us were indicted and charged with a number of counts of conspiracy to violate the laws of the United States. The trial was held in Los Angeles in 1949 and ran into 1950. It revolved around our plane smuggling. The American government must have spent hundreds of thousands of dollars bringing witnesses from Czechoslovakia, Honolulu, and the West Coast. For some reason it seemed important to them to obtain a severe sentence. We consulted our various lawyer friends. Murray Gurfein, one of Tom Dewey's early crime busters, was our main strategist, and very bright he was. Everyone pleaded guilty, and the trial ended with an acquittal on all charges except for a gun-running charge with which Hank had been involved.

F.J.—4

He was convicted on that one count and was awaiting sentence.

At that point our lawyers decided to make use of a peculiar provision in the law. With the consent of the U.S. attorney general, a man pleading guilty to a crime and convicted can go back to his district of origin and be sentenced there instead of the place of trial. The attorney general gave his consent, and Swifty Schindler, for instance, came before a judge in New York and was given a suspended sentence. This happened in nine cases out of ten. The only exception, another pilot, did not follow our lawyer's advice. He could legally have chosen New York, but he chose Florida. A Florida businessman, Chuck had bought three surplus B 17s for civilian use before he had any connection with us. Then Al Schwimmer heard about the planes and bought them on condition that Charley deliver them to Czechoslovakia. This was done, but under cover. It turned out that Florida had a state attorney named Boggs who wanted to give us a hard time. The state was rabidly anti-communist and somewhat anti-Semitic then. The fact that the B 17s were flown to Czechoslovakia was made into a 'Communist plot'. Chuck received a year in jail and served eight months. The others, at worst, had only to pay fines. Hank Greenspun lost his civil rights, but was later pardoned by President Kennedy.

Toward the end, our undercover work had grown so that the F.B.I. closed in on everybody. Al and his people could not stay in one place. They had to move almost every day. The effectiveness of the whole operation was ruined. Finally, they cleaned out everything and in June 1948 went to Israel. Al drove up to Canada (Americans don't need passports to cross that border) and flew from Canada to Switzerland, on to Zatec, and then to Israel on one of our planes. After the war, he returned to the United States and surrendered himself.

Meir Sherman stayed with the mission for a while and was joined by my brother, Paul. Then he went back to the Anglo-African company. He was deeply attached to his wife, Niuta, and initially she was not greatly interested in Israel and felt that we exploited Meir. It wasn't the low pay that worried her – on our scale he was eventually given a lieutenant's salary – for money didn't mean very much to Niuta, who had an extravagant Russian background. But we took Meir away every day of the week, including Saturdays and Sundays, and he never had time to read poetry to her or play with their son, Ronny. It was hard for her to see Meir divide his devotion between his family and his cause. But gradually, as she came to know more about Israel and our problems, she shared Meir's concern.

Meir and I were in constant touch throughout the next decade. I turned to him again and again for help and advice. He always found time, and in 1952 he found a solution to a severe financial problem for us, as will be seen later. Prior to his settling in Israel in 1962, he served for a while as economic minister in our embassy in Washington. In Israel he became director of the Paz Oil Company and a general adviser to the minister of finance. He and Niuta lived first in Haifa and then in Tel Aviv, and Niuta came to love the country. When Meir died in 1969, I felt an irreparable loss.

By the end of 1948, my mission was drawing to an end. In the process, I had learned a great deal about the United States. I had also been to Washington, D.C., and caught some glimpses of the work in our embassy. By the end of my assignment I had made a great many friends through the Friends of Haganah – including people who had influence with the Democratic Party – and, together with my other contacts, I had connections with more people than the embassy or the Jewish Agency did.

When 1948 drew to an end, Zvi Brenner and Aryeh Manor took over from me in New York. I was advised by our legal experts to leave before the F.B.I. got its hands on me, too, and there was not much left for me to do. At Passover, in April of 1949, we had an enormous *seder* for everyone who had worked with us, the whole Israeli mission. It was also my farewell party. I left a few days later and, for the first and only time in my life, crossed the ocean by boat, on the S.S. *America*. It was the close of one of the most memorable periods of my life.

7 America Revisited

In May 1949, soon after my return to Israel, I went to London for a month to meet with Ezra Danin, my long-time friend and our Arab expert, who was there on a fund-raising mission. Ezra, some of our colleagues, and I had come to the conclusion that we had to do something about the Arab refugee problem. We had talked about it before. The Palestinian Arabs were in camps, and we knew that day by day they were establishing themselves as permanent and professional refugees. A few of us feared they would one day constitute the one really insoluble problem in the Middle East. We believed that British companies with interests in the Middle East could provide the refugees with permanent work in Arab countries and thus take them out of the camps.

I had connections with important Jewish businessmen, like Simon Marks, Sigmund Gestetner, and Israel Sieff. Through them and others we approached a few firms that were vitally interested in preserving British influence in the region – mainly oil companies – in the belief that the solution of the refugee problem would appeal to their self-interest. One company, for example, had oil interests in the area between Kirkuk and Tripoli. Another company was building the Syrian port of Latakia. Some of the builders were Quakers, and through the English Quakers I approached them to hire Palestinian refugees for the project. We also talked to other large construction companies active in the Middle East and offered to try and raise funds to build dams on the Euphrates for Syria and Iraq, like those subsequently built by the Russians on the Upper Euphrates in Syria. We pointed out that such dams would create tremendous stretches of irrigated land and would be of great benefit to Syria. One line of argument was: 'If we find you the credit, and you offer it to the Syrians, they will need the Palestinian refugees to settle the land. The Palestinians are good farmers, and Syria is by no means overpopulated. The project would also bring tremendous wealth to Iraq, which now has only a sixth or seventh of the population it had a thousand years ago.' We asked them to consider the truth visible to anyone flying over Iraq: thousands of arid water trenches in the Mesopotamian

Desert, which was obviously fertile, flourishing, and well populated in ancient times.

It was not millions that were needed. Wages were then about two shillings a day; so if we could add a shilling, we could get the refugees to work, provide them with land, and gradually solve our mutual problem. The number of refugees then was much smaller than it is today, since they have since multiplied not only through natural increase, but as the result of propaganda and free food distribution. The few documented proposals I took around aroused hesitant interest.

Ezra and I saw in the refugee problem the greatest potential danger to Israel. We had confidence that defense, frontiers, and other problems could be managed, but the long-term problem would be the refugees. Their plight was a time bomb, and something had to be done before the political situation in our area froze up. But there were few who agreed with our view. We had sent letters and cables to Israel explaining our plan and asking for money, and now we sat in London waiting for a green light. Negotiations had gone pretty far, but there was still no answer from Israel. Finally we cabled Ze'ev Sharef, then the secretary to the government, and asked him to go directly to Ben-Gurion and have him decide one way or the other – but quickly! Sharef's reply was negative. Since we had no support among our own leadership, and we could not carry on as a private partisan enterprise, I went back home.

It was then that I became involved with the establishment of the Israel Bonds project. When I was still with the Haganah mission in New York, I had suggested the sale of bonds on a small scale, and I had even mentioned this notion to Henry Montor, the head of the UJA. Now Montor picked up the idea. Bonds were the only way, he felt, of financing the large-scale immigration beginning at that time, especially from Iraq. (The Jews of Iraq, according to the decision of the Iraqi government, had only a single year to get out.) We were very hesitant about the massive bonds plan because of opposition among the UJA leadership, Hadassah, and practically everyone else. I remember sitting for hours with people who said that bonds would destroy the UJA. Why borrow money when you could get it as a gift?

Even purely objective evaluations of the plan were negative. I went to the States for a few days with Eliezer Kaplan, our minister of finance, to hold a meeting with economists at the now extinct Astor Hotel in Times Square. Altogether about twenty well-known economists were invited, and they were almost unanimous in their pessimistic appraisal of Montor's idea. Their argument was based on an analysis of probability: 'Granted that Latin American countries have issued bonds, but they are established countries, and they are not in the same position as Israel. If any one of them sells $15 million or $20 million worth of

bonds a year, it's a lot. Is that worth your while?' It certainly was not.
By then we were thinking in terms of at least $100 million or $150
million annually. One or two of the twenty advisers said there was a
possibility it might be done. Bonds are normally sold through issuing
houses: Dillon Reed, Stanley Morgan, Lehman Brothers, Goldman-
Sachs. Some of them are owned by Jews, some not. None of them wanted
to touch our bonds. Certainly none of them wanted to underwrite a
major issue for a definite amount of money.

Up to then nobody thought of selling bonds through public meetings.
If the banks would not take us, there was no apparent alternative, so we
decided to create our own sales organization. But in order to do this and
get the public behind us, we first needed the support of the Jewish
leadership. To this end, the American Desk in the Foreign Ministry
organized a conference of Jewish leaders in September 1950 at the King
David Hotel in Jerusalem.

After a few months in Ein Gev with my family, I went to work for the
Foreign Ministry (which was then located in Tel Aviv) as head of the
American Desk. Tamar and Amos moved to Tel Aviv with me. The
operations of the American Desk were very limited then. Esther
Herlitz, who had established it a year before, became my deputy. I
regarded the responsibilities of the department as all-embracing, dealing
not only with diplomacy but with economic affairs, relations with
American Jewry, security matters, visitors, and public relations in
America. This conception ran counter to the ideas of the very young
but already rigid Foreign Ministry, but during my tenure I prevailed.
The conference we organized was a huge success and was the first of
hundreds or maybe thousands of missions that have become an integral
part of organized American Jewish life and were successfully copied by
European Jewry. Montor arrived with a hundred prominent American
Jews. Resolutions were adopted to start the bond issue, and Montor ran
the campaign. I was appointed to go to the United States as minister –
second man in the embassy – and help out from Washington.

The difficulties we encountered in the States were manifold. After the
1929 collapse of the New York Stock Exchange, President Roosevelt
had established the Securities and Exchange Commission to check all
securities offered to the public. To steer our bonds through the American
laws, much legal and political work had to be done. Israel was barely
recognized, and its finances were obscure. The SEC's main demand was
that you had to give the public a clear picture of what they were buying;
'full disclosure', nothing was to be hidden. Our response was a bond
prospectus that really became a handbook on Israel. We held long legal,
political, and community consultations before a very elaborate organization was established in April 1951. It was an experience that gave me
insight into an entirely different facet of American life.

We asked Henry Morgenthau, Jr to become the first chairman of Israel Bonds. His name was particularly important for the Bonds because during World War Two, under his auspices as secretary of the treasury, the United States had for the first time successfully sold its own bonds to the public on a large scale. Morgenthau was over seventy at the time, somewhat formal and dry, but very devoted. He had been secretary of the treasury, but when Truman became president, he had resigned and become active in Jewish affairs, assuming the leadership of the UJA. I believe that what brought a comparatively assimilated Jew like Henry Morgenthau back to Jewish life was that he had seen what had happened to the Jews in Germany more closely than many others, and he had also observed how insensitive even a sympathetic country like the United States had been to the fate of the Jews. This subject came up in the many conversations we had at the UJA office and at his home overlooking Central Park, as well as during his many trips to Israel. He had become head of the UJA before I came to the States, but I helped convince him to take on the bonds.

City managers for bonds were appointed in all major American cities, and we began preparations for the massive drive that was going to begin in May 1951 with a visit by Ben-Gurion. I was in charge of organizing Ben-Gurion's tour, and all the details were well planned in advance. As this was the first visit to the United States by Israel's first prime minister, I felt it was important for as many Americans as possible to see this extraordinary man, who was not very well known then, and thus to see Israel personified. This was especially important because in America people tend to think of issues in terms of the people who represent them. Naturally, we hatched and abandoned a lot of silly ideas inspired by the folkways of American presidential candidates, like having Ben-Gurion photographed at a delicatessen eating a bagel and lox. But we did have a ticker-tape parade down Broadway, through the garment district and all the way downtown, with Ben-Gurion being acclaimed by hundreds of thousands of people who crowded the sidewalks and packed the windows of hotels, shops, and office buildings. The turn-out was far beyond our expectations, and the warm reception was repeated in all the cities we visited. We traveled from one major American city to another in a chartered Pan American plane. Wherever we went, Ben-Gurion was received like a hero, and it was a deeply moving experience. The enthusiasm extended beyond anything we could have imagined.

Our grand opening was in New York – a mammoth assembly in Madison Square Garden, which was packed with 20,000 people. Another 20,000 crammed the sidewalks outside and listened to the speeches through loudspeakers. It was fabulous. He then visited the grave of Mickey Marcus at West Point; held meetings in various Jewish centers of learning, like the Hebrew Union College and the

Jewish Theological Seminary; and met with Orthodox Jewish leaders. These visits were, of course, in addition to the Bond meetings.

In Washington Ben-Gurion called on President Truman at the White House and presented a large bronze *menorah* as a gift. Although this was the first time Ben-Gurion met Truman, there were no burning or basic issues to be discussed. There was no talk of arms supply (that came up for the first time in the Suez period in 1956) and there was no problem over frontiers (they had been settled by the Armistice Agreements – at least for the time being). But the very fact that Ben-Gurion could call on Truman, that the head of the State of Israel met the president of the United States, was in itself significant. Ben-Gurion had very high regard for the president. He thought Truman was honest and straightforward, could bring a matter down to its essentials, and had a strong grasp of historic values. Ben-Gurion was impressed by his understanding of international priorities, as expressed by the Truman Doctrine in Turkey and Greece and later with his decision on Korea, and the decisiveness he had shown in dismissing General MacArthur and thus asserting firm civilian control over foreign policy and military affairs.

From Washington the tour went on to Boston. At the time the Israeli Navy owned all of two ships, and they had arrived in the United States specially for the occasion. Beginning with Boston, they sailed to New York and then all the way down to Miami as part of the Bonds promotion campaign. They were two little frigates, but they had managed to cross the ocean and were the first Israeli naval ships to reach the United States. (Actually, I don't think there were any others there until the Bicentennial twenty-five years later.) Their arrival was a very emotional affair, with our sailors lined up outside the Massachusetts State House when Ben-Gurion arrived. The State House was in session, and Ben-Gurion was unexpectedly asked to address the Massachusetts legislature. He knew something I had not known before – that in 1917 or 1918, the Massachusetts legislature had adopted a resolution in favor of a Jewish commonwealth in Palestine – and inspired by this bit of local history, he made a brilliant five-minute speech. Ben-Gurion was not always a brilliant speaker – certainly not in English – but that was a great and very emotional speech. Later that day Ben-Gurion was invited to speak before the students of the Boston Hebrew Academy. It gave him the opportunity to speak to young Americans in Hebrew.

Ben-Gurion wanted to see the Tennessee Valley, and the governor of Tennessee gave a dinner in his honor. In his speech, the governor emphasized that the Tennessee Valley Authority was in no way a form of socialism, though it was actually the first American project that resembled socialist planning. Still, socialism was a dirty word in the United States then, and the governor was obviously not aware that his guest of honor was the head of a socialist party. As he happily denounced socialism, we began to grow anxious about Ben-Gurion's reaction. To our surprise, Ben-Gurion stood up and made a wonderful speech about development. Afterward he said, 'I could see that you were all afraid I would get up and give that man an education about socialism.' It amused him.

Then we went on to Chicago and Los Angeles, and on the return flight to New York someone found out it was my fortieth birthday, so we had a great birthday party on the plane with cake and champagne. Later, after putting the Ben-Gurions to sleep in New York, we continued the party until the early hours of the morning. In all, Ben-Gurion's trip lasted about two weeks, and it was a tremendous success.

In Washington I held diplomatic status, but I was paid by the Ministry of Finance because I had severed my connections with the Foreign Ministry before leaving Israel. One could say I was assigned to the embassy on a mission for the Finance Ministry. There were several reasons for my dissociation from our Foreign Ministry. First, I was not particularly interested in formal diplomatic affairs – cocktail parties, receptions, and dinners – where the most important thing was to have the right seat and guard your seniority. More important, however, was my belief that the ministry should be more concerned about our relations with world Jewry than anything else. I was convinced that the Jews around the world were our only reliable ally. While Israeli ambassadors and representatives of the Foreign Ministry did appear at meetings and helped Jewish communities and organizations where they could, this was often on the basis of personal initiative, more often they felt less affinity toward their Jewish constituencies than toward their host governments. I thought this was all wrong and that we were copying other nations' patterns of diplomacy instead of creating our own style.

There was also a third reason. I once picked up the Foreign Service Journal of Denmark and saw that ninety percent of it was devoted to foreign trade – obtaining economic and commercial advantages for Denmark in various countries. Obviously the test of a Danish diplomat was whether he was able to bring his country more business. Our Foreign Ministry – at least during its first years – behaved as if it were at the Congress of Vienna under Metternich's guidance. Economic affairs took at least third or fourth place in the list of priorities, and I felt that this very formal, striped-pants style of diplomacy was out of place for us. I had arguments over this approach while still working at the American Desk in Tel Aviv, and I did not want to have any part of it.

Nonetheless, I was formally a minister at our embassy, and in the ambassador's absence I often had to go to the State Department. I was fortunate in having friends there. I had met the assistant secretary of state, Lewis Jones, in Cairo during the war and later when he was first secretary in charge of Middle Eastern Affairs at the American embassy in London. He and his wife, Polly, had been friends for a long time. We went to concerts and the theater together, and through him and some other old friends I had easy access to many people in the State Department. Jones and I were to meet again in Cyprus during the period of Nasser's rule. He was the first to explain to me the significance of the Nasserite revolt, and his insights were invaluable.

We were a small Israeli community in Washington. Abba Eban was our ambassador, but he was also the representative at the United Nations, so he was in New York much of the time. There were four first secretaries in the embassy, including Meir de Shalit ('Memi') and Esther Herlitz. The military attaché was Vivian (Chaim) Herzog – later in charge of Military Intelligence and ambassador to the United Nations. Tamar, Amos, and I had a little apartment on Massachusetts Avenue. Esther Herlitz and my secretary, Ruhama Sapir, lived in the same building, as did the Egyptian minister, but we had no contact with him. In the evenings at home we sometimes played canasta, which was then the favorite game in Washington. We ate a lot of carrots (we were all trying to lose weight), and at a New Year's Eve party I made a deal with Esther Herlitz that for every pound she lost, I would take a dancing lesson. She lost twelve pounds, but I never learned to dance.

When I came to Washington, the embassy was still housed in the old building that had served the Jewish Agency, but was becoming too small. I convinced local friends to put up the money, and we bought the new building, which is still the embassy today. A few youngsters who later became prominent figures in the Israeli foreign service started out as guards in the embassy back then. One of them was Simcha Dinitz, who later became director of the Prime Minister's Office under Golda Meir and ambassador to the United States. One cold winter night he was woken up by a Western Union messenger. He stepped out the embassy door in his pajamas to accept a cable and the door slammed shut behind him. Simcha had been alone in the building and found that he could not get back in, nor did he have any money in his pajama pockets to take a cab. Finally he managed to convince a taxi driver of his desperate situation and arrived at our apartment building, where the doorman didn't want to let a crazy-looking person in pajamas wake up a tenant in the middle of the night. But apparently Simcha had the same powers of persuasion he later demonstrated with Kissinger. I supplied him with a coat, a hot cup of coffee, my set of keys for the embassy – and a double cab fare.

Aside from the Bonds campaign and the special event of Ben-Gurion's visit, I dealt with two major enterprises: technical and economic aid from the United States government and developing ties with various governmental agencies that would be of mutual benefit to our two countries. At the same time, I still had to convince some of our own people, from Walter Eytan (director of the Foreign Office) to Golda, that there was no sense in our remaining neutral and that moving toward the West not only befitted our ideas, but was our only hope.

Parallel to great admiration for the United States, there was still a lingering anti-American feeling in Israel at the time. I had clashed with Golda Meir on this subject back in 1948. In fact, we had sharply contrasting views then about America in general. (With all her greatness, which I fully appreciate, Golda does not forget or forgive; and I suspect that I have been 'included out' of many things since then because of our differences at that time.) She, as a socialist, objected to the United States as capitalistic. She was initially opposed to any economic aid from the United States and believed that neutrality between East and West was of primary importance for us. Her attitude toward the capitalist West was shared by others in the Israel Labor Party at the time. They could not divorce themselves from worn-out slogans. In fact, quite a few government officials harbored impractical, idealistic illusions. Walter Eytan strongly believed that Israel could be a mediator between East and West, provided it accepted no favors from either side. Such ideas evaporated quickly, but many leaders, especially those who had grown up on socialist principles, felt that to accept economic aid would involve us in the East-West conflict – on the wrong side, to boot. The question of alignments was still a very controversial issue in Israel, but I had Ben-Gurion's backing for my viewpoint. We could not ask for $75 million in economic aid and be neutral!

When Ben-Gurion had visited Washington, I accompanied him to lunch with his friend Bedell Smith, who was then head of the CIA. They had first met when Bedell was Eisenhower's chief of staff and Ben-Gurion was in Germany trying to get refugees released from Displaced Persons Camps so that they could go to Palestine. Bedell had been most understanding and was the one who gave permission for Hebrew to be taught in the camps. Ben-Gurion had a strong feeling about the nature of the cooperation between America and Israel and wished the relationship to be based on a mutuality of interests.

When Allen Dulles took over from Bedell Smith, I stayed in touch with him during the many years he was director of the CIA and even after his retirement. Allen and I quickly became good friends. We talked about books and American politics and about the memoirs he was writing (my good friend George Weidenfeld became his publisher). There was never a time I came to Washington that I did not see him. I remember going to his house one snowy night in 1960 and asking him to brief President Eisenhower the next morning before he was to receive Ben-Gurion. Often I was invited to his home socially, not just 'on business'. Sometimes I was the only foreigner present.

Over the years I became particularly friendly with Jim Angleton, whose job in the CIA has recently been fully described in the media. He was head of the counter-intelligence section and very close to all the agency's directors. Jim was a man who felt he had a mission in life – to contribute to the safety of the United States and the free world. He felt that Communism constituted a great danger to Western civilization. I have read the accusations concerning his anti-Communist activities within the United States, which were purported to be illegal because they went beyond the charter of the CIA. From my own experience, I cannot imagine Jim doing anything that was not absolutely proper and clearly permitted, although there is no doubt that he would have been willing to take strong measures against an enemy.

Jim is by no means an ordinary person. He is an original thinker and a man of varied interests, including fishing (which he had in common with Bedell Smith) and orchid growing. He is also an amateur goldsmith of quite some accomplishment, is widely read in poetry, has traveled extensively, and has a broad knowledge of the classics, partly because he had spent years in Italy, where his father had been in business and his sister had married a painter. A very tall, lean man with a hawkish face, Jim was always conservatively dressed and was very calm and thorough in everything he did or said. He loved good food, and we spent memorable times together in the better restaurants of Washington and New York. He liked to sit up talking until four or five in the morning and often spoke in riddles that you had to interpret or feel, rather than analyze with cold logic.

I remember his private visit to Israel soon after I had returned home from my tour in Washington. He came to spend a day with me in Ein Gev, and I still treasure the excellent photographs he took then. The best ones are of no-man's land in Jerusalem, and they give you a strong feeling for the sadly divided city. I believe Jim saw in Israel a true ally at a time when belief in a mission had become a rare concept. He found comparatively more faith in Israel, and more determination to act on that faith, than anywhere else in the free world.

While I was stationed in Washington, the State Department exerted strong pressure on us to send units to Korea, according to the U.N. decision on police action there. We did not want to take part in the war, and it would have created internal complications at home. But neither did we want to turn the U.S. government against us, and the Americans were interested in having all U.N. members participate in Korea. Actually, Ben-Gurion wanted to send a token unit to Korea. He attributed great importance to the U.N. decision to stop Soviet expansion, but the Cabinet overruled him, and in this case I agreed with their decision. I also pointed out to the Americans that if we sent even a token unit to Korea, the Communists might put a stop to the emigration of

Jews from Eastern Europe, which – though only a trickle – was most cherished by us.

In the end, these immigrants proved their value to the entire free world. In 1956, three years after Stalin's death, Khrushchev took the opportunity to broaden the de-Stalinization process by revealing some of Stalin's horrors and crimes. Khrushchev made his famous speech at a closed session of the Party Congress, and it was sent secretly to the leaders of the Communist parties in Eastern Europe. During that period Jewish emigration to Israel from Rumania, Czechoslovakia, and Poland had increased considerably, which actually proved very beneficial. The immigrants passed through Europe on their way to Israel, and in the process the text of Khrushchev's speech made its way into the hands of the *New York Times* and was published in full.

Except for the invasions of Hungary and later Czechoslovakia, there probably has been no single event as damaging to the U.S.S.R. and Communism as the publication of that speech. Until then the Russians had presented Stalin as the light of the world. Now it emerged that twenty million people had died in his camps. The revelation had an overwhelming impact, causing, among other things, the uprising in Hungary and Poland a few months later. I am also certain that it played an important part in the ideological development of Communist parties in the West. The Americans scattered leaflets containing the speech all over Eastern Europe. Millions of copies in many languages penetrated the Iron Curtain and shook Communist morale. The Russians have never fully recovered from that blow, and in his book Allen Dulles presents the obtaining of the Khrushchev address as the outstanding scoop of his career.

The other important subject I dealt with in Washington was American foreign aid. At that time, such aid was divided into two parts. One was the so-called Marshall Aid, the billions of dollars that were provided to rebuild Europe. The second was an idea that Truman had proposed in his inauguration speech in 1949, 'Point Four', which was mainly technical aid. We needed budgetary aid in large amounts, but the State Department classified us among the countries to receive technical aid in the form of experts to advise us on how to develop the country. This could have amounted to $3 million or $4 million worth of assistance – important in itself, but no answer to our problem. We were deeply disappointed when the State Department relegated us to Point Four. We badly needed about $70 million annually in substantive economic aid, a tremendous amount of money at that time. The question of which office administered the aid was also an important point. Marshall Aid was allocated from the White House and was administered by Averell Harriman; the Point Four technical assistance was administered by the State Department.

We felt something had to be done to improve our position and secure the best grants, so I brought in Si Kenen, a former journalist who years later registered as a lobbyist for Israel in Washington, to produce an effective information sheet. He developed good contacts in both the House and the Senate. At the same time Barney Balaban, the president of Paramount Pictures, seconded to us Lou Novins, an extremely bright man who was then handling the company's public relations. We felt that with the new talent at our disposal, it might be possible to convince a majority in both Houses to submit legislation for a large aid program for Israel. The assumption was that the White House and President Truman were sympathetic, the State Department was not, and the president would be reluctant to overrule State unless public opinion expressed itself in favor. And the most powerful barometer of public opinion was and is Congress.

Robert Taft, on the Republican side, and Paul Douglas, for the Democrats, sponsored the aid bill for Israel in the Senate. The two House members were McCormick and Martin, the respective leaders of their parties, both from Massachusetts and both old friends of Zionism and good personal friends. All of them shared the deep conviction that the strengthening of Israel was a primary American interest. We contacted most of the congressmen through our friends in their home constituencies. I took pride in the way our campaign was carried out – without the press, through personal contacts, and without strong pressure, just friends speaking to friends. In a few weeks we had succeeded in enlisting a majority in both the House and the Senate for the special aid bill of $150 million for Israel. The final allocation was $65 million as foreign aid, a typical and satisfactory political compromise since our original objective had been $70 million. It was to be administered not through the White House, however, but through the State Department.

While the Zionist movement had maintained good relations with both political parties in the United States, this was the first example of bipartisan support for Israel as a state. Our policy of cultivating goodwill in both parties was followed consistently until Ambassador Rabin's public – and importune – support of President Nixon during an election campaign broke this tradition. It is an unpardonable error for a diplomat to interfere in the internal affairs of the country that hosts him. Israel would surely never benefit from a Democratic-Republican split. I do not think that his behavior was the result of any deeply thought-out policies but rather the action of an innocent (soldier) abroad. Regrettably, the necessary lesson was not learned, and as prime minister Rabin lent some thinly disguised support to President Ford. That this did not do us serious harm is undoubtedly due to the deep attachment of Americans to Israel.

To say that we were hard up in the early 1950s is an understatement.

We didn't have a penny to our name. And though we hadn't had any money in 1948 either, by 1952 our needs had become even more urgent. Israel had opened its doors to a massive immigration, sometimes up to a thousand arrivals a day. The economic aid was slow in coming, and the state was functioning literally from hand to mouth. Yet we knew we could never fail to meet a single government financial obligation, because one missed payment would destroy our credit. The representative of the Israeli Treasury in the United States was Martin Rosenbluth, whom I had known from my days in London. He was a pleasant and civilized man with a keen sense of humor. I remember when several of us sat in his office taking turns at the phone, because by 3 P.M. closing time, Israel had to have, let us say, $200,000 in the bank to meet an obligation. As the deadline loomed, I would call one person after another begging, 'Lend us $100,000 for a week' – or $50,000 for a day or $20,000. Then, the next day, we would borrow from someone else to pay the loan back.

At one time two ships loaded with economic-aid grain were anchored in New York harbor ready to leave for Israel. The grain was legally ours, but since we were in debt the cargoes could be expropriated. So I had to 'sell' the grain to some friends – from whom our creditors could not seize it – and they sent it to Israel under their names. The situation in Israel became so bad that some of our leaders even suggested that the state declare bankruptcy! I was very much against it, but obviously we couldn't go on with our maneuverings indefinitely.

Then Meir Sherman came up with a brilliant suggestion. Our most bothersome short-term indebtedness ran into about $75 million. It sounds like a ridiculously small amount now, but it loomed like Mount Everest at that time. We wanted to convert these short-term debts from a few months into at least five years. We were paying high interest on these debts, much more than on long-term loans, and managing them was nerve-racking. Sherman's idea was to approach banks in the major American cities and arrange for loans to the local UJA chapters, to be repaid by the UJA over the next five years. These loans would be at a reasonable rate of interest and would eliminate the short-term debts. It took a long time to persuade the banks. Their main question was : 'But what if the State of Israel disappears? Where is your security?' The answer was that our security was the Jewish community in the United States, which would never let Israel down.

We finally held a meeting with leaders of the Jewish communities and organizations, and Sherman's idea was accepted. Quite a few major figures in Jewish life became involved. One was Senator Herbert Lehman, an outstanding liberal Democrat who had been governor of New York for ten years. He came from a Jewish banking family but was not a Zionist. His greatest achievement had been as head of the United

Nations Relief and Rehabilitation Administration (UNRRA) after
World War Two, and that was when he became much more conscious of
Jewish affairs. I met him briefly when he returned to the United States
after leaving the UNRRA position. In 1949 I invited him to Israel, and
we traveled on the same boat. But we became close friends only during
my tour at the embassy in Washington, when I often visited him in the
Senate. Having served as head of UNRRA, he later headed the UJA,
which added greatly to its prestige.

In later years an eminent historian wrote a biography of Lehman. I
had lunch with the senator in his New York home shortly after the book
was published, and I remember the argument we had because in that
biography – the story of an American Jew and his political career, from
his support of Al Smith to Roosevelt – Israel was not mentioned once
and American Jewry hardly at all. The historian apparently did not get
the feeling that Jewish affairs meant much to Lehman. It seemed a great
pity, particularly as I knew Lehman's real deep Jewish attachment.

David Dubinsky, the head of the International Ladies' Garment
Workers' Union, was another one of the early supporters of Israel and
Israel Bonds. He had the workers and the union buy our bonds and
established the tradition of union support for Israel. He also helped us
politically through his important connections. Another man who helped
substantially was Sam Leidesdorf, probably the foremost accountant in
the United States at the time. He had befriended Albert Einstein on his
arrival in the United States, had taken care of him, and helped build the
Princeton Institute for Advanced Studies and later the Einstein School
of Medicine. He was also the executor of Einstein's will. Sam's career
began when, as a young man, he gave his guarantee for some deal that
didn't work out. Although he was a man of limited means at the time,
he paid the entire sum, which was considerable, from his own pocket.
By that act he earned himself an honored name in the business world and
the boundless trust of the banks.

I think that the man most helpful in persuading the UJA to agree to
Sherman's idea was Bill Rosenwald. The Rosenwalds, a family with a
long tradition of philanthropy, had started Sears Roebuck. Bill's older
brother, Lessing, headed the anti-Zionist American Council for Judaism,
but Bill and his sister, Adele Levi, were Zionists. Bill was unlimited in
his devotion. He was also what is called a 'character' and an overwhelmingly fastidious man. At that time it was still common to travel long
distances by train. Whenever Bill took a night train, the Pullman
Company was informed in advance, and his linen had to be washed in
soap, not detergents. He used three pillows and always wrapped himself
up carefully for fear of catching cold. But despite all this caution, he
would run anywhere to help us. And, of course, his name was good with
any bank.

Between them, Rosenwald and Leidesdorf persuaded first the banks of New York and then others all over the country to help us. We succeeded in borrowing the desired $75 million and extricated ourselves from the daily morning agony of trying to find the money necessary to repay a debt by evening.

The largest bank in the United States at that time was the Bank of America. By sheer accident, I stumbled into an acquaintanceship with its president. In 1946, when the Anglo-American Inquiry Commission visited Palestine, I came to know one of its leading American members, Bartley Crum, a Republican Catholic lawyer from San Francisco. (He subsequently wrote *The Silken Curtain,* a book that describes how the British Colonial Service prevented outsiders from penetrating behind that curtain into the real situation in Palestine.) When I headed the Haganah mission, I went to San Francisco to visit him and also met his partner, Philip Ehrlich, a Jewish lawyer who represented the Bank of America. About a year later, I was sitting in a boat on the shore of the Sea of Galilee in Tiberias when I saw two men walking along. One was Philip Ehrlich, but I didn't know the other. Even though I was wearing working clothes, I impulsively rushed over to the two well-dressed tourists and – like Stanley's 'Doctor Livingstone, I presume' – greeted them with a hearty 'Mr Ehrlich!' For a moment he did not recognize me, but then we renewed our acquaintance warmly. The man with him just happened to be the head of the Bank of America, and the introduction turned out better than if I had been in striped pants and cutaway. The fishing-boat atmosphere lent color and interest to the occasion. When I returned to the States in 1952, we received substantial loans from the Bank of America for the first time. I like to believe the pleasant informality of our meeting on the lake shore had something to do with it.

That was not the only time chance lent a helping hand. One day in 1950 we were at our lowest. We desperately needed $20 million and we had to have it within about forty-eight hours! The United States government had undertaken to give us this sum, but procedures were slow, and we needed it fast. I was on a plane from New York to Washington when by pure coincidence I noticed that Averell Harriman, then director of the Mutual Security Agency, was in the seat in front of me. I had met Harriman when he had visited Israel a year earlier and once or twice through friends who worked for him, but I was not exactly chummy with him at that time. Still, we needed the money, so I approached him and asked, 'Mr Harriman, may I sit next to you and tell you my troubles?' I told him of the $20 million and why we would perish without it. Not the very next day but soon enough, we got the money. Saved again!

Besides trying to keep the state afloat, I was also interested in helping build our economy at home by availing ourselves of American knowhow.

On one of my trips back home, I ran into Moshe and Ruth Dayan. Ruth had been working for the Jewish Agency organizing women in new-immigrant settlements to make use of their skills in embroidery and the weaving of textiles and carpets. She had sent some samples to stores in the United States with poor results, despite the interesting work. Ruth poured out her troubles to me. So back in Washington I arranged for her to come to the States on a UJA mission and at the same time found her what I believed she needed – the advice of a marketing expert. She came to the States, made public appearances for the first time in her life, and more than earned her expenses. In fact, she was a great success. On the last day she came to Washington and I drove her to Mount Vernon to show her George Washington's house. On the way I asked if she had seen the marketing expert about her carpets? 'No,' she said, 'I just didn't have the time.' I had gone to a great deal of trouble to get her to the States and made that appointment to advance her work, and she had had time for everything else but that! I lost my temper – it is short at best of times – and slapped her on the knee. Ruth burst into tears and didn't speak another word all the way back to Washington.

A year later, the slap forgotten, we met with U.S. aid administrator Bruce McDaniel, who allocated $5,000 for the purchase of wool and other basic materials. The government-owned Maskit company was created, and for the first few years I served as chairman of the board. Ruth made a world-famous success of the Maskit handicraft products – rugs, shawls, scarves, skirts, pottery, and ornaments. Maskit was a particular blessing in the 1950s for the masses of new immigrants pouring in. It provided employment and adapted their skills to modern designs.

After a year and a half in Washington, I felt that my work there had been completed, and I decided to go to Harvard and study economics. I planned to register first for two months in summer school, which anyone can attend, hoping that if I did well I would be accepted to study for a year. Credits were not particularly important to me, and I had no clear plan for the future. I just felt that after all the turns my life had taken, I was entitled to a year of study. Tamar and I rented an apartment in Brookline, Massachusetts, and enrolled Amos in school. But all that came of the plan was a beautiful vacation, one of the very few Tamar and I have ever taken. We drove for two weeks, first south of Washington, then north. I had barely arrived in Boston when Ben-Gurion contacted me. He wanted me to return to Israel immediately to become the director-general of the Prime Minister's Office. I had a long argument with him over the phone. I simply did not want to go back yet, and Tamar was behind me. It took a number of days, but Ben-Gurion finally convinced me that if a head of state makes a request, personal preferences should be set aside. So we returned to Jerusalem.

8 'What Are You Doing Here?'

In the summer of 1952, I became the director-general of the Prime Minister's Office, which in those days was quite different from what it is today. It comprised many departments that had nothing in common except the fact that they were not part of any other ministry. Among them were the Broadcasting Service, the Department of Statistics, the Government Printer, Scientific Civilian Research, the Intelligence Service, the Press Bureau, the Civil Service Commission, and the adviser on Arab Affairs. The Prime Minister's Office also tried to act as a coordinator between other ministries.

Ben-Gurion had little or no interest in some of the departments that had been attached to his office, and some were left entirely to me. Once a year he had to make the budget speech in the Knesset to explain the activities of his office. It was the only speech we would ever write for him. Then he would cross out most of the items and talk only about what interested him: defense, foreign affairs, absorption of immigration, education, scientific development, settling the Negev, World Jewry. He had no interest in the Department of Statistics or the Tourist Department we established later, and he gladly left the radio to others. The Intelligence Service (Mossad) was not under my jurisdiction; its head dealt directly with Ben-Gurion. Only two of the permanent departments I handled really interested Ben-Gurion: the Research Council and the Scientific Translations Project. So I would often approach Ben-Gurion and say, 'I want to do this and that,' and he would say, 'Do it.' He did not ask about details, and he gave me a free hand and backing when necessary. His tremendous prestige enabled us to get a great deal done.

Only a limited number of people were close to Ben-Gurion. Yitzhak Navon came into the office six weeks after I did and became Ben-Gurion's secretary. He had worked closely with Foreign Minister Sharett, who was happy to have his own man in the Prime Minister's Office. But Yitzhak became truly devoted to Ben-Gurion. Nehemya Argov, a founding member of Ein Gev, was the prime minister's military secretary. He was the closest of all to Ben-Gurion. Whatever

Ben-Gurion said, that was that; Nehemya never asked questions. It seemed to me that I argued with Ben-Gurion more than the others, but he generally took it well.

Entering into our relationship was his wife, Paula, a remarkable personality who took a liking to me and even more to Tamar. Paula and I got along, but it was not always easy. I did not like her *'schnorring'* (which in a polite translation means 'soliciting funds'), even though I *'schnorred'* myself, having gradually developed a faculty for that art. Still, it is different when a prime minister's wife does it. She was always fund raising for Pioneer Women and other fine causes, and at times it could be embarrassing. Paula knew about everything – sometimes by remarkable intuition; sometimes because Ben-Gurion told her; sometimes because she ambushed everybody stepping out of Ben-Gurion's study and asked what they had discussed. Sometimes she sat in on Ben-Gurion's talks at home, which took place often. She was a self-appointed peacemaker between Ben-Gurion and Levi Eshkol, Pinhas Lavon, and others, and sometimes she actually succeeded, at least temporarily. She prided herself on having sounder judgment of people than Ben-Gurion, and she certainly had a sharper eye for character.

Ben-Gurion was not always lucky in the selection of his co-workers. Of course, many were not selected by him. They were pushed in by the party, or by the army, or by circumstances. But he was no great judge of people, possibly because he was so much more interested in issues. Sometimes he was attracted to individuals who had little to contribute, and Paula's warnings often proved correct. She never hid her opinions, and she was very blunt, telling people what she thought right to their faces. In the end everybody took it more or less graciously. She would also ask personal questions : 'Why don't you have children ? How much do you pay your maid ? How much did you pay for that dress ? Why didn't you invite so-and-so to your home ?' – and surprisingly often she was given a reply. Paula was honest and neither mean nor particularly self-seeking. She wanted the truth, often for its own sake or for Ben-Gurion's. That made a difference. Even so, she upset people.

Paula also took great physical care of Ben-Gurion. She ruled over his diet, made him take a rest, and did not allow anybody to disturb it. She would insist on knowing in detail why somebody rang late in the evening – whoever it was – and unless she was convinced that the matter was important, she would not wake Ben-Gurion. But despite her strong opinions, she always deferred to him. In fact she was an ideal wife for Ben-Gurion. The fact that Tamar and I got along well with Paula made it easier for me. Ben-Gurion's secretaries ruled his time jealously, and it was not always easy to knock on his office door and just drop in. I could come to their house and talk things over when the office was overcrowded.

Despite the 'guards' at Ben-Gurion's door, the emphasis in the Prime Minister's Office was on informality. Soon after my arrival, I broke the glass top on my desk by banging on it because my new secretary, Shoshana Fiedler, kept calling me Mr Kollek. Thus the use of first names was established. Ben-Gurion himself added to this atmosphere by indulging his instinct to tease people. On different occasions, when it was perfectly obvious why someone had entered his office, Ben-Gurion would look straight at him and say, 'What are you doing here?' (as if to say, 'What are you *really* doing here?'). He did this often, though I don't know why. Perhaps he had been in another world and someone's appearance suddenly brought him back. Those around him got used to it, but other people were often offended : 'What does he mean? He knows who I am and why I'm here! Why does he ask a question like that?'

Sometimes Ben-Gurion would come into my office when I was meeting with people and ask : '*Nu*, did that book arrive?' I would show him what had come in recently, and he would look at them and say, 'What else? And what's new, Teddy? *What are you doing here?*' I would tell him that we are working on improving the landscape, and he would say, 'Really? What are you improving?' I would explain this and that, and he would say, 'Really? Very important! What else do you do?' I would say, 'We have the consultant on Arab affairs coming . . .' and then Ben-Gurion would make a gesture with his hand. He felt it was hopeless to deal with the Arabs in Israel as a separate issue because he tied the problem in with the situation in the Arab countries. He didn't see the Israeli Arab and the rest of the Arabs as separate elements, as many people do. So I would ask, 'Do you want coffee, BG?' And he would answer, 'Why are you so fat?' I would say : 'Because I love to eat. Look, your secretary, Yitzhak, is fat too.' And Ben-Gurion would say, 'That's right, you're both gluttons. You eat too much. One should only eat two meals a day, not three. And why don't you take walks?' I replied, 'I'm busy, I can't take walks.' Then Ben-Gurion would look me straight in the eye and say, 'What are you busy with? What do you do all day? What are all these telephones about? What's going on? *What are you doing here?*' He said it with a kind of humor, sheepishly, a little because he liked to needle, a little because he really wanted to know. But it was in good spirits.

After working at the Prime Minister's Office for a while, I gradually came to realize that we would not be going back to Ein Gev. It wasn't an easy fact to face, neither for Tamar nor for me. I felt really at home in Ein Gev. When we founded the kibbutz, I believed I had arrived at the place where I would spend the rest of my life. Ein Gev was breathtakingly beautiful, and it was a great achievement to settle barren land and make it flower; to start from the beginning and plant every tree, build every house – and to do all this on the frontier, under conditions of danger. This is what we had educated ourselves for, what we had aspired to. At the same time, we were surrounded by the tranquility of nature – the lake and the mountains. Everything combined into a feeling that is difficult to describe, but I felt I belonged to Ein Gev. I remember riding with another member of the kibbutz in the nearby mountains during World War Two and discussing our innermost feelings. It was before El Alamein, when the Germans were advancing in Africa and we expected the Arabs to side with them if they saw any profit in it. The Italians were in Syria, and the fate of our kibbutz was cloudy. We said one to the other : 'Whatever happens, we will not run away. This is our home, and nothing will drive us out. If it's the end, it's the end ; but it's here !' That was the way I felt about Ein Gev.

Leaving Ein Gev was a gradual process. I had taken on various jobs during the war and left the kibbutz for shorter or longer periods, but each time I came back. These periodic absences went on for more than a decade, from 1940 to 1952, but I never once thought there would be a final parting. For most of these periods, Tamar stayed in Ein Gev. She was even more attached to the kibbutz than I. I wasn't particularly interested in working with my hands, but I didn't shirk such work. When it came to carrying sacks of sand, I could compete with anyone. It was the same with sailing a boat. And certainly I was always willing to take my share on guard duty or tasks of a similar nature. But I found no particular satisfaction in working with my hands, while Tamar did. I was also gradually attracted to things that were beyond Ein Gev's horizon. For a long time this attraction expressed itself in reverse : many people who otherwise would probably never have come to Ein Gev did come there to visit me, and it added something to the kibbutz. But I felt I wasn't pulling my weight in Ein Gev. My membership was more in theory than in practice, and a kibbutz is not a club in which you can pay dues or work for a day and be regarded as a full member. I feel that many people who fill fairly important full-time positions in the country and spend their weekends in their kibbutz really play a game. I couldn't do that. Occasionally I would decide to drop everything and stay at Ein Gev. But it never worked out that way. I did what my job required – as I do today.

So I had to make up my mind. It was even more difficult for Tamar to leave than it was for me. For her, leaving meant only joining me ; she wasn't particularly attracted to the life I had chosen. For me it was the job that counted. I had no great ambitions, but I wanted to do what I thought I could do comparatively well. That mattered more to me than my own personal satisfaction or a quiet, pleasant life. After a year or two in the Prime Minister's Office, I knew I wouldn't go back to Ein Gev. The thought of returning to the kibbutz was only a pipe dream.

When I began my job, I had a strong feeling that the government wasn't really in control of things. From the beginning the Israeli administration was just a loose federation of feudal baronies. Matters were brought up at Cabinet meetings and laws were passed by the Knesset (our Parliament), but the management of the ministries and their projects was controlled by the budgetary process that took place in the Ministry of Finance. In the United States, the Budget Office was situated in the White House, and through the budget the president was able to direct policy, while the secretary of the treasury still had extensive influence and plenty to do. I suggested to Ben-Gurion that we adopt that system and transfer the Budget Office to the Prime Minister's Office. He was not quite convinced. Ben-Gurion felt sure that if he made decisions, they would simply be carried out, and he really had no idea of the practical workings of government machinery. Nevertheless, he called a meeting with Finance Minister Levi Eshkol and several others and gave me the opportunity to try and convince them.

I knew, of course, that I had no chance of persuading a Cabinet minister to relinquish control and part of the power of his ministry. But everyone went through the motions, and the results were as might have been expected. The Budget Office stayed in the Ministry of Finance, and the prime ministers of Israel continue to have little real control over anything beyond foreign affairs and defense. They certainly do not determine priorities in social and educational or urban matters.

Some of the areas in which I assisted Ben-Gurion were formerly not part of his office. For instance, contact with world Jewry, in which I was experienced. I helped to formulate an important agreement with the non-Zionist American Jewish Committee and its leader, Jacob Blaustein, whom I knew well. The American Jewish Committee in itself was a small group, but it reflected the feelings of a great number of Jews who were pro-Israel but not Zionists. In meetings with Blaustein, we worked out a formula on the major controversial issue : Israel would not attempt to interfere in internal American Jewish affairs and did not regard the Jews of America as owing national loyalty to the State of Israel. From time to time, accusations had been made that Israeli Cabinet ministers or Jewish Agency officials had attempted to exercise undue influence on American Jewry, and a reconciliation was called for. Getting the full confidence of the widest spectrum of American Jewry was always one of Ben-Gurion's major interests. The Zionist movement felt that not all Jews, but only Zionists, should be partners with Israel. Neither Ben-Gurion nor I agreed. On the other hand, one of the biggest fights Ben-Gurion had about the role of the Diaspora in Israel's affairs was with Rabbi Abba Hillel Silver. Ben-Gurion's position was that the Diaspora could not determine policy for Israel; only those living in Israel could make decisions for the country. He fought hard to establish that policy, and eventually he succeeded.

I dealt with American Jewry on many levels and tried to persuade different Jewish groups to come to Israel to get involved. One of the semi-Jerusalemites whom I very much liked was Nelson Glueck, the head of Hebrew Union College in Cincinnati and a great archaeologist. Glueck had been in Palestine during World War Two where he ran the American School of Archaeology and traveled around the desert in the steps of the Nabateans. He was the first to locate Etzion Gever, King Solomon's port near the present-day port of Eilat. In the early 1950s he conceived the idea of building a school of archaeology in Jerusalem connected with the Hebrew Union College. I suggested that it should be a rabbinical college and that every rabbinical student of the Reform movement should be required to spend a year in Jerusalem before ordainment. I obtained the most beautiful plot in the city, not far from the King David Hotel and overlooking the Jaffa Gate, and the Reform movement employed an outstanding architect, Arthur Rau, to build one of the city's most handsome buildings. The school gradually grew – in fact, it is still in the process of growing – and became a fine institute of archaeology. Eventually the Reform movement decided that every rabbinical student should indeed spend a year in Jerusalem before completing his studies. So both Nelson's dream of the archaeological school and our joint understanding about the Reform rabbis became reality.

In the first few years at the Prime Minister's Office, I also dealt with American and U.N. Technical Aid, which was a familiar subject from my days in Washington. We received aid from both Point Four and the U.N. Technical Assistance Program. Technical assistance programs in many countries did not succeed very well, mainly, I believe, because the donor always decided what the recipient needed and was often wrong. But we knew what we wanted, and we asked for it. The economic aid continued on the same scale every year, according to strict rules. We had to submit budgets and prove our needs. There were controls, but no strings of a political nature were attached. The only restrictions were economic, so that the money would bring the widest benefit.

One of the really exciting ideas that came up during President Eisenhower's administration was the Jordan River irrigation project, which concerned mainly Jordan and Israel, but to some extent Lebanon, too. The premise behind the project was that if the Arava, the lower Jordan Rift Valley on both sides of the Israeli-Jordanian border, were irrigated and people could live there, peace between the two countries would follow. This was an American idea, and the United States was willing to put up the necessary money for the project. They felt it would stabilize and save Jordan and help us.

Eric Johnston, who had been chairman of the U.S. Chamber of Commerce and later chairman of the American Motion Picture Association, was assigned to look into the idea, and with him came a number of water experts. He visited Israel a few times in 1953 and 1954 and then went to Jordan. Negotiations continued for months, with Johnston commuting between Israel and Jordan. There were endless arguments about volume and storage, how much water would evaporate from the Huleh Lake in the northern Galilee, and whether the water conserved would be ours or Jordan's. Every little spring was measured. In the end, the project fell through when Johnston approached Nasser, who categorically vetoed the idea. We were outraged. 'What does Nasser have to do with it?' we asked. 'The Jordan River is not a part of Egypt!' But the Americans could not persuade the Jordanians to proceed without Egyptian approval. As a result, we were eventually given some help in building a central pipeline within Israel to carry water from the north to the Negev, and the Jordanians were given money for irrigating their lands from the Yarmuk to the Dead Sea. But the joint scheme, which should have gradually brought about an easing of the political tensions, never came about.

It was Israel that eventually initiated the termination of the U.S. Technical Assistance. We had developed enough knowledge and expertise of our own, and the kind of experts we still did need could not be provided within the framework of Technical Aid, which paid its people modestly. Another reason for giving up the technical assistance when we did was that many new countries had appeared on the map, especially in Africa, and we felt that the experts and money were needed more urgently there than in Israel. By that time we ourselves were offering expert technical help to developing countries. Our initiative both in ending the aid programs and starting ours was much appreciated by the Americans.

U.S. assistance came to a complete end in 1961, and we gave a big party to express our appreciation. Both the Americans and the U.N. officials commented on the high efficiency with which we used the aid. We directed U.S. aid to agriculture, arid-zone research, hydrological problems, many industrial projects, and teaching business administration. The U.N. aid was allocated to aviation control, among other things, and U.N. assistance – both receiving and giving – continues modestly until today.

Yet formal governmental assistance was only a part of our concern in the economic sphere. We also tried to get money from other sources. I believe it was in 1954 that we approached the Ford Foundation. The president of the foundation was a lawyer in San Francisco, Rowan Gaither, a fine and intelligent person and a close friend of Barney Balaban. I approached Balaban, and together with a colleague of his, Mendel Silberberg, he won the foundation's favorable consideration for our request. Eventually Balaban's assistant, Lou Novins, who had been my co-worker when we organized congressional support for our economic needs, came to Jerusalem and suggested an arrangement by which Israel would receive a few hundred thousand dollars a year. This was initially directed to agricultural research but later came to include social and educational projects. It was Israel's first successful attempt to draw on private non-Jewish sources for research funds.

I have already described my position in the Haganah mission as a kind of 'traffic cop'. In many ways, however, I now functioned as what Israelis call a 'cork', filling in for all kinds of jobs whenever a need arose. It calls for a lot of flexibility – and it can be hard on the nerves at times – but it was never dull. One of my 'cork' jobs was to serve as a sort of national 'host' for visiting personalities. For instance, when Adlai Stevenson came on a short visit after his defeat by Eisenhower in the 1952 presidential elections, I accompanied him on his rounds.

Most of us were very impressed by what we had heard about Stevenson, though he had worried us as a candidate. We never felt he was a decision-maker. The times called for the kind of common sense and strength that Truman had displayed – we were naturally biased toward Truman – yet Stevenson was highly attractive in his articulateness, wit, intelligence, and attitudes. But when he came to Israel, nothing seemed to click. For instance, I accompanied him to the temporary quarters of the Hebrew University (the Givat Ram campus did not exist yet) to see its president, Professor Benjamin Mazar. Through the windows, across the nearby border, we could see Mount Scopus, where the original campus was. We had been cut off from it since the War of Independence. Mazar commented, 'That's where we have our library, our books, our land; and we can't get to them.' Stevenson replied, 'Well, I suppose that is how the Arabs feel when they look over here from their side.'

Ben-Gurion and Stevenson could not seem to develop any rapport. People of all kinds, from all parts of the world, had been greatly impressed upon meeting Ben-Gurion – by his strength, his generosity, the charm with which he mingled biblical, political, and scientific elements in his conversation. Stevenson sat like a man reluctantly listening to a salesman. He asked needling questions that displayed little sympathy with Israel as a whole.

Stevenson was at the end of a tiring world tour that followed a tiring and unsuccessful election campaign, and we tired him a lot more. We took him down to Eilat and, instead of letting him have a swim, dragged him on to the Timna copper mines, where there was absolutely nothing to see. But we were so proud of the first mine in the country, and that we had found copper where Solomon mined it, we couldn't resist. It was a blistering, unbearably hot day. But if Eilat was hot, Stevenson was cold. Communication seemed almost impossible.

At his departure, when I gave him a small gift (an ancient Jewish oil lamp) and we stood talking about its background, he seemed moved and for the first time amicable. Nonetheless, I was more than astonished when I met him in New York a few weeks later. I was in an elevator at the old Savoy Plaza when Stevenson walked in and said, 'What luck! I just heard you arrived and I've been trying to trace you for the past two hours.' We went to his room, and while he was changing for dinner he told me the following story. The day before, he had been to Washington at the invitation of John Foster Dulles, the secretary of state, who asked about the impressions he had brought home from his world trip and then rather abruptly proposed that both political parties cooperate on an anti-Israel policy. Stevenson had vigorously refused, and he wanted us to know what the administration was up to.

I was very surprised by Stevenson's candor, especially because he went on to say that he did not like what he had seen in Israel. Ben-Gurion, perhaps angered by his coldness, had been rather aggressive during their meeting. In general, Stevenson did not like our self-assertiveness. He was a remarkably honest man, but over-sensitive, I think, for successful statesmanship – certainly for politics. Yet with all the differences concerning our affairs, I found him very attractive and likable.

Another example of the scope of my activities was the hand I had in the acquisition of the Dead Sea Scrolls. In 1954 an advertisement in the *Wall Street Journal* offered several Dead Sea Scrolls for sale in New York for $250,000. The first four scrolls had been purchased from an antiquities dealer in Bethlehem on the eve of our independence by Professor Sukenik, Yigael Yadin's father, for a few hundred pounds. The rest were not bought because Sukenik simply did not have the extra few pounds that were needed. Yadin was in the States and succeeded in obtaining a gift of $150,000 from Sam Gottesman, the paper manufacturer. With Sharett's recommendation, I borrowed the additional $100,000 from the Israeli Treasury. I signed a note to Eliezer Kaplan, then minister of finance, stating that I would be responsible for payment of the loan. Then we sent the money to Yadin, and when nothing happened for a while I cabled him: '*Nu?*'

Yadin was having long and difficult negotiations in New York with the bishop of the Assyrian Church, who had brought the scrolls from Jordan. There were many other problems as well. How would the Jordanians react? More important, were the scrolls real? It was a tremendous sum of money to pay for something we were not sure of. Yadin went from one expert to another to help him decide, and all this took time. But finally the scrolls arrived. They were packed in sacks and had been sent through the diplomatic pouch, because their export classification was a tricky question. It seems that there was a question about whether they had been taken out of Jordan legally in the first place – never mind that Jewish scribes had written them in Hebrew in the first century A.D.!

We took the scrolls to the office of Ze'ev Sharef, then secretary of the Cabinet, and they were opened. Sharett and President Yitzhak Ben-Zvi, himself a scholar, came in to watch. It was an auspicious moment. Today these scrolls would be worth many millions of dollars on any market. But more important, they are the Jewish people's most important historic and religious documents and authenticate the articles of faith of the Judaeo-Christian beliefs. They are now beautifully displayed in the Shrine of the Book, a special structure at the Israel Museum that is architecturally one of the most interesting buildings in Jerusalem.

Years later, in a drawer somewhere in the Prime Minister's Office, I came across a piece of scroll the size of a hand. When I showed it to Yadin, he was delighted and relieved. It was a missing piece of the Dead Sea Scrolls, and he had been searching for it for years. Apparently it had dropped off the day we opened the scrolls in Sharef's office. So one mystery was solved, but another point stands open to this day: I suppose that, legally, I still owe the State of Israel $100,000.

My own interest in collecting antiquities predates the purchase of the Dead Sea Scrolls by at least a few years. Since my father had been a collector, I may have been influenced in that direction as far back as my childhood. At any rate, shortly after my return from the United States, I paid a visit to a wealthy collector in Tel Aviv. Eisenhower had just been elected, and I came up with the idea of sending him a Hebrew coin on behalf of the Israeli government. (Bedell Smith had told me that Eisenhower liked to play with something between his fingers.) At the collector's apartment, I discovered a wealth of coins, jars, and ancient glass, and I became interested. He gave me a *shekel* for Eisenhower and a glass cup from the first century for myself. It was then that I started collecting. Later, whenever I went to Cyprus, I bought antiquities for my Tel Aviv friend and for myself. In the beginning I thought of acquiring a small collection, mainly in order to be able to give special people interesting gifts. But I soon became hooked on collecting antiquities, and I am until today.

Although, strictly speaking, it was not one of my duties, I continued to be involved in many of the contacts we had with the United States. In 1955, a year before the Sinai Campaign, for example, the Americans attempted to arrange a personal meeting between Ben-Gurion and Nasser and negotiate peace between Israel and Egypt. At the close of the War of Independence, we had signed Armistice Agreements with the Arab States; now the Americans were hoping for a final peace treaty. This was also after the first Egyptian-Czech arms deal, through which Egypt was receiving alarmingly large shipments of weapons to build up its armed force. The Americans told us that Nasser felt he could now make peace. Having received the Czech arms, he could negotiate as an equal, not as an inferior. CIA representatives in Egypt – high ranking officials – believed him (one of them, Miles Copeland, later published a book describing this episode, *The Real Spy World*, which was not very accurate in its details). So President Eisenhower, John Foster Dulles, and Allen Dulles decided to undertake a major diplomatic initiative and to probe whether there was any basis for the negotiation of a Middle East settlement.

To arrange the Ben-Gurion – Nasser meeting, the president picked Robert B. Anderson, previously secretary of the Navy and deputy secretary of defense and later secretary of the Treasury and Eisenhower's personal candidate for the presidency. This was one of the original shuttle exercises. When Anderson arrived in Israel (ironically, his plane landed at the little-known airfield in Petach Tikvah – 'Gate of Hope'), I looked after him. We had undertaken to keep the Anderson mission secret, and I handled the political side of it.

We secured an apartment for Anderson opposite the prime minister's home in Jerusalem, and he met with Ben-Gurion and Foreign Minister Sharett. I also took part in these meetings, as did the late Ya'akov Herzog, who kept the minutes. Anderson flew back and forth between Egypt, where he met with Nasser, and Israel, to talk with Ben-Gurion. At the president's request, those meetings were kept secret even from the American ambassador. Anderson maintained close contact directly with the White House and John Foster Dulles.

The atmosphere of the meetings in Israel was warm. For Ben-Gurion it was a great opportunity to meet with a man coming directly from Nasser. Anderson was able to give him a first-hand report on the Egyptian leader, his ideas, and his thinking. Ben-Gurion wanted to know everything possible about Nasser, down to how he looked and how he talked. Now he could really evaluate information about Nasser, and he concentrated on it with tremendous single-mindedness. He was seeking a token of sincerity. What Ben-Gurion really wanted was to meet Nasser in direct talks, not through intermediaries. So Anderson went back and forth between Jerusalem and Cairo trying to arrange a meeting.

First Nasser raised objections to the site of the proposed meeting – an American destroyer. When Anderson reported that Ben-Gurion agreed to come to Cairo, Nasser made other demands. When these were met, he frankly told Anderson that he was scared. He believed he could make peace with Ben-Gurion in one meeting, but the next day he would be assassinated. The negotiations never proceeded to the point of Nasser agreeing to a meeting. It was Ben-Gurion who said he'd meet Nasser any place. Nasser kept raising the ante and eventually drew a map as a possible basis for negotiations. His demarcation line was a few miles south of Beersheba, tens of miles inside Israel and far to the north of the old international boundary.

The Anderson mission had great influence on Ben-Gurion's decision to join the French and the British in the Suez action and launching the Sinai Campaign. By 1956 he saw that Nasser had no intention whatsoever of making peace. The campaign opened at the end of October 1956. It was a well-guarded secret, and even I was not told about it beforehand. But I was in good company within Israel and abroad. The Americans were likewise kept completely in the dark. When it was all over, I argued about this approach with Ben-Gurion. I realized immediately the effect the news must have had on the American administration and felt it was a colossal blunder not to have notified the Americans at least a short time before the action. I could imagine Eisenhower's anger, hearing about it suddenly as he stepped out of his plane in some small city during the election campaign. And from a practical, military point of view, closing the Americans out worked to Israel's disadvantage. 'If the Americans had been told even an hour beforehand and not felt slapped in the face by their friends and allies,' I argued, 'two or three days might have been gained in the field before we were stopped, and maybe Nasser would have fallen.' At that time our primary objective was to overthrow Nasser, and if the Americans had understood that – instead of being insulted – the history of our region might have changed and for the better.

I was, of course, also annoyed about not having been told myself. I was sure I would have prevailed on Ben-Gurion to inform the Americans, and I almost resigned my position over this incident. After the campaign, the argument about closer cooperation with the Americans continued, not so much with Ben-Gurion as with Golda. I later learned that the reasoning presented to Ben-Gurion about keeping the Suez plan from me was that I wouldn't keep it secret! I still believe that in the long run we could have improved relations with an immeasurably important ally.

Immediately after the Sinai Campaign – and after Ben-Gurion prevailed on me to stay in office – I was sent to the United States to explain our position to the Americans. I called on John Foster Dulles at the State Department and put forward our reasons for launching the campaign. Apparently I was overtired, because I remember that after giving him my account I briefly fell asleep right there in his office. (This was before I started taking an occasional energy pill.) In any case, Dulles' attitude toward Israel was more understanding than that toward his formal allies, the British and the French, but I cannot claim that I fell asleep because the atmosphere in the room was warm and cozy.

While I was in Washington, I also held talks regarding the radio transmitter in Cairo, which the Americans regarded as also instrumental in disseminating unsettling propaganda throughout the Middle East. The Cairo transmitter was the most powerful in the Middle East, and I proposed the possibility of installing comparable transmitters in Israel dedicated to Arab broadcasting. I had always been impressed by the competence of the BBC. Unlike almost any other organ of information, the BBC both during and after World War Two had achieved a reputation for credibility beyond any other broadcasting service.

Our equipment for Arab broadcasts was skimpy – a miserable little transmitter that functioned less than an hour a day. During the Sinai Campaign, Ezra Danin was called from his farm to take over Arab broadcasting. Ezra faced terrific odds. The Arab world was far ahead of us because, with nearly ninety percent of its population illiterate, the only way the people could be reached was by ear. The transistor radio had created a social revolution, and the Egyptians were exploiting it to maximum effect. They broadcast at all hours on many channels, and with powerful equipment threatened to jam our little transmitter. Ezra needed a new, expensive, powerful transmitter to compete with their broadcasts and achieve some balance over the air. The money was not available.

The response to my suggestion was to give us both the money and the equipment, and we increased our broadcast scope enormously. Ezra did not use this new power in the hysterical and misleading ways practiced by the Arabs. The real point about this American contribution was that they believed we had something to offer each other. It wasn't a one-sided bargain.

With the installation of the new equipment, our Arabic broadcasting became very important. The staff increased from six to 120, and the broadcasting time increased to eight hours a day. The new transmitter, of course, meant that Israel was heard in a much wider area and more clearly than before. The station became influential in Arab countries; of that we had overwhelming evidence. Yehuda Tajer, an Israeli who had been in an Iraqi prison for ten years, was released soon after the new transmitter went into operation. His companions in jail had been political prisoners from various periods – a few of Nuri Said's ministers, some communists, and so on. Tajer told us how they listened, together with the wardens, to every word of the Israeli broadcasts and how we, unlike the Arab stations, were regarded as reliable.

We arranged for a listeners' survey in Lebanon, and the report exceeded our most optimistic expectations. Another test came in summertime, when many middle-class Arabs went to Europe on vacation. From there they could send us letters they wouldn't dare mail from their native countries, and we received thousands of notes expressing their appreciation and asking for some particular program.

The radio served many good purposes. We kept pounding away at basic political truths, citing events our listeners had experienced to demonstrate how force begets force and terror propagates terror – and neither brings peace. We also played games, for instance, by correcting Nasser's Arabic – his grammar, syntax, and choice of words. It seems that we got through to him, because he tried to avoid similar mistakes on later occasions. More important, we played back our recordings of earlier speeches by Arab leaders and pointed out the inconsistencies with more recent statements. There is no way of measuring it, but our 'games' must have cut deeply into Arab morale.

We also added to our credibility by inserting minor facts reported from Egypt by a foreign visitor, or by chance. Perhaps there was a fire in a village or an accident on a train – an incident unreported on the Egyptian radio because it was trivial or against policy. We broadcast every tiny item, like gossip in a small-town paper. The local listeners were impressed. 'It's true! I saw it! It happened to my brother-in-law! But our radio said nothing about it. How do the Israelis know?' We developed a substantial audience, and a sense of Israeli power was created. Whatever we said, important or not, had credibility. Directly or indirectly, our broadcasts influenced Arab policy. Certainly they proved to Nasser that we commanded the attention of our neighbors.

After the Sinai Campaign, I also pushed for the legislation to create a public broadcasting authority. I wanted radio (there was no TV yet) to be taken out of the Prime Minister's Office, where it received haphazard treatment, and be administered by a public body. In a sense, I was responsible for broadcasting, but only on rare occasions was there reason to intervene – and then only in connection with foreign affairs. Occasionally, I would suggest to the director of broadcasting how to handle a matter, or Yitzhak Navon would tell him what to broadcast and what not. Ben-Gurion scarcely ever intervened, despite what some people believed. In fact, I remember only three occasions when he did.

Once the radio announced that Ben-Gurion was intending to make a trip to Canada, although according to our agreement with the Canadian government, the announcement was to be made just before departure – at most. Ben-Gurion decided to phone through to Kol Yisrael (the Voice of Israel) personally. Paula placed the call for him, and when he took the receiver the broadcasting staff did not believe that it was really the prime minister. They thought someone was pulling their leg. 'You're Ben-Gurion?' they replied, 'I'm Ben-Gurion, too!' Finally he contacted Yitzhak Navon, who prevented repetition of the announcement.

The second occasion was when the radio management introduced a combination of a news bulletin and columnist's interpretation. 'I want to hear straight news. Let them give the interpretation separately and at another time,' Ben-Gurion complained. He definitely wanted that stopped, whereupon the press rose against him ('Dictatorship!' they cried) and, of course, the matter was raised in the Knesset. But Ben-

Gurion kept repeating, 'I just want to hear the news.' I arranged a radio and news media working meeting with the prime minister, and we sat down and discussed the conflict calmly. By then the public had expressed so much criticism of the combination news-and-interpretation bulletins that even the broadcasters agreed it should be discontinued.

The third time Ben-Gurion issued orders to the radio was when a political commentator insulted de Gaulle personally on the air. Kol Yisrael was still a government division in the Prime Minister's Office, and Ben-Gurion issued instructions that as long as he, as prime minister, was responsible, insults to foreign governments – even when they represented the personal views of a commentator – would not be permitted. I don't recall his ever protesting or taking action when our own government was criticized. In fact, he didn't even show much interest. Some of us did resent it when the radio mocked Ben-Gurion too crudely, but we kept our resentment to ourselves.

Aside from these three incidents, all other orders to the radio came from me or from Yitzhak. But I was convinced that the radio had to be an independent unit, like the BBC. As a government department, it would eventually lose its credibility. After much discussion, Ben-Gurion finally accepted the idea. He submitted to the Knesset a law making the radio a public authority, and it was passed in 1962.

In addition to broadcasting to the Arabs beyond our borders, we also had to give our attention to the problems of our own Arab citizens. For that purpose, there was an Arab Department in the Prime Minister's Office. Some of the good things we did for Arab villages made their inhabitants more dependent upon us. We accustomed them to a different standard of living, and they were no longer quite so much a part of the old Arab world beyond the frontier.

But there were still important questions outstanding. One of them we tackled at the time was compensation. Some Arabs had returned to their homes in Israel a few weeks or months after the 1948 war, and years later they still had not received their papers. In addition, there were many who had papers, but their land had meanwhile been settled by Jews, and they were entitled to other property or compensation. We finally put through legislation to compensate the Arabs living in Israel and settle large numbers of claims. This was done partly with the help of Finance Minister Eshkol, who had a close feeling for Arab farmers as one farmer to another. The trouble was that the compensation paid out was not always generous enough. It was fixed by what is now the Israel Government Land Authority, and they saved the state a few million pounds. But the sum cannot be measured against the ill will the Lands Authority created. It has never been quite forgotten, even though the years since the establishment of the state have brought tremendous prosperity to the Arab population in Israel.

Alongside the claims of our own citizens was the ever-present shadow of the Arab refugee problem. In 1955 Ezra Danin and I became involved in another attempt to solve it. This time we negotiated secretly with Arab parties about settling the refugees in Arab countries. First proposed in discussions that Josh Palmon held in Europe, the idea was to create a series of housing and construction projects in underdeveloped areas where, aside from local workers, refugees would be hired on a large scale. Thus the refugees would be released from the debilitating idleness of the camps and would become productive again – an asset to themselves and to the host country.

We had a rather elaborate plan that seemed practical for an Arab country in North Africa, where many villages had been deserted by European colonists after World War Two. These villages had once been productive and could be made productive again. Our plan, which had to be kept secret for fear of provoking hostile Arab reaction ahead of time, was to allocate a sum that would roughly total the monetary value of the claims held against Israel by the refugees. With this money, we would buy land in and around the empty villages, using a Swiss insurance company as a front, and provide conditions that would make that land acceptable to the refugees as compensation for their claims. The conditions would include using Lebanese and other construction companies in the rehabilitation of the villages and the farm areas.

This time the government was behind us. Golda Meir, then foreign minister, was particularly in favor. She accompanied Ezra Danin to see Finance Minister Eshkol in early 1956, and Ezra asked for advance money. Eshkol answered, 'Why make it hard for me? Don't press me now. You have my word that the money will be there when you need it.' Ezra went to Europe for the legal transfer of the first parcel of land to our Swiss corporation. He left Israel on a Thursday, and on Friday an Israeli newspaper announced that Ezra Danin and Josh Palmon were about to complete a large land transaction in an Arab country. The item was immediately picked up by the *New York Times*. It exploded our elaborate plan to avoid hostile Arab publicity by buying the land secretly, and the whole project collapsed.

The news had somehow reached the ears of an Israeli reporter. When we later asked him how he could have destroyed the whole project in this way, he said, 'With a scoop like that, you wanted us to keep quiet?' (We all value the freedom of the press, but sometimes I feel there should be some intelligent defense mechanism to protect the public interest.) Anyway, several years later the land we were going to acquire for pennies was worth billions of dollars : oil was found on it. One Arab still writes us from Europe to repeat how wretched we had made him feel by not completing that deal.

In the late 1950s, I was for a long time on the wrong side of the fence and supported the continuation of a military government in Arab villages. There were two considerations behind the military government. One was security; the other was that through the military government Arab votes were secured. The second argument gradually disappeared as the country matured. But I still favored military government for security reasons. There were many restrictions that seemed necessary. For example, Arabs were not allowed to move around freely in the frontier districts, and for a time I felt this was right. Isser Har'el, the head of the Mossad, was an outspoken proponent of this viewpoint. And in this case, not only Ben-Gurion, but many others were influenced by it, myself included.

The opponents of military government in the Arab sector were numerous and vigorous, and once there was a very narrow contest in the Knesset. Most of the parties were against Mapai (the leading Labor party) on this issue not because they wanted to help Arabs or because they felt that the security measures were unnecessary, but because they wanted to deny Mapai the possible extra votes. Only through an alliance with the ultra-Orthodox Agudat Yisrael Party did Mapai carry the vote to continue the military-government regulations.

In the end, the political price Mapai had to pay in various concessions to small coalition partners – which became a habit in the Israeli system – was too high to maintain the existence of the military government. We knew that in the near future we would probably not be able to carry a majority. Moreover, within the Mapai Party itself, quite a number of people asked themselves whether it was really necessary. Finally we came to the conclusion that it was not. So the military government was abolished with no ill effects to security. It could have been done years earlier.

For the first thirteen years of statehood, the emphasis all around was on pushing forward: growing, building, developing, and trying to clear away any of the problems that might block our way. Then, in 1961, there was a sudden, jolting intermission in this thrust as the whole nation paused to remember. That was the year we brought Adolf Eichmann to trial.

Much has been written about the motivations that caused Israel to hold this trial. Eichmann had been in hiding in Argentina under a false identity until Israeli agents, directed by Isser Har'el, caught him, smuggled him out of the country, and brought him to Israel to stand trial. Over the years, whenever we received reports that Eichmann had been spotted, there were long arguments in the government about whether or not he should be brought to trial. Ben-Gurion's reasons for wanting a trial were historical – in a sense, I would say, educational. Unlike the Nuremberg trials, this one would not be carried out while the impressions of war were still very sharp. Through it, Ben-Gurion wanted to impress upon the world what had happened to European Jewry. He was particularly interested in reaching the younger generation of Jews, who had not known Hitler, and Jews from the Arab countries, who had not experienced what had happened closely.

When Eichmann was finally caught, the technical arrangements for the trial were delegated to the Prime Minister's Office. Together with the police and the Ministry of Justice, I was made responsible for these arrangements. I vetoed all suggestions of building temporary huts or structures specially for the trial and instead pressed for the completion of a building that had been under construction for a long time. Here was a chance, as a by-product of this sad business, to complete a cultural center that the city of Jerusalem had begun years earlier but did not have the money to finish. There were other problems. For the first time we expected hundreds of foreign journalists and had to arrange for facilities. As the Press Office was part of the Prime Minister's Office, this also became my responsibility. During the weeks preceding the trial, while Attorney General Gideon Hausner prepared the case, I often went to the building to watch the preparations of everything from the prison cell to the public galleries and the press facilities. During the trial itself, there was tremendous pressure for tickets. Many people came specially from abroad to attend the trial, and not just journalists.

I only went to the trial once. I was torn by my feelings about that event. I fully agreed with the purpose of the trial, but I kept away. I just couldn't bear it. It was too terrible. I couldn't bear listening to the stories and the outflow of emotions. That's just not my style, although I do have the same reactions any other Jew had to the horrors of the Holocaust. The importance of the trial was that it concentrated the story on an individual. The public could not grasp the murder of six million people, even if the number was divided into camps: Treblinka, Auschwitz, Dachau, and so on. The story that had made the strongest impression up to that time was *The Diary of Anne Frank*, although there was comparatively little visible cruelty in it. But that story was personal. You could envision the individuals, you identified with them; they were you. And here, by seeing one criminal, by watching the surviving victims of his crimes facing him in the dock, the story had a better chance of reaching young Jews in Israel, Jews in the Diaspora, and the world as a whole. I agreed that remembering was of inestimable importance. And those goals were indeed achieved – for a time.

Eichmann's trial was important also because it showed that an insignificant individual – who could well have ended up as a petty clerk – could have done all that damage to humanity. But the effect of the trial cannot be maintained all the time. I go to the Yad Vashem memorial center every two or three years, and each time I am shaken all over again, for every one of us forgets. In a sense, I believe that the most significant event in our modern history was not the creation of the State of Israel, but the extermination of six million Jews. One is a positive event and the other negative. But if it's possible to compare the two at all, the latter – a terrible tragedy for our people – probably had the most profound influence on the course of our history. Still, you can't hate historical events, and there is no use in hating individuals. I had no strong feelings about Eichmann as a person. On principle I don't hate anybody. I can get extremely angry or frustrated, but I've never felt hatred – even toward anti-Semites. During World War Two, my rage was more against our own impotence than against the Nazis. We just couldn't stop them.

Over the past decade, and even earlier, I had been invited to Germany for meetings of mayors and conferences of all kinds – often as a guest speaker – and I always declined. But when the Catholic Academy of Bavaria invited me to Munich in March 1975 to receive an honorary award, I saw in this a recognition of the unification of Jerusalem by an important Catholic body. That was important enough a reason for me to go. Then I was invited to Berlin in November 1976 to open a Jerusalem exhibition there. At the same time, a library in the city was named Jerusalem library. Jerusalem had been a divided city, Berlin still was, and on various occasions the city of Berlin had shown outstanding solidarity with us. For instance, on the second day of the Yom Kippur War, the lord mayor of Berlin, Klaus Schutz, phoned me from a mass meeting that had been called specially to express support for Israel in its hour of difficulty.

I was in Berlin for a day and a half. Among other things I visited the Jewish community center. It was built on the site of a synagogue that had been destroyed by the Nazis. In order to walk in you have to pass through a few stone arches, remnants of the old building, and outside the building there is a wall with the names of all the camps on it, similar to the floor in Yad Vashem. A ceremony was held there, with the mayor of Berlin and many guests, Gentile and Jewish, in attendance and many wreaths of flowers. I made a brief speech saying that we must never forget, but I felt oddly detached and unemotional about the whole affair. Later I went to visit the Berlin Wall, which made a strong and depressing impression on me. I also went to a few social functions and received a great deal of attention everywhere. After all, I had come from Jerusalem, where the dividing wall had fallen and the city had been united again. With all the differences, the similarity was obvious. Jerusalem gave the Berliners hope.

The next morning, before driving to the airport, I visited a local Jewish kindergarten. It was a very well-maintained, pleasant place, with about 120 children. I spent some time there talking to them, and then it suddenly struck me that it was children just like these, a million of them,

who were killed by Hitler's Germany. I suddenly couldn't bear it. All I
wanted to do was get away. But the fact is that none of us can run away
from our own history. The Holocaust will remain a part of every one of
us for as long as we live.

9 A Bit of Everything

I suppose everyone can divide his daily rounds into two categories: duties and loves. Tourism was one of my loves. From the start, I believed it had even greater importance and potential for Israel than for other countries. It could be much more than a dollar earner for us. Tourism could explain Israel to the world better than any public relations firm and could win friends for us far beyond any propaganda. Every tourist becomes an emissary from Israel to his own country. He relates his first-hand impressions to everyone he meets, and his report will not be doubted.

From the very start of my public work, way back in the youth movement, through my present office as mayor of Jerusalem, I have always regarded myself first and foremost as an emissary of the Zionist cause. I believe it is of utmost importance to explain Zionism to the world, and it comes naturally to me. If I had had the power to make changes in government offices, I would have concentrated all the bodies dealing with public relations, explanatory functions, media, and tourism in the Prime Minister's Office. They are fundamental and should be directed and coordinated by the man in charge of Israel's policy.

Tourism in Israel, however, was in very inept hands in those days. It was an obscure part of the Ministry of Commerce and Industry, which was run by a kind old gentleman, Dr Peretz Bernstein, and his party, the General Zionists. The department was tiny and was housed in an ugly little slum building. The simple fact of the matter was that tourists were not coming; and over the years, quite a number of people from all parties had asked me to take an interest in the subject.

During the period when there was a feud between the General Zionists and Moshe Sharett (then prime minister), and the General Zionists were consequently out of the government for a while, I persuaded Sharett to transfer tourism to the Prime Minister's Office. I started to take charge of the department, and then I had a brilliant idea: to create a special department of the Tourist Office for the restoration of historical sites and the development of the landscape. I offered that department to Yaacov Yanai ('Yan'), an exceptionally able man who had been chief signal officer during the War of Independence. After the war he had gone to the States for a short time to study, and upon his return he entered the automobile business together with Joe Boxenbaum, who had meanwhile immigrated to Israel.

Yan was not really interested in business, however. His real ambition was to become director-general of the Ministry of Posts in order to deal with communications. In the meanwhile, he and Joe had parted company, and I asked him to join me in the effort to develop tourism instead. He finally took over responsibility for restoring ancient sites and has been doing so ever since, very thoroughly and with first-class results. Yan started early in 1956 by restoring Beit She'arim, a large Jewish necropolis not far from Nazareth. Since then he has restored about thirty historical sites and parks, the most important undoubtedly Masada, where, together with Yigael Yadin, he developed a method of preserving excavations while the dig was still in progress.

Yan's work has been invaluable, but that alone did not solve our problem. In 1956, for example, we were expecting 45,000 tourists – and then came the Sinai Campaign. The United States immediately put a ban on travel to the Middle East, and tourism dropped absolutely – almost to zero. The King David Hotel in Jerusalem closed, and the Accadia in Herzliya was practically shut down. In fact, all the hotels faced bankruptcy, and the American tourist blockade continued relentlessly. I became deeply involved in the tourism crisis, and we began to move in various directions. First we persuaded Hadassah to schedule its annual convention in Israel and fight the State Department for permission. They succeeded, and it was the first convention ever to be held in Israel, but it has been followed by many others. Israel – and particularly Jerusalem – has actually become a popular convention center.

At the same time, we initiated a wide variety of activities for tourists. But we still needed something extraordinary to put Israel on the tourism map. It was not only the hotels that were down. The mood of the whole country was low, despite the military victory in Sinai. Immigrants who had been moved out of temporary tent camps and settled in permanent housing did not like their apartments, their streets, their neighbors. There was a general economic slowdown. Something grandiose was desperately called for, and I found what we needed in the coming Tenth Anniversary of Israel as a state. The date was no secret, of course. But at the time many people both inside Israel and abroad still regarded the fate of the state as uncertain. People knew little about Israel, and this included both many people at home – who were not really sensitive to the tremendous achievements of the first ten years – and people abroad – who were mostly in the dark about the real character of the country. We felt that, properly planned, the Tenth Anniversary celebrations could remedy this. I aimed at creating a celebration by Jews all over the world to be centered in Israel. It would also be a means to increase tourism considerably. The Prime Minister's Office was charged with the responsibility for organizing the events.

Meyer Weisgal agreed to become chairman, and I was the executive director of the whole affair, while 'Memi' de Shalit took responsibility for activities abroad. We opened an office in Tel Aviv, and I sometimes spent three or four days a week there in connection with preparations for the celebrations. During this period, I spent a good deal of time with the Dayans and the Yanais, who were neighbors and used to go to the movies together on Saturday nights. I often joined them, and that was actually the only period in my life that I saw films.

We had a year and a half to prepare for the great event. It was hardly time enough, so we made maximum use of each day. The main point of the festivities was to show the world we were here to stay. Senator Herbert Lehman became the international chairman, and Tenth Anniversary committees were established on every continent, wherever there were Jews. These committees, in towns large and small, industrial or agricultural, commercial or academic, sparkled with great names.

In Israel streets were cleaned, cities were spruced up, the achievements of the first ten years were retold in schools, and a major exhibition of achievements in all spheres – from agriculture to industry, health to education and culture – was mounted in Jerusalem's National Convention Center. We introduced Israel's first gold and bronze commemorative coin and it caught on; in fact, it sold out. (Since then, Israel has issued many other handsome coins and medals, administered by a state-owned company that I initiated and that is financially solid and unfailingly profitable.) We used fireworks, for the first time, with imagination and drama. We also built movable outdoor stages all over the country and invited performers from all over the world. And as a special extra, Israeli wine was sold on the streets at giveaway prices.

Some of the best ideas were Meyer's. While he did not deal with details, he was bubbling with enthusiasm and energy. It was Meyer who obtained from the government the budget we needed to execute our plans. He persuaded the ministers that the money was well invested, as in truth it turned out to be. Almost everyone in the world knows Meyer. He is the Weizmann Institute's founder, president, and everything else. He started building the institute very soon after Weizmann's death. Before that he was a journalist, an impresario who worked with Max Reinhart, and a well-known Zionist leader. Meyer is a man with absolutely relentless good humor and more drive and more friends in the world of art and literature than anybody else I know. He is also the world's greatest 'schnorrer', and I learned a great deal from him.

The greatest success of the celebrations was the result of an idea

brought to me by Ora Herzog (Chaim's wife). She thought a competition held like a spelling bee but testing one's knowledge of the Bible
might be interesting. It sounded good but somewhat limited. Then we
realized the stunning possibilities it had. We opened the contest to the
world and invited the finalists to meet in Israel for the championship
match. The idea caught on like wildfire, and what a marvelous finish!
The final round took place in the Hebrew University open-air theater in
Jerusalem, and Ben-Gurion and Ben-Zvi were all but doubled up with
laughter at some of the answers given.

I remember that Ben-Gurion enjoyed the occasion tremendously, but
afterward something annoyed him. It was damp in the stadium, and at
the end of the program *Hatikvah*, our national anthem, was played.
Apparently because of the dampness, the strings were a little off tune,
and the national anthem sounded different. Ben-Gurion said furiously,
'What are they doing to *Hatikvah*? Why are they changing *Hatikvah*?'
He had no ear for music, but *Hatikvah* he knew!

At any rate, the winner of the contest was an Israeli, Amos Haham, a
phenomenal scholar and so poor that he didn't even have running water
in his home. He was also a cripple who stammered, and that, of course,
made him even more of a hero. He moved our little nation to tears.
Amos Haham's poverty was alleviated. In addition, his victory – or perhaps the contest itself – led to the establishment of a Bible circle in
Ben-Gurion's home, and suddenly Bible circles were cropping up all over
the country and all over the world. The real payoff of the celebrations,
however, was that well over a hundred thousand tourists came in 1958.

The day following Independence Day, I called everybody in and told
them that the Tenth Anniversary office was closing down within two
weeks. And so it did, including selling – at a profit – the office space we
had bought and submitting detailed accounts. I cannot remember any
other occasion in Israel when an organization voluntarily disbanded!

The most famous 'tourist' of all during the period I served in the
Prime Minister's Office was one we least expected. Suddenly at the end
of 1963, Israel had to prepare for the pilgrimage of the new Pope,
Paul vi. The announcement came as a surprise, but we later found out
that two priests had come, wandered around the Holy Land, and, without talking to either the Israeli or Jordanian governments, returned to
Rome and reported to the Pope. The Vatican promptly and simply
announced the pilgrimage for January 1964. It also came as a surprise to
all the Catholic Church dignitaries, both in Israel and abroad. Levi
Eshkol, who was prime minister by then, placed responsibility for all
arrangements in my hands.

We were hardly given any time, so after we looked at the itinerary,
the preparations were sometimes close to frantic. For instance, we
hastily built a road up the hill to Mount Zion, in Jerusalem, so that a

visit to the Coenaculum (the room of the Last Supper) would be possible. Many details had to be attended to : telephone and telegraph lines, radio circuits, facilities for reporters from all over the world (our experience with large numbers of reporters at the Eichmann trial helped).

We were particularly concerned about security. The Vatican planned to ship its own automobiles to Amman, where the Pope and his entourage would be picked up and driven across the Jordanian-Israeli border. Our government officials would meet the Pope's party in the morning at Megiddo (the site traditionally associated with Armageddon) near the usually sealed frontier. From there the route would be Nazareth, the Sea of Galilee, Jerusalem, Mount Zion and the Coenaculum, and return to Amman. Our security people were worried about the cars. What if somebody in Jordan put a bomb into a car carrying some cardinals, or even the Pope, and it went off on our territory? In the uncertain atmosphere of those days, that would be all we needed to add a Christian crusade to the already existing Arab *jihad*!

To settle the question, I went to Rome with Yosef Nahmias, the inspector general of police, and Nahmias met with the Vatican representatives. In reply to his question on security arrangements, they said, 'We have no security, except for the Swiss Guards at Vatican City. For the purposes of this trip, we have handed security over to the Italians.' The Italians said, 'Why don't you go to Amman and check the cars?' They had no conception of the situation or how to handle it. There was nowhere else to go. Security did not seem to concern the Italian Foreign Ministry, so we offered to supply our own cars for the Pope and his entourage at the border. Under no circumstances would the Vatican agree. We obviously offered to buy the best cars – same size, same make, same color – but the Vatican stood fast. Fortunately all went well, and there were no incidents involving the cars – or anything else – during the visit.

While the Pope was en route from Rome to Amman and my colleagues and I were frantically making the necessary final arrangements, the ideologists of Israel were raising questions. Should the Pope be officially received? In fact, since the Vatican had not recognized Israel, and the Pope had not requested an entry permit, should we let him in at all? Chief Rabbi Nissim decided that if the Pope was going to call on the Patriarchs in East Jerusalem, he should call on Rabbi Nissim as well. The chief rabbi categorically refused to go to Megiddo to greet the Pontiff. In the end, however, it was concluded that by the very act of his visit, the Pope did recognize Israel. 'Do we want to advertise to the world that he does not recognize us?' we all asked ourselves. So the president and members of the Cabinet went to Megiddo to welcome His Holiness.

At the entrance to Jerusalem, the Pope was greeted with the traditional presentation of bread and salt. Chief Rabbi Nissim did not show up. As a matter of fact, there was such a long list of people who wanted to shake hands with the Pope that I, too, could quietly absent myself. That made it easier for me to refuse others the opportunity – which was obviously necessary. President Shazar came to see the Pope off at the Mandelbaum Gate before he crossed back into Jordan. Later the Pope sent the president a set of beautiful silver candelabra. When it was all over, I was annoyed by the farewell message the Pope sent the president of Israel from his return flight. It was addressed not to Jerusalem, the capital, but to Tel Aviv – in a sense, a gesture of non-recognition of our capital.

Every aspect of the Pope's visit was quite atypical of the way we hosted most of our more famous guests. As a rule, our hospitality tended to be far less formal. Starting in the late 1950s, and particularly after the Tenth Anniversary, Israel began to draw famous entertainers from abroad, mostly from the United States. Danny Kaye came to Israel on a UNICEF mission and gave a concert at Ein Gev, where we met for the first time. Since then he has become deeply involved with Israel. During times of war – unfortunately too often – Danny comes to visit wounded soldiers in the hospitals and entertains them in his own inimitable fashion.

On his first visit, I took Danny to see Ben-Gurion in his office. Danny dressed well for the occasion, while Ben-Gurion, as usual, wore a short-sleeved shirt – no jacket and no tie. He immediately asked Danny, 'Where are you going? What are you going to see?' Danny replied, 'Tel Aviv, Jerusalem, Haifa . . .' 'Tel Aviv, Haifa?' Ben-Gurion broke in, as if that were so unusual. 'That's not Israel! Israel is the desert. You must go to the Negev.' So we took Danny to the south, and on the way back from Eilat we stopped to visit Ben-Gurion at his kibbutz, Sdeh Boker. All of us were dirty and covered with dust from the trip, but Ben-Gurion was well dressed. He looked at Danny and said, 'That's the way you come dressed?'

Danny was one of the few people who managed to penetrate through to Ben-Gurion with humor. Perhaps Ben-Gurion thought he was a little crazy, but Danny amused him. I remember Danny's first meeting with Paula. She immediately asked him, 'Are you married?'

'Yes.'

'Are you married to a Jewish girl?'

'Yes.'

'But you, are you Jewish?'

'Of course, I'm Jewish! What are you talking about?'

'You don't look Jewish,' she said.

Danny says this is the first version he ever heard of the famous story where a lady in a train says to a young man : 'Are you a Jewish boy?' He says : 'No Ma'am, I'm really not.' She says : 'Don't be ashamed, you're Jewish.' Finally he says : 'Fine, all right, okay, I'm Jewish.' Then she says : 'You don't look it.'

Though Danny and I are bound by our devotion to Israel, there is another, almost as close, bond between us : our interest in food. Danny, as is well known, is not only a great musician and entertainer, but also a fantastic cook. For years he specialized in Chinese cuisine. Whenever I was in Los Angeles, I visited his home in Ysidiro Drive and would sit in the garden enjoying his wit and watching him cook his specialties. (He later widened his interests to French and Italian cooking.) On various occasions he also took me out to good restaurants. Danny complained that I always fell asleep between courses; I was too tired to talk, but *never* too tired to wake up and eat. Once he took me to a little vegetarian place in New York and explained at length that it was strictly vegetarian and, as it was located in the Garment District, it was frequented by many Jews who ate only kosher food and were certain they would get it there. To prove his point, Danny commented in a loud voice : 'What excellent lobsters!' You could hear the sudden nervous clatter of knives and forks all around and people calling the owner to find out whether he had changed his ways.

Danny is one of the brightest people I have ever met. We all enjoyed the discussions he has had in our apartment with historians, archaeologists, and politicians on basic philosophical issues, the basic foundations of the State of Israel, and its immediate political problems. He was the first American star to tour the country and became immensely popular in Israel, creating great excitement everywhere he went.

In 1960 I went to Cyprus during the filming of *Exodus* in Famagusta. Otto Preminger was there with Paul Newman, and Joanne Woodward, and Peter Lawford (who was married to Pat Kennedy at the time). Our ambassador gave a party for the whole *Exodus* cast in Nicosia, and the entire Cypriot Cabinet came – with the exception of President Makarios. For me it was an occasion to discuss cooperation in tourism. Because the book *Exodus* generated so much interest in and support for Israel throughout the world, it also helped boost tourism to the country, as did the film.

Exodus was a fabulous public relations success, but in the long run I believe it had also a negative result. It created an exaggerated image of Israel as a place where everybody was a hero, a demi-god, extremely clever, and courageous – in short, a nation of exceptional people. Ever since then, each mistake made, each criminal act committed in Israel, every failure is exaggerated a hundred times, because the expectations are so great that one never can live up to them. This effect of the book was later further magnified by the Six Day War and penetrated even the

Israeli Cabinet. I feel that the leaders who created a feeling of absolute superiority after 1967 – the sense that we could beat the Arabs every time, that we could stand up to the entire world, that we were the strongest power between Europe and Japan – were far more responsible for the Yom Kippur War than any of the Intelligence officers or the chief of staff. The exaggerated belief our leaders placed in our military potential was the real blunder, not the mistaken reading of troop movements or war preparations on the other side of the cease-fire lines. The ugly truth is that we became slightly arrogant, slightly fat, and – most damaging of all – slightly careless. The tragedy is that it cost us a few thousand of our young men's lives – our most precious commodity – to come to grips with the distortions in our self-image, and I'm not sure that many people in Israel have really woken up yet.

There was another aftermath to *Exodus*, of quite a different sort. I had met Leon Uris in 1957, while he was researching the book, when he came to the Information Center in the Prime Minister's Office. Afterward I heard from him from time to time, and he sent me each of his new books as they came out. Then one day he turned to me with an urgent request. A German doctor he referred to in *Mila 18* as a man who had conducted horror experiments in a Nazi camp was suing him for libel. Uris asked me for help in gathering material to prove his accusation. I put him in touch with the people who could help him and we did the best we could, not only because of our sympathy for Uris, but because the basic issue was an important one. The outcome of the trial was that Uris was fined a token half-penny, having been found technically guilty but morally just. He later described these events in another book, *QB VII*.

Among the many film stars who have come to Jerusalem to work and visited our home were Paul Newman and Joanne Woodward, who identified strongly with Israel. Their first visit was at a time when great American liberal ideas and ideals had not yet been tarnished by the Vietnam War and its consequences. Paul in particular felt that many of these ideals were being fulfilled in Israel. Later, during the period of the Lavon Affair, he wrote me a letter filled with disappointment. He felt we had betrayed our own ideals. I have seen him from time to time in the United States, and on one occasion he had grown a full beard. I asked whether this was for a particular role, but the purpose turned out to be an entirely different one : to enable him to walk in the street without being harassed.

Kirk and Anne Douglas also came to Israel on several occasions. Kirk played the role of Mickey Marcus in the film version of *Cast a Giant Shadow* and two of his sons were working on the set. The other stars were Yul Brynner and Frank Sinatra. Toward the end of the shooting they threw a party in the house they had rented near Tel Aviv. I drove down from Jerusalem with the liquor, Kirk cooked an excellent meal, and Yul supplied the cigars. It was a jovial occasion, and we all got a little drunk. Sinatra even tried to convince Kirk to run for governor of California. That party marked the beginning of my friendship with both Douglas and Sinatra.

Ed Murrow was no film star, but he was certainly just as famous and, without question, one of the most unique men I have ever known. He first came to Israel in 1957 to do a one-hour documentary. We had not met before but, because of a mutual acquaintance we had in New York, he came straight to our Jerusalem apartment from the airport. Our introductory meeting was the beginning of a friendship that I valued highly then and treasure even more in retrospect. Ed went to Ein Gev during that visit, and his camera crew filmed our fishermen at work on the Sea of Galilee. They did not do well that particular night. The nets were almost empty; all they had caught were a few meager sardines. But they had loads of fish that had been caught earlier in the day. Our fishermen suggested filling the nets to give him livelier footage, but Ed turned them down flat. What he saw was how the camera would tell it. He returned to Israel again and again, and we also met whenever I was in the States. I especially remember a sparkling dinner with Ed and Marlene Dietrich in New York for it was the first time I met that remarkable woman. Ed also brought his thirteen-year-old son, Casey, to Israel for an extended stay, and I think he enjoyed that visit the most.

The last time I saw Ed was in 1964. I had come to New York on the eve of a legal holiday and could not do any work the following day. So I went to Isaac Stern's Connecticut country house, which was near Ed's farm in Pawling, New York, and spent a few hours with Ed. He was already very sick by then, with lung cancer, but he believed he would recover. He had resigned from his job with the government and told me he had taken sad leave of President Johnson. That day he felt well and asked about Israel and our problems. Then he said, 'You know, the president told me that when I come back I can have any job I want. I don't really want a government job; I'd rather do some writing. But there is one job I would take. You're still not out of the woods in Israel. You exist, all right, but the real trouble is ahead of you. The only country on which you can eventually count is the United States, and a lot will depend on what people in the United States think about you. You haven't got too many friends here, and one day the role of the U.S. ambassador to Israel may be decisive to your future. If I'm ever well enough, I'd like the president to give me that job.' That was our last meeting. Soon after his condition worsened and he passed away.

The books, films, and documentaries certainly stimulated interest in Israel and made more people want to come and see for themselves. Another aspect of our desire to bring tourism to Israel was the creation of the Israel Festival. In this connection I made my first visit to Edinburgh in 1962 to attend the Edinburgh Festival, and that allowed me to see an old and dear friend. The first thing I did upon arrival was to phone Lorna Wingate, who was living outside Edinburgh, and we met the next day. She had remarried and looked a little older but was still a very beautiful woman. We arranged for her nineteen-year-old son, Jonathan, to visit us in Israel, and he turned up a few months later. It was his first time in Israel, and we took him around. He didn't mention his father once, but he was intensely interested in everything. Many years later, on his honeymoon, he came back again. By then he had become a gunner in the British Army, like his father.

Over the years we repeatedly tried to talk Igor Stravinsky into coming to Jerusalem and participating in the Israel Festival. He finally did come in August 1964. The man who really persuaded him was Aharon Propes, the director of the festival. The additional attraction that may have helped convince him was that we organized an exhibition of paintings by his wife, Vera, a gifted artist in her own right. Stravinsky had written a special piece of music for us, 'The Sacrifice of Isaac', which Bob Kraft rehearsed with the orchestra and was first performed in Caesarea. I took Stravinsky down to Caesarea on one of the hottest evenings I can remember. Our car broke down and we were stuck on the road for over half an hour. We barely made the beginning of the concert. He was already eighty-four at that time, but he kept up remarkably. Stravinsky had a great capacity for whiskey and champagne and was the most enjoyable and high-spirited companion imaginable. Like many great artists who reach an advanced age, when Stravinsky stood up holding his baton and started conducting, at least twenty or thirty years fell off his shoulders, and he behaved like a young man. I introduced him to Chivas Regal, a whiskey he had never tasted before. Afterward he wrote me a note, in good Russian, saying that Chivas Regal was the best whiskey he had ever come across. I sent the note as a birthday gift to Sam Bronfman, the owner of Seagrams, who was only a few years younger than Stravinsky.

Many world-renowned artists began coming to Israel in those days, but one visit by Isaac Stern stands out particularly in my mind because it took me back to Ein Gev. Actually, I visited Ein Gev fairly often while serving in the Prime Minister's Office. But Isaac was drawn to the kibbutz not by memories and old friendships but by the music shed, which was used for concerts and festivals, particularly at Passover. The idea for a music festival at Ein Gev dated back a long way, practically to the first days of the settlement's existence. The kibbutz had a friend named Dr Sommerfeld, from Tel Aviv, who came to Ein Gev with four or five other musicians every Passover and played classical music for the members each night of the week-long holiday. This beautiful tradition came to an end in 1941, when Dr Sommerfeld drowned, but the love for music remained. In 1951, when I was in the States, I helped Ya'akov Steinberger, a friend from Ein Gev and an organizer of cultural activities, to obtain a gift from Ethel Cohen and the Esco Foundation in order to build the shed. Ya'akov was the moving force behind the Passover festivals that became a continued success.

When Isaac Stern was expected, I promised to pick him up in Tel Aviv and drive him to Ein Gev for his performance. At 6 A.M. the radio announced a revolution in Syria and fighting on the Golan Heights. My telephone in Jerusalem rang. 'I assume the concert is cancelled,' Isaac said from his Tel Aviv hotel. 'Why?' I asked. 'The revolution in Syria. You have to drive to Ein Gev along the Syrian frontier. Who will come to the concert?' I assured him he would have his usual full house, and of course the concert hall overflowed. Thousands of people came in trucks from the entire border area. Isaac couldn't believe it.

That night we left Ein Gev at midnight. On our way back, at about 2 A.M., we dropped in on Ezra Danin to get a political appraisal of the revolution. All we knew of it was the sound of distant shooting we had heard while our car moved along the quiet shore of the Sea of Galilee – too distant to disturb the music of Isaac's violin. When I think about it now, both the bullets and the song of Isaac's strings were signs of those times.

10 Larger Than Lifesize

I HAD my finger in dozens of pots during the years I worked in the Prime Minister's Office. My schedule was not only crowded but often diffuse. Yet there was one thread, one force, that bound all my activities together. For most of that period, the prime minister of Israel was Ben-Gurion, and everything I was doing in the ministry was woven around him. Ben-Gurion was a man whose presence was always felt. He probably had a greater influence on me than any other individual I have met in my life.

It was sometimes hard for the people close to him to appreciate Ben-Gurion. He was not an outgoing person, no hand-shaker or back-slapper. But he was always eager to discuss, to argue. It didn't have to be with somebody important. He would answer a child on the street or a parent who had written a letter. The subject of discussion need not necessarily concern your job. You could discuss anything with him: Zionism, the Jews, the Bible, science, Buddha, history. He had a scholarly temperament and loved to explore almost any subject. And he would never pull rank on you or claim he knew better because he had more experience.

Ben-Gurion was deeply interested in philosophy and science, particularly the frontiers of science. The human brain fascinated him. I remember the many evenings of discussions with Israel's outstanding scientists, the late Amos de Shalit and Aharon Katzir, and the arguments about the brain versus the computer. Ben-Gurion deeply believed that the singularity of the human being could never be replaced by any mechanical contraption, however sophisticated and advanced. He was also very interested in the cosmos and in whether we have any right to believe that the rules and laws of our particular solar system prevail throughout this tremendous universe. Many of the ideas that had recently come up in astrophysics occupied him and, according to the scientists he talked with, his questions were always original and provocative.

I was one of the people who provided Ben-Gurion with books. In fact, some friends in the States put a small fund at my disposal for this particular purpose. The search began with books on the history of Palestine and the Middle East, an interest we had in common. He was always after books – Greek books, history books, philosophy books – and on his visits to Europe and the United States, he always found time to go to bookshops. In fact, Ben-Gurion would make a special trip to Oxford to visit Blackwell's. On many such occasions I went along, and while I was hunting according to my own interest – old travel books on the Holy Land and the Middle East – I also enjoyed his search immensely. He would also spend considerable time going through catalogues and ordering books. In the end, he stopped reading fiction for lack of time, but until the early 1950s he read a lot of fiction, even thrillers.

There was a period when Ben-Gurion was deeply interested in Indian philosophy and particularly in Buddhism. I remember that for years people in the Prime Minister's Office were trying to find all the volumes of the *Sacred Books of the East* until finally we gave up on one of the volumes, which was absolutely unobtainable. In the end, we borrowed it from the New York Public Library, photographed every single page (this was before Xerox machines), and had them specially bound in order to complete Ben-Gurion's set. This interest culminated in Ben-Gurion's accepting Prime Minister U Nu's invitation to visit Burma and spend some time in a Buddhist monastery trying to meditate.

When we received a grant from the United States government to translate the great books of the classics into Hebrew, a committee was appointed to compile lists of basic books. Ben-Gurion and Martin Buber were involved in what seemed like an interminable argument over the question 'What is a classic?' For Ben-Gurion, classics were only the works of the Greeks: Aeschylus, Sophocles, Euripides, Plato. But Goethe? He wasn't so sure. Schiller? Even less so. He thought in terms of the ancients – Greeks, Romans, Buddha, Confucius – and, of course, the Bible, which didn't have to be translated. Ben-Gurion believed that the two most universal philosophers were Plato and Buddha and that theirs was the purest and clearest form of thinking. He regretted that the Greek philosophers of the fifth and sixth centuries B.C. didn't meet with the Jewish prophets of the time. The world, he thought, might have been a much better place if they had.

It was very difficult, however, to impress Ben-Gurion with more recent European literature. Buber and he would argue long into the night. The other members of the committee had equally strong opinions, and the meetings were very lively. Buber would become exasperated at the firmness and resourcefulness with which Ben-Gurion insisted that the word 'classic' had a specific meaning and that it was important to define and respect that meaning. Ben-Gurion had been inspired by the University of Chicago 'One Hundred Books'. I don't think he agreed with the full hundred that were chosen, but he liked the idea of a number like one hundred and thought that a list for the Jews and the Hebrew-reading world should be chosen in Israel. This all seems so long ago, for today thousands of the world's classics are available in Hebrew, and Israel is the country with more publishers, bookshops, books, and news-papers read per capita – and more readers per piece of printed matter – than any other country in the world.

It was the same drive to inquire and discuss that brought Ben-Gurion to seek how great minds in the Jewish world related to the subject 'Who is a Jew?' The question arose when decisions had to be made about how to register religious affiliation on an Israeli identity card. There was a heated discussion in Israel about 'Who is a Jew?' and the Law of Return, which permits every Jew to settle in Israel and automatically become a citizen. So Ben-Gurion reached out. While he naturally wrote to rabbis, he also ranged far and wide and sent letters to historians and jurists. The historian and political scientist Isaiah Berlin, for example, sent a long, very scholarly dissertation in return. In fact, Ben-Gurion received many scholarly opinions from Jewish savants in both the Diaspora and Israel. These were confidential; he had given his word not to publish them. I don't think he personally conceived of a division between religious and national identity in Judaism. He felt that you cannot belong to the Jewish people if you profess another faith. A man needn't be actively religious. But in a Jewish nation, one who worships Buddha or Christ or Mohammed should not be called a Jew.

Oddly enough, Ben-Gurion the atheist often brought God into his discussions. He brought in the Almighty in his own way – and he often surprised his listeners. It happened that Ben-Gurion was in New York when David Remez died. Remez had been a contemporary of Ben-Gurion's, and they had worked together both in the Histadrut (Labor Federation) and the first Israeli government. Remez was a calm, balanced man, not a firebrand like Ben-Gurion. But with all their differences, Ben-Gurion held him in high regard. A memorial service was held at the Israeli consulate, and Ben-Gurion spoke. Emotionally he said something about 'meeting up there', lifting his eyes toward heaven, and it certainly surprised most of those present. But I remembered back to 1951, when Ben-Gurion and I were driving to the first Bonds meeting in Philadelphia and stopped in Princeton for a few hours with Albert Einstein. The conversation centered entirely on whether there was some higher force directing the universe. Both agreed that there was such a force, some central power, and that was basically a religious concept.

On that same visit to New York, there was an occasion when it was deemed inappropriate for Ben-Gurion to be near a synagogue on a Saturday and not attend services, so he went. Nonetheless, he had no feeling for formal religion, and he certainly fought all his life to establish the principle that Israel was a state governed by civil law, not the written and oral religious tradition. It was notable, however, that despite his lack of feeling for ritual, Ben-Gurion gave much thought to religious questions. I remember his going twice to Bnai Brak, an Orthodox district near Tel Aviv, to meet the Hazon Ish, an outstanding religious thinker. They spent many hours discussing their different concepts of the Jewish people, though there was no meeting of minds.

Art didn't interest Ben-Gurion. When a friend of his once brought him a rare edition of Plato, some 300 years old, Ben-Gurion looked at it and said, 'I have this already!' 'But this is a rare edition,' his friend exclaimed. 'What rare!' Ben-Gurion said. 'I have it in clearer print in Penguin.' When I took him to see ancient sites we were reconstructing, he walked through in complete indifference. He simply didn't understand why we were doing it. 'Why don't you take it down and build something new and beautiful?' he said. But there was an acute difference between his aesthetic sense and his attitude to nature. I remember the first day after we moved to the new Prime Minister's Office in Jerusalem. The area surrounding the building was still completely bare. Ben-Gurion stood at the window of his office and stared out. His face was gloomy. 'Why aren't there any trees here?' he said to me. 'Can't we have trees?' The next day I had little green twigs planted all around the building. He thoroughly enjoyed the horseback trip in the Golan but walked impatiently and reluctantly through Caesarea or Old Jaffa.

In 1965 I took him to see the Israel Museum before it was completed. I could imagine it complete; he was totally bored. His face expressed his boredom so strongly that it made me miserable. But later, at the opening, I think he enjoyed himself – not so much because of the museum per se, but because of the occasion. Then he began to comprehend that something of value had been added to Jerusalem, to Israel; something it didn't have before. But for art in general he had no feeling.

At the same time, anything historical about Israel fascinated him – how the first settlements started, especially how the first pioneers left Jerusalem in the 1880s to establish Petach Tikvah. He saw the beginning of the State of Israel in those settlers of Petach Tikvah and Mikveh Yisrael in the nineteenth century, not in the old community that came to Jerusalem to pray and die and not just in 1948. For Ben-Gurion, history stopped with the destruction of the Second Temple in A.D. 70 and started again with the modern return to Palestine. I never agreed with his view. I cannot accept cutting out parts of history as if they never happened. Ben-Gurion's attitude may have been conditioned by his coming from a very Jewish *milieu* in the Diaspora and resenting it, while I came from a more assimilated background and therefore could have a more detached view. He wanted to skip the Diaspora altogether, and sometimes he grew vehement in his feelings on this subject.

One case in point took place in May 1961, when I accompanied Ben-Gurion on a state visit to Canada. I have one interesting memory from the trip. On the way we stayed overnight in New York at an airport hotel. About a month earlier, Ben-Gurion had made a long speech at the Zionist Congress in Jerusalem that included one or two sentences to the effect that a Jew living outside Israel is like a 'man without a God', a quotation from the Talmud. His intention had been to urge religious Jews to come to live in Israel, but the *New York Times* and other papers reported it and created an uproar. As a result, before Ben-Gurion's trip we received urgent messages to prevent his repeating such statements, in order not to harm the relationship between Israel and Diaspora Jewry. On the evening of our arrival in New York, I had a heated argument with Ben-Gurion on this subject. Five or six other people were present. I had actually expected Abe Harman, our ambassador to Washington, to warn Ben-Gurion against offending the American Jews and Zionists and alienating them further, but he didn't.

As this was our last meeting with Ben-Gurion before starting the tour, and therefore the last chance to settle the matter, I felt the need to speak up. I remember that it was a rather bitter argument, with Ben-Gurion shouting and my shouting back. Nobody else interrupted. I felt pretty uncomfortable. It's true that I had had many arguments with Ben-Gurion before, but never with other people present. I felt so uncomfortable, in fact, that later the same evening I told Ben-Gurion I was going back home. The next morning, however, he came into my room and asked me to stay, and so I did. And though nothing was resolved during our argument, Ben-Gurion was very diplomatic throughout his visit and said nothing to anger the Jews of North America.

On the way back from Canada, we stopped in New York again, and Ben-Gurion met with President Kennedy. One of the reasons that prompted Kennedy's interest in that meeting was the American suspicion that Israel was either producing an atomic bomb or stockpiling potential bomb material, and the United States was then negotiating atomic controls all over the world. The U.S. was anxious to have control over our activity in that field, and that meeting was a *tour d'horizon* of the Middle East and Israel.

I somehow had the feeling that Ben-Gurion was not very impressed with Kennedy. He did not feel that the president had strength or vision. The rest of us were impressed with the grace, panache, and elegance of the general goings-on in 1961. But I think Ben-Gurion could relate with greater ease to the more experienced, older statesmen of the time. He had more respect for de Gaulle than for Churchill. Churchill, he felt, had merely given great expression to his people, reflected their mood. He led the nation to victory, but it was a nation that was willing to fight from the start. De Gaulle had to drag the French to heroism and brought them through against their will. Through all the great issues and crises – his decisions regarding Germany, Algeria, and so forth – de Gaulle had to fight the will of his own people, and he prevailed. He was a great leader in the truest sense of the word. After the Six Day War, when de Gaulle took a stand critical of Israel, Ben-Gurion, then three years out of office, wrote him a long personal letter explaining his view of Israel's position. De Gaulle responded immediately with an account of his own feelings. They remained friendly until de Gaulle's death. It was a relationship based on mutual respect.

Perhaps that was generally the most comfortable type of relationship for Ben-Gurion. He was the most impersonal man I have ever known – burning, but far away. The only one I knew who spoke intimately with him was the devoted Nehemya Argov, his military secretary. And yet, read Ben-Gurion's letters to his wife Paula or Ruth Dayan's account of how she would come storming over to him with her personal problems. In all our years together, I myself never discussed anything personal with him, and rarely did he show any interest. The conspicuous exception was his attitude to individual soldiers and, even more, to bereaved parents. He was a compassionate man and it was hard for him to send soldiers on a military operation where he knew there might be casualties.

As for the six million killed by the Nazis, he reacted not only to the individual suffering but also to the loss of great strength for the Jewish people. He regretted the loss of the particularly sharp intelligence that developed among East European Jewry, especially because he knew what it would have meant for Israel if it could draw on that intellect. Ben-Gurion felt our political problems would have been solved if there were two million more Jews here, that their presence would have determined our history. He always put the Jewish people first. The Jews conceivably could exist without Israel, but not vice versa. This historical attitude was typical of him. He would overcome the sentimental issue and see only the final, permanent result.

On a few occasions, I did try to move across into his personal feelings about others. Once, in 1959, I tried to iron out the very strained relations between Ben-Gurion and Moshe Sharett, whom I regarded highly. I invited both of them to our home a few times. Right before the latest visit, Ben-Gurion had spoken disparagingly in public about Sharett's part in obtaining arms for the Israel Defense Forces, saying that Sharett did not believe in armed strength. This was the cause of the final break between them. Sharett had already been out of office for a few years. All I hoped to do was to dissolve the personal bitterness.

When I invited them, Ben-Gurion responded, 'Of course, I'll be there.' Sharett agreed very reluctantly. I brought them to our apartment, put them in a room, closed the door, and left them alone. But they could not communicate. Afterward Ben-Gurion kept saying, 'Moshe? I have nothing against him. He's a good man. Devoted. Just wasn't right for the Foreign Ministry, that's all.' He had offered Sharett the Ministry of Education and other positions as well. But Sharett was insulted and boiling: 'Ben-Gurion does not even understand what he has done to me!'

When Sharett left the government in 1956, it was the first time, I believe, that a major Cabinet member had resigned his position without moving quickly into any other clearly defined activity. One purely practical outcome was that Sharett had to leave his official residence. He had long before sold his private apartment, had no car, and had no means beyond his pension, and some of us felt personally responsible for him. We arranged for someone to buy an apartment and place it at Sharett's disposal. We also helped him in other ways until he was elected chairman of the Executive of the Zionist Organization and the Jewish Agency, a post he maintained until the last day of his life.

A similar situation, incidentally, came about years later when Ben-Gurion was out of office. He went to live at kibbutz Sdeh Boker in the northern Negev, but no transport, secretarial service, or other facilities were put at his disposal. The security service decided that Ben-Gurion still had to be guarded, so the car following him was paid for by the government; but the one in which he himself traveled – he was then a man of close to eighty who had never learned to drive – and the driver were paid for by his friends. Only some years after Ben-Gurion's resignation did I persuade the minister of finance to put certain facilities – like postal services, secretarial services, and a travel allowance – at the disposal of retired presidents and prime ministers.

I did not read Moshe Sharett's diaries, which were published posthumously by his son Ya'akov (Koby). (The first installment of the serialization in one of our newspapers upset me, and I was certain that Sharett himself would not have published them in that form.) But many people reported to me that I was practically the only person mentioned in that difficult period of Sharett's deteriorating relationship with Ben-Gurion who came out unblemished in the diary account. Actually, I had made it clear to Sharett that in the substance of the argument between them, I was entirely on Ben-Gurion's side. I once explained at a public meeting that I believed in a system similar to that in England, where a prime minister can ask a Cabinet minister to resign, and that Ben-Gurion had exercised that right with Sharett. The following day, Koby Sharett wrote to me complaining that as a civil servant I was forbidden to take sides on a political issue. He explained that his father had been very offended by my remarks. I went to Sharett, explained my position in principle, and then went to Ben-Gurion and offered my resignation. Sharett understood and wrote me a letter to that effect – nor would I otherwise have fared as well in his memoirs – and Ben-Gurion did not accept my resignation.

Although I supported Ben-Gurion on his position of principle, I nonetheless thought that on many occasions he had been inconsiderate and had offended Sharett unnecessarily. In December 1953, when Ben-Gurion resigned to go to Sdeh Boker and study a number of national problems in relative peace and quiet, Sharett became prime minister against Ben-Gurion's will. The party had decided on Sharett; Ben-Gurion wanted Eshkol. Sharett had become foreign minister because he had been in charge of the Political Department of the Jewish Agency before the state was established. But Ben-Gurion never believed Sharett understood foreign-policy strategy. He thought Sharett was an appeaser who believed in conducting foreign policy through good personal relations, a method Ben-Gurion firmly rejected. Sharett felt that only orderly diplomacy based on accepted procedures would further the interests of the state. There seemed to be no middle ground on which these two men, with different political philosophies and temperaments, could meet in agreement.

A short time before Sharett's death, when he was still active as head of the Zionist Organization Executive, a Zionist Congress took place in Jerusalem. Sharett had intended to give the keynote address. Unfortunately, he was hospitalized and incapable of attending the impressive ceremony on the opening night. IIis address was to be read. At the last moment, I decided to spend the evening with Sharett at Hadassah Hospital and listen to the radio broadcast of the proceedings with him, rather than to go to the convention hall. I expected to find many friends in his room, but his wife, Zippora, and I were the only ones there.

Whatever Sharett might have believed, I don't think Ben-Gurion singled him out for abuse. In fact, Ben-Gurion offended many of our leaders, though I never saw him act unkindly to an ordinary citizen. It would exasperate me to see him short tempered with men like Sharett, with Zionist leaders like Nahum Goldmann or Abba Hillel Silver. After all, he had a soft spot for some people who had behaved inconsiderately toward him, like Golda Meir and Zalman Aranne. It's true that he sometimes behaved offensively to these people, too, but never with malice. I remember occasions when he sat with Golda, Shimon Peres (who was like a red rag to a bull for Golda), Moshe Dayan, one or two others, and myself. With all his regard for Golda, Ben-Gurion would continually give preference to the younger people, like Peres and Dayan, in such small matters as who should speak first. Or he would pay no attention to where people sat. He was completely insensitive to such details, but they were important to others. This often added fuel to a situation that was already difficult.

One of the great figures in Zionist history was Ze'ev Jabotinsky, an

excellent writer and probably the greatest orator the Zionist movement
ever had. Jabotinsky had formed the Revisionist movement, a right-
wing group that had some anti-Labor – and we believed even fascist –
tendencies in its makeup. In spite of this, in the mid-1930s Ben-Gurion
had worked out a set of agreements with Jabotinsky to ease the friction
between the Histadrut (the trade union movement, of which the Labor
parties were the ideological backbone) and the Revisionist Labor
movement that Jabotinsky had created, but Ben-Gurion's own party
rejected the proposals. After that, the Revisionists moved further
toward the right and finally spawned the two terrorist movements, the
Irgun Zvai Leumi and the Stern Group.

Jabotinsky died in the United States during World War Two and in
his will requested that when a Jewish state came about, his remains
should be transferred there by official decision. Ben-Gurion refused to
carry out this last wish of his adversary. I tried but failed to change his
mind. When Eshkol became prime minister, he also refused, partly
because he was still anxious not to clash with the retired Ben-Gurion.
But even the younger Mapai people were politically nervous. 'His grave
might become a place of pilgrimage, a shrine. It could increase the
strength of Jabotinsky's followers,' they claimed. Peres was particularly
opposed to such a move. I felt their attitude lacked sagacity. Jabotinsky
was part of our history, no matter how much we may have disliked his
political testament and heirs. In spite of Ben-Gurion's opposition,
however, I finally persuaded Eshkol to bring the matter before the
Cabinet, and today Jabotinsky is buried on Mount Herzl in a spot that
we chose together with a committee of his disciples. The feeling of
injustice that would have been created by stubbornly clinging to the
original refusal would have brought more strength to the Opposition
than what we actually did.

Strong-willed though he was, one of the many traits I liked in
Ben-Gurion was his basic personal modesty. Although he may have
been distant and impersonal, he was deeply democratic. He had all the
qualities that make up an honest man and no pretenses to being super-
human. Ben-Gurion made his share of mistakes, but he also had unequalled foresight, time and again. One of his Cabinet colleagues, Pinhas
Rosen, who was originally from Germany, called this sense *'unheimlich'*.
'Uncanny' is an inadequate translation.

We disagreed on many things, and Ben-Gurion was ultimately proven
right. He believed in the potential of American Jewry and the prowess
of Palestinian Jewry. How right he was when he packed in immigrants
at the rate of 120,000, 130,000, and 200,000 a year, when many of us
thought, 'Let's do it slowly. Thirty thousand a year, forty thousand.' I
thought the creation of a viable social and economic entity should be our
main concern and that too much stress was placed on political and

military matters. Ben-Gurion was the only one who foresaw that time was running out, that if the Jews in Iraq and Syria did not come then, they would never be able to get out. He had never recovered from the historic impact of the six million dead. He felt that the strongest branch of the nation had died in the Holocaust, and that such destruction could repeat itself in the Arab countries. He was the one who insisted on bringing these Jews out quickly. Ben-Gurion also regarded the proper integration of immigrants as crucial many years before others recognized the seriousness of the problem. He expressed this belief in the form of slogans. 'When we have a Yemenite chief of staff, then we shall have reached unity.' He dedicated a lot of thought and care to this problem.

His decisiveness about a State of Israel, his pressing sense of urgency when wise men like General Marshall said 'Take it step by step,' was magnificent. Ben-Gurion replied: 'This is our one opportunity. This combination of events may not come again in a thousand years.' He believed we would win our struggle and our war; but win or not, the chance must be taken. It was greatness combined with humility.

Ben-Gurion truly respected democracy. I doubt if all his opponents did. Many of them relied strongly on machine politics. They, or somebody acting with their knowledge, 'bought' so and so many local party secretaries and so and so many Histadrut clerks in so and so many places. These people all knew where their bread was buttered and that they would advance only if some party official close to Pinhas Sapir, strong man of Mapai and eventually minister of finance, recommended them. Ben-Gurion's followers never enjoyed any similar advantages through him. That was the reason why he was eventually outvoted in his own party. The members of Mapai knew he would never back a candidate for personal reasons. Ben-Gurion would back only a cause, not an individual – even if that individual had supported him. In the civil service, Ben-Gurion's appointments were based entirely on his estimate of a man's qualities. He often did not even know a man's political affiliation, and he surely never cared. He was flawless in the consistency with which he kept government and party politics apart. That does not mean, of course, that he was always successful with his appointments.

He also had respect for the Knesset, our Parliament – and certainly much more respect than people in government showed in later years. He believed deeply in parliamentary procedure. He and I shared the belief that the election system should be changed. I discussed the concept with him before the first elections, and we both favored regional elections, similar to those in England. It couldn't be done at that time, and later I approached Ben-Gurion with the familiar compromise to increase the blocking percentage, which would create larger parties but not create direct representation. I admitted that this was not what we wanted, but

I felt it would be an improvement by creating a majority and an opposition and eliminating the uncertainty of government by coalition. Ben-Gurion said, 'No. I don't want that. If anything at all, then the English system. No compromise.'

I think that one of the things that may have gotten in people's way was that Ben-Gurion didn't really have a sense of humor. He didn't enjoy jokes and certainly never told any. Once we listened together to a broadcast of 'Three in a Boat', a radio program of political satire, and he did not react. He simply had no feel for satire and went against his enemies with a heavy sword. But if Ben-Gurion had no sense of humor, he certainly was not a cold person. He was particularly warm toward children and always interested in what they had to say, how they perceived the past, and to what extent they lived and experienced history. When our son, Amos, was small, Ben-Gurion would always ask him what he was studying in school and who his favorite biblical figure was. Hebrew was also very important to him. He taught our daughter, Osnat, that to be exact in Hebrew you had to say 'certainly' instead of 'sure'. At the age of three, she would recite this every night before going to sleep, like a lullaby.

On October 29, 1957, a crank threw a grenade in the Knesset. Ordinarily, Ben-Gurion was accompanied wherever he went by Nehemya Argov, Yitzhak Navon, or both. But at this particular time Yitzhak was in South America, and Nehemya, a man who lived and breathed only for Ben-Gurion, happened to feel unwell and therefore did not come along. Fortunately, Ben-Gurion was only slightly wounded in the foot. But during the first few days that Ben-Gurion was in the hospital, Nehemya committed suicide. I remember our looking for him all over Jerusalem. He was found in his home in Tel Aviv, where he had shot himself. Our first thought, naturally, was that he had done it because he was shaken at having failed to be with Ben-Gurion to protect him. But the facts were more complicated. Shortly after Ben-Gurion had been wounded, Nehemya had struck a pedestrian while driving. Whether Nehemya, grieving and distracted, had lost control at the wheel, no one will ever know. He apparently thought his automobile victim had been killed; actually the man suffered no serious injury and recovered quickly. But now Nehemya was dead. It was tragic.

Ben-Gurion, still in the hospital, did not seem to be recuperating well at first, and we did not want to upset him with this news. We called all the newspapers – Ben-Gurion was an inveterate newspaper reader – and asked them to print a special copy of the next day's edition for Ben-Gurion without the report of Nehemya's suicide. Together with Moshe Dayan, I took Danny Kaye (who was on one of his visits) to see him in the hospital. We thought Danny might improve Ben-Gurion's mood a little. But sooner or later he had to be told. And the following week, when he was convalescing, Yigael Yadin and I went to break the news about Nehemya's death. When we told Ben-Gurion, he did not say a word. He turned to the wall and cried.

As long as I can remember, Ben-Gurion hated being prime minister. Throughout the years, again and again, he would say, 'This is the worst job anybody could have – much worse than hard labor in prison. The day I leave here, I will be relieved.' I didn't know at the time whether he would really feel that way after leaving office. But while he was in office, he certainly felt he was carrying a terrible burden, beyond any normal person's capacity. And when Ben-Gurion eventually resigned, he did feel great relief.

11 Lost Battles

I HAD little, if anything, to do with party politics during the years I worked in the Prime Minister's Office, but I learned a lot about the people who moved through those rooms. One of my most interesting observations was that Ben-Gurion was often quite unaware of the seething power struggles going on around him. For instance, he had a politically and economically open attitude toward Germany, despite his deep sensitivity to Israel's natural emotional bias (which he could not help sharing, of course). As a statesman, however, he was ready to deal with the Germans. This open attitude was used by the people who wanted to overthrow him.

Golda Meir, who succeeded Sharett as foreign minister, was sincere in her anti-German feelings and often attacked Ben-Gurion's 'pro-German' policy. Levi Eshkol was not at that time actively against Ben-Gurion and definitely did not want to step into Ben-Gurion's shoes. Eshkol was modest and too frightened of the responsibility. But essentially the 'Big Three' – Eshkol, Golda, and Zalman ('Ziama') Aranne – were all against Ben-Gurion from the late 1950s onward. They were the leaders of the 'Second Echelon'. All of them were of Ben-Gurion's generation in the Mapai Party, and their hostility developed when Ben-Gurion began to favor the 'youngsters'.

When I say the 'youngsters', I am speaking generally of members of my own age group and a few somewhat younger. During the first decade of the state, I was not politically active. As director-general of the Prime Minister's Office, I did not have Cabinet rank but was the highest-ranking civil servant in the country. That prevented me from being drawn into the political line of fire. In addition, I didn't have a taste for politics and actually avoided involvements. But Ben-Gurion appointed Shimon Peres as deputy defense minister and helped Moshe Dayan, Abba Eban, and others to reach high office; and he did so without consulting the Second Echelon. That must have raised the fear that he would bypass them, appoint more young ministers the next time round, and eventually squeeze the older generation out. The Second Echelon had been edgy about Ben-Gurion even before 1959. Some complained that he never invited them for coffee and a chat. The fact is that he never invited anyone else, either; but they were offended just the same. They didn't exactly organize against Ben-Gurion, but they created a feeling of uneasiness.

Years earlier, shortly after the establishment of the state, I told Ben-Gurion that for all her great qualities, Golda could cause the country untold harm – and I have stuck to this opinion all through the years. That does not change the fact that Golda is an admirable and likeable woman, perhaps the most impressive woman I have ever met. She has a truly regal appearance, is a proud representative of Israel, and as a fund-raiser has an unequalled gift for turning emotion into cold cash. She was also an enormously hard worker, and nothing could deflect her from her duty as she saw it. Golda is not an original thinker; she is a popularizer. As a woman, she must have had a more difficult struggle to assert herself than a man in her position would have. That, of course, only increased her determination and strength of character. Since Ben-Gurion passed away, she has said often enough that nobody in their generation could be compared to Ben-Gurion for extraordinary foresight and political imagination. But she differed with him greatly in her fundamental concept of statehood.

To Ben-Gurion, the principle of statehood came before anything else. He was almost alone in the view that the party, the Histadrut, and everything else had to be subordinated to the principle of statehood. Ben-Gurion had emancipated himself entirely from the clannishness and parochialism of the Jewish *shtetl* of Eastern Europe, with all its familiar warmth and humanity. That was an atmosphere in which leaders like Pinhas Sapir and Levi Eshkol thrived, and Golda was also a party to preserving it. Too often, and even in critical situations, the party and the Histadrut came first for Golda. She believed them to be the most vital instruments for the state, and at such moments the very needs of the state itself were overshadowed. I believe that this attitude, which many others shared, is at the root of much internal strife today.

In 1952, just after I had returned from Washington to begin work in the Prime Minister's Office, I brought Ben-Gurion along to an informal meeting of several government officials from our close circle. I believed it was important for him to hear our evaluation of the way affairs were being conducted, and I personally expressed severe criticism of Golda's approach to some important problems. Ben-Gurion had called her back from Russia, where she had been our first minister, to become the country's first minister of labor. As such, she was in charge of the immigrant camps, and I thought that her handling of the immigrant problem was fundamentally wrong. These newcomers were being taught to expect something for nothing but the asking, just because they were

Jews and they had suffered in Iraq, or in Kurdistan, or in Yemen. Their
suffering had been quite real – one cannot deny it. It was a state they had
been born into for generations. But even so, I didn't believe that entitled
them to automatic compensation from the State of Israel. I knew that
one day we would pay dearly for this policy, and I believe we are reaping
the fruits now – in the ports, at the airlines, in our labor and social relations throughout the country. The notion that you could close the social
and economic gap not by individual hard work, but simply by demanding
more and counting on acquiescence from the other side, was and is
ultimately self-defeating. Work, not charity, was the solution. Worse
than that, we not only educated the people that they didn't have to work
in order to get what they wanted, but they came to expect that the party
– in this case, the Labor Party – would answer all their needs. When
their expectations rose and the party was not able to meet them all, the
people turned against it. The elections of May 1977 provided staggering
proof of that.

As far back as 1952, I told Ben-Gurion that Golda – with her 'Jewish
mother' nature, dogmatic adherence to obsolete slogans, and ability to
see only black and white – was not furthering our independence. I also
forecast that she would one day be among the first of his closest colleagues to fight him. But Ben-Gurion did not believe me. He was fond of
Golda and thought she was an outstanding figure. In fact, he continued
to think so until the end of his life – even during the great rift between
them, when he was out of office and was treated almost as an outcast.

Ben-Gurion had enemies among the younger generation, too. These
were people to whom he had given power and were greedy for more. In
time, they all joined forces. In Golda's case, conflicts sometimes became
particularly intense because she disliked Peres, and Ben-Gurion used
Peres for dealings with Germany and France (which she, as foreign
minister, rightly felt should have been carried out through her). None
of this troubled Ben-Gurion, however. He may not even have been
aware of the problem he created. Hierarchy was not important to him.

Lurking in the background while political rivalries were ripening
throughout the 1950s were the seeds of Israel's most dramatic political
controversy: the Lavon Affair. It was the instrument that would eventually deflect and debilitate Ben-Gurion's political career. The incident
out of which it grew goes back to 1954, when Ben-Gurion was out of
government, Moshe Sharett was prime minister and Pinhas Lavon
was defense minister. Agents planted in Cairo had been instructed to
create incidents that would lead to enmity between Egypt and the U.S.
and other Western Powers. They planted bombs in the USIS Library
and other sensitive places, but the whole operation was so poorly
planned and executed that they were quickly caught by the Egyptians.
An action of this kind should certainly require the prime minister's

approval, but in fact it had not been authorized on such a level. An argument later arose as to whether it was ordered by the chief of Intelligence, Benyamin Gibli, on instructions from Defense Minister Lavon, or whether Gibli had given the order on his own. The fact that Lavon had planned and authorized several other adventurous operations without consulting the prime minister strengthened the suspicion that he was involved in this one as well.

After the blunder in Egypt, Sharett appointed a two-man committee (consisting of former Chief of Staff Ya'akov Dori and Supreme Court Justice Yitzhak Olshan) to investigate the matter and decide who had been responsible. But Dori and Olshan could not reach a conclusive decision. As a result, Lavon resigned his position, and Ben-Gurion returned to government as defense minister (soon afterward he became prime minister as well).

Then in 1960, the whole matter came up again when a district court – judging an unrelated case – found reason to believe that documents had been forged and Intelligence officers had committed perjury in their testimony before the Olshan-Dori Committee. Lavon, who was then secretary-general of the Histadrut, turned to Ben-Gurion and demanded that his name be cleared forthwith. Ben-Gurion said he was not in a position to either accuse or acquit anyone. Lavon then took his case to the Knesset Foreign Affairs and Security Committee, stating that he had been a victim of false accusations and lying witnesses. That was when the entire affair became public knowledge, and the country was in an uproar.

Lavon continued to cry 'foul' and demand that his name be officially cleared, but Ben-Gurion believed that only a judicial body had the powers to investigate or pass judgment in such a case. In the hope of reaching a compromise, Levi Eshkol stepped in and proposed the establishment of a ministerial committee to review the facts and decide whether an independent state inquiry commission was really necessary. This ministerial committee has become known as the Committee of Seven (because it was composed of seven ministers, including Eshkol himself), and some of the procedures it adopted in collecting evidence and hearing testimony were open to question. It seems that Eshkol's primary aim was to put the affair to rest. Getting at the real truth took second place to simply getting the nasty business out of the way. The committee's unanimous conclusion, submitted in December 1960, was that Lavon had not given the order for the misguided operation in Egypt. In spite of its investigation, however, the committee neglected to mention who had given it.

Ben-Gurion remained convinced that only proper legal procedures could establish the guilt or innocence of a person, and there was no reason why a high ranking officer or a Cabinet minister should be an exception. That was why he was opposed to a decision by ministerial committee. It simply didn't end the controversy that had shaken Israel's political life – and to some extent even its foreign relations. The entire country quarreled. The less anyone knew of the facts, the freer he felt to support his choice of the conflicting rumors. Many acted with passion that grew into hatred and degenerated into sheer malice. For years the catchword was: Who gave the order? Even more than the Kastner affair, this incident brought about a loss of confidence in the country's leadership, a skepticism that continues to play a central role in our public life. Ben-Gurion felt he could not compromise on this point and submitted his resignation. Thereafter, he relentlessly pursued his demand for a proper judicial investigation, even at the cost of inconvenience and embarrassment. He felt that Eshkol (whom Ben-Gurion had recommended to succeed him as prime minister) had let him down by not agreeing to have the case tried properly. The relationship between the two men deteriorated rapidly, and my attempts to bring them together were useless.

Years later, Pinhas Rosen, the chairman of the Committee of Seven, revealed how, in his view, Eshkol had misled him into making a political decision instead of a judicial one. Eshkol had said to him: 'Lavon is a wild man, and he will not acquiesce; but Ben-Gurion is wise and will understand if we take this course.' The implication was that decisions are made not according to proper legal procedures, but according to how people will react to them. It illustrates one of the basic differences between Ben-Gurion and Eshkol.

The Lavon Affair is still probably the most publicized and least understood political controversy in Israel's brief history. What is clear is that it provided Ben-Gurion's enemies with the means to end his days as prime minister. I believed – and continue to believe – that Ben-Gurion's stand on the issue was right, but he handled it badly. In fact, it was handled badly from the very start by all of us – Col. Chaim Ben David (Ben-Gurion's military assistant), Yitzhak Navon, and myself. We could not stand up to the onslaught. Ben-Gurion won a few skirmishes, but he lost the battle. And as a result, the country lost a few more years of his leadership, which would have served to consolidate the state to a greater extent.

Suddenly there was a flood of resentment from people who felt that Ben-Gurion had slighted them. They simply could not live with a man who was, in a way, a little larger than lifesize. Some people tire of a man who is always a step ahead and naturally resent a man who too often has his own way. Ben-Gurion tended to ride roughshod over the opinions of others, even in his own party, and he frightened some of his colleagues with his refusal to compromise. Even his unlimited faith in Israel's military capacity was a threat to some party members. So Ben-Gurion's political opponents within the party and without latched on to the opportunity to put him down. They were joined by the great fighters for freedom among the professors at the Hebrew University, who were as far removed from real life then as most of them are today. I don't think we really understood the situation at that time. I personally was so deeply conscious of what this country owed Ben-Gurion that I couldn't quite comprehend the vehemence of the backlash. I never learned the lesson of similar examples – if you can compare this experience with what happened to Churchill in England or, at one period or another, de Gaulle in France.

One of the reasons why the Lavon Affair has been misunderstood is that so much emphasis was placed on Ben-Gurion's behavior that the real issue was lost in the shuffle. Ben-Gurion's point was that nobody should be above the law. Nobody. He insisted that only the courts could rule. This was not some freak, isolated issue for him. It was part and parcel of his general belief that Israel would continue to exist only if we preserved our moral qualities as a nation of virtue. His greatest fear was of levantinization, and again he saw many years ahead. Ben-Gurion often believed that once he had formulated and analyzed a problem, it was up to others to deal with solving it. So the fact that he took the Lavon Affair completely on himself – whether or not he handled it properly – proves how seriously he took the problem.

If we laughed then at the concept of a nation of virtue, we lived to see how profound his vision was and how important it was to follow his lead. Ben-Gurion knew we would always be only three or five percent of the surrounding Arab population, and if we failed to maintain our moral and intellectual integrity, we would not be able to stand up to our adversaries. But in the case of the Lavon Affair, he failed to convey this issue to the public. He often gave the impression that he was trying to settle a personal score with Pinhas Lavon, and his enemies within the party saw to it that this impression was magnified. As Ben-Gurion lost ground, he became increasingly frustrated and less articulate. Those of us around him were unable to change that pattern.

The Lavon Affair lingered and brought about a change in Ben-Gurion. He lost a lot of his self-confidence and his contact with people, as though he had lost the ability to talk to them. He knew his cause was just, but when he saw that he was unable to convince others, he became exasperated. In his fury of frustration he began to attack his opponents personally, and that finally brought him down in June 1963. No one liked hearing him speak that way. No one liked seeing him descend to such depths. It was embarrassing. People couldn't accept his attacks – particularly the lashing out at the men he himself raised, like Eshkol. And every time Ben-Gurion attacked Lavon personally, he lost support. The bickering over the Lavon Affair continued for more than two years and gradually isolated Ben-Gurion within his own party. I believe he resigned for good in 1963 because he felt he had lost the support of his old political comrades. That was the basic underlying reason. But what triggered his resignation at that particular time had a lot to do with Isser Har'el, then head of the Mossad.

For years I had taken a strong stand against the way business was conducted between Isser and Ben-Gurion. Isser would report directly and confidentially to Ben-Gurion and to nobody else. There was no way of checking the validity of his intelligence evaluation, since everyone else in the government – without exception – was kept in the dark. Even Ben-Gurion's unlimited faith in Isser did not seem to justify such a practice. Others who knew Isser well shared my opinion. But this wasn't really a matter that concerned Isser personally; it was a question of proper procedures. I continually insisted that a responsible third party should be present at all meetings between the head of Intelligence and the prime minister. I felt there ought to be some check on facts and especially the validity of conclusions.

The break between Ben-Gurion and Isser Har'el occurred over the so-called German scientists who were reported to be preparing advanced atomic weapons in Egypt. Isser had made a purely personal and almost hysterical appraisal of this particular situation. This was largely because for months and months he had concentrated all his forces on finding a child, Yossele Schumacher, who had been abducted from his parents by a group of Jewish religious extremists, the Neturei Karta. (The Neturei Karta were connected with the child's grandparents, who wanted to give him an ultra-religious anti-Zionist education.) Ben-Gurion was rightly concerned that kidnapping could not be tolerated, and the child was traced all over the world until he was finally found in New York. In the process, however, various other important activities had been neglected by the Mossad for lack of manpower. The alternatives had never been put to Ben-Gurion. It may well be that had he been told the search for Yossele would be at the cost of proper surveillance of enemy activities, he would have decided against it – or at least given it lower priority. When Yossele was finally found – and how could Isser afford not to find him after he had successfully traced Eichmann? – Isser was suddenly confronted with stories of German scientists in Egypt, and they frightened him.

When Ben-Gurion did not accept his estimate of the Egyptian situation, Isser ran around trying to convince other members of the Cabinet. But Ben-Gurion, who had received direct assurances from a reliable German source, still did not accept the evaluation. This had never happened to Isser before, and his response was to resign. That increased the tension between Ben-Gurion and his colleagues to such an extent that it ultimately led to Ben-Gurion's resignation as well.

One afternoon I stretched out on the couch in my office for a few minutes. The door opened and Ben-Gurion came in. He didn't let me get up but sat on a chair beside me and started talking about the relationship between the prime minister and the Intelligence services. His concern was to find the best way to define a clear line of command and responsibilities. I suggested that he appoint a committee to work on these ideas, and he did so only a few days before he actually resigned. The committee consisted of Yigael Yadin and Ze'ev Sharef. Their recommendation to appoint a special adviser to the prime minister for Intelligence affairs was submitted when Ben-Gurion was no longer in office. Levi Eshkol, who had succeeded him as prime minister, did not want to enforce the committee's recommendations and searched for a compromise. While I had nothing to do with this side of the prime minister's duties, I had forebodings, and this particular chapter was one of the main reasons I myself eventually decided to leave the Prime Minister's Office.

On June 15, 1963, the Saturday night before Ben-Gurion resigned, I brought Golda to Ben-Gurion's home. The conversation was about the German scientists in Egypt and other aspects of our relationship with Germany. I didn't think that Ben-Gurion would make the decision to resign that night, but I saw his despair at not being able to convince Golda about that matter. The conflict over the subject was probably so sharp because there was already a rift anyway, not because this particular problem was insurmountable. Their conversation didn't end with an explosion. It was more like an estrangement, an abyss in their thinking. Ben-Gurion did not accept the appraisal he was given of the matter. He didn't think the situation was dangerous, and he didn't believe the scientists – if, indeed, there were any – were working with the backing and approval of the German government. Ben-Gurion had met with Carlo Schmidt, the chairman of the German parliament and a key figure in the Social Democratic Party, who had always been a friend. When he came to Jerusalem bearing a message from Adenauer and swore there was no truth in the accusations, Ben-Gurion knew he could believe him. But a whole campaign had been organized by Ben-Gurion's adversaries through the Press Office. It included sending reporters all over the world to speak out against Germany and the scientists, and that made Ben-Gurion furious.

The morning following that meeting with Golda, Uri Lubrani (who had temporarily replaced Yitzhak Navon) came into my office very alarmed and said Ben-Gurion was about to gather the party leadership and announce his resignation. I was dumbfounded. Of course, I knew Ben-Gurion was unhappy, but I hadn't thought he was actually planning to leave. During the day I tried to persuade him to reconsider – as did many others – but to no avail. He would not be moved from his decision.

Perhaps a great many people in Israel and all over the world, common citizens and statesmen alike, were relieved that the stubborn old man was leaving and now there would be an easier regime. They may have hoped that some badly needed young blood would be injected into Israeli politics. But being well acquainted with Eshkol and the group surrounding him, I knew this would not happen. Israel was losing a great leader, and there was no one to take his place. The next generation of leadership – Eshkol, Pinhas Sapir, Zalman Aranne – none of them 'young blood', had no real understanding of what statehood was about. They still acted as though they were living in an enlarged *shtetl* and dwelled on the old concepts they had brought with them from Eastern Europe. Perhaps if Ben-Gurion had stayed on for a few more years, the third generation – Dayan, Peres, and their contemporaries – politically more sophisticated men – would have taken over. But by the time that generation finally did take over, things had already become much worse.

I don't know to what extent the people in Israel realize even today that the battle Ben-Gurion fought over the Lavon Affair was for a principle no democracy can exist without. With all the attention focused on corruption now, I doubt that if a similar incident occurred it would be treated any differently. I am afraid that most of the people in this country have not yet grasped the importance of Ben-Gurion's stand. Basically, it is the same principle that I invoked in my long battle against what I call 'Sapirism'.

I believe the long-time minister of finance and sometime secretary of the Labor Party, Pinhas Sapir, was a bad influence on the state. With all his good intentions and his tremendous record of practical achievements, he never seemed to cross the threshold between the early days when we were ruled by a colonial power and living up to the responsibilities of statehood. In the Palestine of 1936, when we worked for the Public Works Department of the British mandatory administration, certainly we stole tools, falsified 'overtime', and took more money home to the kibbutz. From whom were we taking? From a foreign government that did not sympathize with our purposes and in fact kept frustrating them. To whom were we giving? The community, the future. None of us profited individually and there was no greed. We were engaged in a struggle for future independence from a power that was out to protect its own interests first. Under British rule we all felt entitled to cheat. Why should we pay even low taxes when we could smuggle and not pay any? That attitude spread. Men felt they had a license to steal as long as they did so for the public purse. All this was, of course, based on an earlier inbred attitude toward the governments of Poland, Russia, and so on, which had dealt ruthlessly with their Jewish populations.

Then, when the state was founded, some people could not adjust to the difference. One of Ben-Gurion's noteworthy characteristics was that from his first day in Palestine, he understood the needs of a state. At times he seemed to be the only one that did. Eshkol once quoted the Biblical phrase 'Thou shalt not muzzle the ox when it threshes out the corn' in reference to minor cases of officials misusing their positions for their own profit. A man high in public office should not have said that, certainly not to a people who have lived for centuries as second-rate citizens and have yet to develop a firm tradition of 'good citizenship'. I was told that Eshkol later regretted having used this quotation.

Because too many of our leaders were incapable of drawing the line between outwitting the oppressor and cheating our own government, Israel is suffering today from a kind of Levantine corruption. It's not that on occasion someone takes a bribe, although such cases certainly exist, as we well know. It's a general decline of public or civic morals. Take wage arrangements, for example. In order to have their salaries raised without having their taxes go up proportionately, Israelis were given tax-free mileage allowances for cars they didn't run. They were told, 'In order to increase your salary by IL100, we would have to give you IL500 to cover your income tax. So instead we will give you extra paid mileage.' There were also tax-free allowances for professional books, whether they were bought or not. In this way, employees received added income without any record of salary increases. The purpose of the system was to stave off demands for salary increases in other industries and services and to prevent rises in the cost-of-living index, thus benefiting the economy. But it was crooked thinking, a throwback to all the practices of Eastern Europe, where the government was an enemy. This is what I call Sapirism.

Sapir had been director-general of the Treasury, then minister of trade and industry, and later minister of finance and the Labor Party secretary, the two jobs which made him a tremendously powerful political figure. His last appointment was as chairman of the Jewish Agency. He was a big, tall, bald-headed man who looked a lot like Kojak. I, on the whole, rather liked him. Furthermore, it is quite rightly said that there was practically no development town, no development scheme, no industry, and no institution of learning that Sapir had not been involved in and had not helped. No man got up earlier and worked harder or with more consistency and more devotion. He was indefatigable, and economic progress in Israel was his main concern. He was a great fund-raiser, and people had confidence in him.

It is very difficult to be critical now, so soon after he died in harness. But without analyzing the influence he had on the country, it will be impossible to understand many things that have happened here and even more difficult to repair them. For a long time even before his death, Sapir had been a controversial figure, and during the last few months of his life much of the disastrous economic situation and low morale was blamed on him. There were accusations against the 'Sapir system' and the 'Sapir Fund' and many other facets of the economy. My own relationship with Sapir was an ambivalent one. I had the greatest admiration for his work capacity and for his ability to cut through red tape, make quick decisions, and make them stick, so that his officials could not revoke them. But I did not feel this qualified him to set the direction for the workings of Israel's economy. And while Sapir's practical achievements were noteworthy, the legal, orderly, and moral basis of his transactions was regrettably lacking.

I criticized Sapir openly on various occasions, frequently in his presence. (I must say that this did not affect the personal relationship between us, and even when he was most occupied, I had free access to him.) My argument with Sapir was not personal; it was over the 'Sapir system'. He judged many matters not on their merits but by who had brought the problem before him and how it had been presented. Thus an important matter might be pushed aside because the 'wrong' person advocated it; a poor policy may have found favor because it was advocated by someone who was close to Sapir and willing to call on him in his modest home and implant the idea over a glass of tea on a holiday afternoon. It was also a method by which Sapir personally made decisions on an *ad hoc* basis, and the Ministry of Commerce and Industry and the Ministry of Finance lacked clear guidelines and standards for dealing with big business. Thus industrialists had far more to gain by currying the favor of ministry officials, or of Sapir himself, than by trying to improve their production or cutting down on their labor costs. It was easier to make a profit this way than to work hard and achieve increased sales or lower costs.

This same attitude also led to some give and take in connection with the 'Sapir Fund', which must inevitably have led to some abuses – though I was sure that as far as Sapir personally was concerned, it was absolutely aboveboard.

Sapir was linked with some unsavory incidents, although he himself was of the highest personal integrity. There is not a soul, not even among his most violent critics – most of whom have halted their criticism since his death – who believed that he stood to gain personally in these dealings. But that is not the point. The issue was not the man, but the system. And the system is not restricted to the minister himself.

Basically I always believed in approaching people to donate money for a specific educational or civic project. That would allow the donors to see the results of their generosity. Under Sapir, however, government officials dealt with people who were investing and building in Israel, so that the very same people were offering gifts and applying for certain concessions. When you combined donations and the Sapir method of conducting business, disaster was inevitable. It was impossible to establish priorities when the methods befitted the small-town leader who knew everybody's problem and could conduct business out of his waist-coat pocket. A minister of finance, even in a small country like Israel, must be a statesman.

As to Jerusalem, Sapir supported many of its institutions but not the city itself. Whenever I claimed that Jerusalem was not getting its share, he showed me long lists of industrial and educational institutions that had been showered with funds. He had no understanding of the fact that when you invest hundreds of millions of pounds in a university, for example, you also have to invest an appropriate amount at least in building the roads leading to it. The same surely is true about the new suburbs going up around the city and a parallel strengthening of the central city. We have not yet entirely overcome this negative tradition. It was very difficult to fight Sapir, and it is astonishing that we did make progress in getting some governmental support, in spite of his attitude.

Perhaps the gravest danger of all, however, was not to recognize immediately after the Yom Kippur War that the time had come to bring home to the people the need to lower sharply our standard of living. Sapir saw the solution in going out and collecting more donations from the Jews all over the world, rather than in changing policy at home. I am perfectly convinced that in a few years' time nobody will be able to understand how we survived for years and years under Sapir's short-sighted economic dictatorship.

It was principles of this kind that played a major role in the Lavon Affair, the battle Ben-Gurion undertook and lost. When he resigned in June 1963, Levi Eshkol was Ben-Gurion's choice to succeed him, and naturally Ben-Gurion's friends wanted him to be successful. I had known Eshkol a long time and had worked closely with him while he was minister of finance. I usually called on him on Saturday mornings to discuss the affairs of the week and bring about some coordination between Ben-Gurion and his chief lieutenant in the Cabinet. We had many talks during the Lavon Affair. He felt that Ben-Gurion was exaggerating its importance but supported him because of a sense of loyalty that came naturally. He knew it would be tough for anyone to follow Ben-Gurion, and those of us inside the Prime Minister's Office tried hard to adjust to Eshkol and help him. Yitzhak Navon, Ben-Gurion's personal secretary, had gone to Latin America on a mission when Ben-Gurion resigned. Uri Lubrani, who had been working on Arab affairs in the Prime Minister's Office, had temporarily replaced Navon and continued to act as Eshkol's private secretary during his first few weeks in office. But soon it became clear that Eshkol had to have people of his own choice.

Eshkol brought in some people recommended by Ya'akov Arnon, the director-general of the Finance Ministry, and I remained with my vague and many-sided role as director-general of the Prime Minister's

Office. But the whole style of things was completely different. As the months went by, Eshkol began to take a much greater interest in the details pouring into the Prime Minister's Office than Ben-Gurion ever had. His interest went beyond deciding on policy or principle; he intervened in the smallest decisions. Moreover, you might arrive at a decision with him and the next morning, having talked to someone else, he had changed his mind. Sometimes he even forgot to tell you so. Still, it was impossible to dislike Eshkol, and we remained on good personal terms for the rest of his life.

After he became prime minister, Eshkol remarried (he had been a widower). There were quite a few candidates, but Miriam was the lucky one. It was a sudden marriage ceremony squeezed into an overburdened schedule, as Eshkol had become a very busy man. A rabbi was provided for the wedding on a few hours' notice. I remember that at the last moment Eshkol said jokingly, 'Maybe we should postpone it?' He always hated making crucial decisions. 'You'll have to decide one day,' we said almost in unison. Finally, at eleven o'clock, it was decided to hold the wedding at noon. I rushed home, Tamar grabbed half a cake and a bottle of champagne, and we rushed off to what was a very small and pleasant wedding party at Eshkol's home. It became a happy marriage indeed.

Miriam had a strong influence on Eshkol, and I think she directed him on to the wrong course in his rift with Ben-Gurion. She apparently felt that Eshkol should assert himself and be a strong prime minister and that this was the only way he could demonstrate leadership to the country. It may have been a legitimate attitude on her part, but left to his own devices, Eshkol might have found ways to compromise with Ben-Gurion. Such accommodation might have lessened the tensions that eventually led to the split in Mapai, which had a long-term negative influence on Israel's affairs. Even though the party was reunited a few years later, the wound was not entirely healed. Sometimes a little stone on the tracks can derail a large train.

My final break with the Prime Minister's Office resulted mainly from the continuing argument about secret, absolutely personal reports from the head of Intelligence to the prime minister. Eshkol appointed Meir Amit, a former general and deputy chief of staff and an extremely intelligent and capable person, to head the Mossad. I tried to persuade the prime minister to implement the Yadin-Sharef committee's recommendations by appointing a permanent liaison in the Prime Minister's Office. I even wanted him to make this a condition of Amit's appointment. But Amit opposed the idea as not being in the tradition of the service, and Eshkol gave in.

I believed that this situation might one day cause disastrous results, as it had in the past. Although I had no direct connection or responsibility in this sphere, I did not want to remain in the Prime Minister's Office if the loose arrangements of the past were perpetuated. I finally decided to leave. Eshkol made several attempts to persuade me to stay (in general he didn't like upheavals), but I felt that my usefulness had come to an end.

Some time after the changeover from Ben-Gurion to Eshkol, I had a long conversation with Isaiah Berlin on the difference between the two regimes. Isaiah tried to explain to me that it was time to bring the 'heroic period' to a close. We could not go on demanding heroism from the people all the time, as Ben-Gurion did. The country should be able to relax a little, and whatever our personal feelings were, we should be happy that a shift toward relaxation had taken place. I tried to convince him that our roots were in many ways still very shallow, and another four years with Ben-Gurion as prime minister would have been tremendously advantageous. Now, many years later, I still believe that.

12 Two Victories

WHEN I left the Prime Minister's Office on January 1, 1965, the Israel Museum was in the last stages of construction. I had become involved with it while still working for Ben-Gurion. It hardly came within the scope of my 'official' functions (for one, it was a private institution), but the idea of a great art museum in Israel, in Jerusalem, excited me beyond anything I had undertaken until then. I suppose that excitement was rooted in my childhood. I had grown up in a beautiful city, and as a boy I loved looking at the miniatures, pieces of glass, and little silver snuff boxes my father collected. He often took me to the museums of Vienna, and although I never had had any artistic talents, beautiful surroundings were part of my life. I couldn't conceive of a country existing without them.

The story of the Israel Museum goes way back to the American aid we received in the early 1950s. At that time, the United States Economic Aid was accumulating what are called counterpart funds – Israeli pounds that were paid to the American government for supplies and services. The Americans were very generous in allocating these funds to Israel's benefit. For example, Israel had no foreign exchange reserves whatsoever. In 1952 we couldn't even buy books, records, or newspapers abroad. On the other hand, a substantial number of books from Russia and other countries behind the Iron Curtain were shipped into Israel free. They were in English and German, the languages most widely read in Israel, and they filled the bookshops. But we had no foreign currency to buy from the Western world.

This was the period when the Cold War was at its height, and the Americans wanted to balance this influx of books from Communist countries with material from the West. Other countries, like India, were in the same position. So the Americans initiated a program for which they initially allocated $10 million, if my memory serves me correctly, and we started getting large quantities of American books, periodicals, and records. All the money accruing from the sales of these items was put into a special account destined to be used only within Israel for cultural purposes.

Then the program was withdrawn from Israel, partly because our small population bought more Western books and periodicals than the combined populations of all the other non-dollar countries involved, including India and Pakistan. And by the time it was over, we were earning enough foreign currency of our own to allocate money for things other than the bare necessities. But during that period of two or three years, the equivalent of $5 million or $6 million had accumulated in the special account of Israeli pounds. In 1954 or 1955, Bernard Katzen arrived from America to distribute these funds to various cultural projects in the country.

Katzen had been appointed by John Foster Dulles as a kind of U.S. cultural fairy godmother. He announced to the world that he was coming here to give away money, and immediately everyone in Israel was after him. Before long matters got out of control, and we were afraid that much money would be wasted on unsound programs. So we decided to submit to Katzen a program on behalf of the Prime Minister's Office. I met him two days after his arrival and he seemed very relieved when he looked over our suggestions. He had made some previous commitments for a few thousand Israeli pounds, but the rest was allocated according to our program. It was divided between the translation of classics into Hebrew, in which Ben-Gurion had a great interest; the Weizmann Institute; the Hebrew University in Jerusalem (none of the other universities existed); the Mann Auditorium in Tel Aviv; and various projects in towns and villages. But the largest single amount went to the Israel Museum, and that was how we were able to start.

From the beginning, the museum was conceived as an independent project. I felt that Jerusalem had to have a great museum. First of all, important archaeological finds were brought to light every day. Whenever a new village was built, wherever a plow started turning up the soil, new artifacts were found; but there was no place to display these finds. I also believed that we should have a great art museum in our country. Most young people in Israel were unable to travel abroad and were deprived of seeing the beautiful works of art with which the children of Europe, for example, were familiar. I felt that a museum to display the greatest artistic achievements of civilization from all corners of the world, even in small samples, was important. I also hoped that many of the outstanding collections of Jewish-owned art abroad would eventually find their home in Jerusalem – once a good building existed. Such a museum would be an antidote to the cultural insularity of a small nation. Moreover, I believed that a good museum, particularly the archaeological part, would become a great tourist attraction.

We received a quarter of the counterpart funds for the museum – a tremendous amount of money then – and plans for the project advanced quickly. I talked to Eshkol, who was minister of finance at the time, and we obtained a plot of land owned by the government between the Hebrew University and the Valley of the Cross. Then, when I left the Prime Minister's Office, I spent most of my time helping to bring the museum to completion and guiding its early activities. I had been a member of the museum board from its establishment, and I continued to work for the museum full time until June 1965.

For years I had been talking about my concept of a museum with the only school friend I had from Vienna, a man by the name of Gad (originally Goldberg) whom we all called Hego. Hego had become an outstanding architect and had settled in Tel Aviv. Together with his wife, Dora, he specialized in interior architecture. In fact, immediately after the declaration of the state, I had raised the money to acquire a building for the official residence of the foreign minister in Tel Aviv and had asked them to renovate it and furnish it. Hego and Dora had done a splendid job, and from there they had gone on from achievement to achievement.

I sat with Hego and Dora from time to time and discussed my dream of the museum. I conceived of it as being built on a hill in Jerusalem like a Mediterranean village, so that pavilions could be added whenever new collections were acquired and more money was available. Hego passed away very young. His last work, together with Dora and a Haifa architect, Professor Mansfeld, was the interior of two small Israeli passenger ships and finally the great *Shalom*. I was against these wasteful passenger ships; I didn't think they added anything to tourism or that they would amount to much for Zim, our largest shipping company. To my regret I was proven right; but the ships were certainly the most comfortable and beautifully equipped sailing the ocean at that time. At any rate, when the architectural competition for the museum was announced, I rang Dora and said, 'Why don't you participate? We discussed such beautiful ideas with Hego.' Finally she and Mansfeld entered their ideas for the museum. I was not on the jury, but when I was shown the winning design, I knew who had done it.

Construction began in 1961. The first art collector I approached was Billy Rose, who had amassed an important collection of sculpture. Rose had been approached a long time before by Nahum Goldmann and Gershon Agron. But when Agron was mayor of Jerusalem, there was no museum, not even a site. Now we had the site, the money, and the authorization, and Billy responded. His contribution required space, and we agreed to give him five acres of the eighty we had. Considerable expense would be involved in preparing the ground, and several meetings were held with Billy in New York and in Jerusalem. He wanted other donors to share his interest, and eventually he gave not only generously but the choicest pieces of sculpture from his collection. Billy commissioned Noguchi to design the garden, and we were on the way.

On May 7, 1965, the Israel Museum in Jerusalem had its grand opening ceremony. A few days before, things looked so chaotic that people were betting the museum would not be ready in time. I was sure it would all come together and took every bet. And I won them. Everything clicked into place, including the May sun and breezes. It was a glorious affair, the best of its kind I had ever seen. We had a limited number of seats on the museum's plaza – about a thousand – and at least five times as many requests for invitations. The very fact that thousands wanted to come and could not be accommodated created great curiosity, excitement, and a feeling of great anticipation. Crowds arrived in Jerusalem from all over the country and from abroad. People were willing to go to extraordinary lengths to be there. All this for a museum. It was glorious.

We had planned everything down to the smallest detail. The invitation card, for instance, could be folded into the shape of a hat to shade the guests from the sun. On the eve of the opening, the Israel Philharmonic gave a festive concert at the Convention Center in Jerusalem. On the opening night itself, we presented gold medals to everyone who had contributed in a major way, from Samuel Bronfman (whose children had given over a million dollars to the archaeological wing), to a construction worker who outdid himself (and is now a contractor in Jerusalem). Even the speeches were brilliant. Eshkol spoke beautifully, and Bernard Katzen's introductory speech was eloquent. And we received a long, splendid message from President Johnson. (It was much rarer then to receive a message from the president of the United States, particularly for the opening of an art museum in another country.)

We opened with an exhibition of fifty great works illustrating scenes from the Bible, from Rembrandt's Moses carrying the tablets down from Mount Sinai to a beautiful sixteenth-century enameled cofanetto from Limoges depicting scenes from Joseph's life. The works, from every part of the world, were on loan from some of the best museums, as well as from private collections. The loans we received from Vienna, New York, Philadelphia, Chicago, the Netherlands, Germany, and Washington were generous – all masterpieces – and their impact was indescribable.

It happened that elsewhere in the world, two other museums opened during the same week or so. One is probably the greatest museum created in our generation: the Mexican Museum of Anthropology, an ethnographic museum designed by the great architect Ramirez Vazquez. Set in an impressive park, it was created with a grant from the Mexican government. The other, the Los Angeles County Museum, is located in one of the richest cities in the world and was designed by Pereira, a well-known California architect. It is also a very fine museum, but I think ours may be proudly compared to both. I should also add that the Israel Museum was built at a much lower cost than the other two.

Altogether, we spent a little over $8 million for the part that was com-
pleted. The Los Angeles Museum spent over $16 million, and the
Mexican Museum spent very much more. The setting of the Israel
Museum, on the hill overlooking the Monastery of the Cross, is second
to none. And for the quality of its art and archaeological objects, our
museum is of the highest distinction.

I attribute this status to the principles we adopted from the start.
First of all, only first-rate quality, regardless of the artist's race or
religion, was acceptable. In the beginning, pressures to place emphasis
on works by Jewish artists were strong – and there are some great
Jewish artists : Modigliani or Chagall, for example. But they are not
great because they are Jews; they are essentially European artists. If we
had given preference to Israeli and Jewish artists, the museum would
have become a parochial affair, and its standards would have dwindled
into obscurity. Nonetheless, the arguments about how much and what
Israeli art to exhibit continued over the years. We were finally able to
build several – but still too few – pavilions for a permanent collection of
the works of Israeli painters and sculptors, as well as provide temporary
exhibitions. Had we stressed Israeli art out of proportion, however, the
great gifts we have received or have been promised – which are some of
our country's great national treasures – would never have come to
Israel.

It was necessary to construct an outstanding building for another
reason. Here I must go back to the early 1950s, when Tamar, Amos, and
I were living in Washington. At that time, two well-known American
Jewish art collectors happened to pass away, Maurice Wertheim and
Sam Lewisohn (a distant relative of Tamar's). Wertheim bequeathed
all his paintings to the Harvard Fogg Museum; Lewisohn left his to the
Metropolitan Museum in New York. Though Wertheim had been
interested in Israel, was a personal friend of Ben-Gurion's, and had been
chairman of the American Jewish Committee, he had never thought of
leaving a single painting to us. Similarly, Sam Lewisohn's family were
major public benefactors (among other projects, they built Lewisohn
Stadium in New York), but it never occurred to him to set aside even
one painting for Israel.

At first I wondered about this. But as I came to know some of the
collectors better, I discovered that a collector's attitude toward his
paintings is almost like a father's toward his children. By the time he has
put together a collection of importance, his own children are probably
grown and have left him. Anyway, he cannot tell them what to do. With
the paintings, however, he has absolute rule. He wants for them the
same things he would like, say, for his daughters : to settle down in a
nice neighborhood, marry fine boys, and be surrounded by the best company. That is the reason a collector will not give his paintings to a

second-rate museum. He would like them to be in the company of other good paintings – the best. And just as he would like his family to stick together, he wants his paintings to remain together – a strong and note-worthy group – and thereby have his name preserved, just as he would like it preserved by fine and faithful sons and grandsons. This brings me to my second point: the singular importance of a first-rate museum building – beautiful, modern, with good lighting and the temperature and humidity control necessary for works of art. These standards were especially important at the start, before we had established a reputation for only the very best.

Meeting these two criteria – a flawless basic art collection and an impeccable museum building – takes time. But we were faced by an additional fact of life that refused to wait. Many of the potential bene-factors were growing old, and for men in their tax brackets the inherit-ance tax is practically prohibitive. Family members who inherit a fine art collection also inherit devastating taxes, which they often cannot afford. The only alternative is for the collector to give or will the collec-tion to public institutions. One thing was certain: most of the present collections, certainly in countries like the United States and England, would end up in museums. It was important that our museum be one of the public institutions that would benefit. Therefore, we needed the building urgently. Another ten or fifteen years would have been too late. The argument that is always put forward – it's best to wait until we are over the particularly grave problem of this particularly difficult week, or month, or year in our history – is a futile one. Israel needs to absorb immigrants and it needs arms, but it also needs expressions of culture and civilization. Otherwise we will not be able to survive.

When I returned from the United States in 1952, I examined the museum question. Others had thought about it. Mordechai Narkiss, the curator of the modest Bezalel Museum in Jerusalem (which concentrated mainly on Jewish ceremonial art), had tried to add some paintings of general interest, but with limited success. Archaeologists like Benjamin Mazar and Yigael Yadin had discussed an archaeological museum, for we had some very interesting finds from our excavations but no place to show them. And, of course, there were the Dead Sea Scrolls, which were exhibited in the basement of the Hebrew University. In addition, some of our orientalists wanted to gather and display Islamic art.

Gradually we formed a working group composed of Narkiss, Mazar, Yadin, the orientalist Professor Leo Ary Mayer, and myself. We invited Gershon Agron, then mayor of Jerusalem, to join us. We met, talked, planned, and eventually developed the idea of a universal museum em-bracing samples of the finest that human genius had created anywhere in the world, including a large wing concentrating on Biblical archaeology. To that concept, Karl Katz of the Bezalel Museum added an emphasis on attracting the youth of the country and through them reaching that part of the older generation which is indifferent to art or had never visited a museum before.

During the early 1950s, our national leaders did not place high priority on the first stirrings toward an art museum. They felt that in that comparatively early phase of national renaissance, art was a luxury. It did not occur to them that a museum was a vital organ in the body of a society. As our society struggled through its formative years, the museum performed many roles beyond being a repository of great art. Children came bringing parents who had never heard the word museum. Suddenly these people saw beautiful dresses from Morocco, a beautiful ancient Torah scroll from Yemen or Iraq, an old Hanukkah lamp from Tunis or Kurdistan, all exhibited with the same care and elegance as Dutch paintings and French sculpture. It gave them pride and a sense of belonging to see objects familiar from their native lands displayed in such a setting.

In 1960 Charles Bronfman arrived from Canada with Leo Kolber, a high-level executive of Seagrams. I had met Charles several times in the States with Samuel Bronfman, his father and founder of the Seagrams liquor empire. Sam had always been very active in Jewish affairs and was the recognized leader of Canadian Jewry. Through Seagrams, he had a wealth of interests all over the United States. I came to see him for the first time in 1950 or 1951, when he helped us contact some of the congressmen and senators who supported our foreign aid application in Washington. Since then I had kept contact particularly with Sam and his wife, Saidye, but I had also come to know the children. Charles and the other three Bronfman children, Edgar, Minda, and Phyllis, wanted to give their father a joint gift for his seventieth birthday. This was the hand of fate. Our little group wasted no time in pointing out what to give a man who has everything: 'Has he got an archaeological wing in a museum in Jerusalem?' we asked.

The Bronfmans responded to the idea instantly. They were considering giving us two or three times the million and a half dollars we finally received if the whole museum were named the Bronfman Museum. But in the end we all saw that it would not be wise, if only because that might make other donors reluctant. So we decided to call the museum what it really intended to be: the Israel Museum. Then, properly and proudly, we could dedicate the Bronfman Wing, the Crown Plaza, the Goldman Hall, the Gruss Gallery, the Billy Rose Art Garden, and so on. Of course, the success of the museum depended ultimately on the excellent group of highly qualified curators, headed initially by Karl Katz and then by Elisheva Cohen, who later continued as the museum's general art adviser.

With Marc Chagall, the museum had an unhappy romance. He had done some beautiful things for Jerusalem. I first met him in the early 1960s when he was working on the twelve stained-glass windows for the synagogue in the Hadassah Medical Center. Later he did the beautiful tapestries for the Knesset building (which he recently permitted us to reproduce on postage stamps). Chagall and I got along very well most of the time. The difficulty began when we wanted to create a special Chagall pavilion. Chagall was not even consistent about his rejection of the idea. At one point he said he would consent if we gave him a separate building. We agreed, and then he changed his mind.

Chagall is a complex person. He appeared angry at the museum opening, despite the prominent display of his paintings (which we had borrowed from other institutions), and I have a suspicion it was because we had a similar display of Jacques Lipchitz sculpture. On the other hand, while he could not tolerate a Jewish competitor, he never wanted to be narrowly classified as a Jewish artist. He undoubtedly was proud of being a Jew, and he knew that his roots were in Jewish tradition; but by coming too close to Israel, he feared that he would be jeopardizing his position as a great universal artist. Whatever the world's judgment of Chagall will be a few decades from now, Israel will appreciate him more than any other country. He has portrayed for posterity one of the most poignant experiences of our recent history, the little Jewish *shtetl* in Russia, a way of life that has entirely disappeared. It exists in the descriptions of some of our writers, but only in Chagall's paintings is it visible.

Chagall was also angry, and rightly so, because his windows were not well placed. The small synagogue building at the Hadassah Hospital in Jerusalem did not satisfy his expectations. The windows were too close together, and for years we tried to find remedies for this miscalculation, but we could not convince Hadassah to give up their windows. Together with Chagall, we made propositions and counter-propositions : he could create smaller, more suitable stained-glass windows for Hadassah, and the windows of the Twelve Tribes would be installed in a specially designed synagogue. But we got nowhere. Still, the windows themselves are as beautiful as ever.

The attitude of the sculptor Jacques Lipchitz toward Israel was much less complicated. He regarded himself first and foremost as a Jew, and during the later years of his life he became a follower of the Hassidic Lubavitcher Rebbe. Lipchitz felt that the fountainhead of Jewry today was in Israel. He spent much time in the country, and his last, not quite completed work of art was a plaster cast for a twenty-foot sculpture to stand by the restored Hadassah Hospital on Mount Scopus. He regarded this as the crowning achievement of his career. Finally, after much labor by his wife, Yulla, this sculpture is being completed, and Jacques' last request will be carried out. The Israel Museum is the proud owner of several important Lipchitz sculptures, several drawings, and, even more important, 130 bronze maquettes that were models for his sculptures. These were donated to the museum by Jacques' brother, Reuben, and in a sense they are sometimes more interesting than the sculptures themselves, because you can actually see the thumb mark of the master on them. This comprehensive collection of a great artist of our time is a great attraction at the museum.

The English Rothschilds also made a significant donation in those early days. They had seen and liked the museum and shared our conviction that we must set an uncompromising standard of quality from the very start. They backed their conviction with five great paintings – two Van Goghs, a Cézanne, and two Gauguins. These paintings had been willed to a distant and poor relative, and the English Rothschilds bought them back for the Israel Museum.

A similar conviction was expressed a few years ago by Baron Edmond de Rothschild in Paris, a very close friend. He and his wife, Nadine, gave our museum one of our most outstanding single gifts – an eighteenth-century French Period Room, which is considered the best of its kind outside France. Period rooms (and this was the first of several donated to the museum) have special importance for the many Israelis who do not have the opportunity to travel abroad. Edmond is the chairman of the museum's International Board of Governors and chairs our annual meetings in Jerusalem with great efficiency. His involvement naturally lends considerable prestige to the museum, and his knowledge as a collector allows us to avail ourselves of his excellent judgment.

After a decade as mayor, I am still the chairman of the board of the museum and go into my office there almost every day. It is like a second home to me. But I am getting slightly ahead of myself. I've grown so accustomed to being mayor that I sometimes forget I wasn't always so comfortable in my role. In fact, how I came to be the mayor of Jerusalem is an unusual story in itself.

After I resigned as director-general of the Prime Minister's Office under Eshkol, I was unemployed for a while – except for my work as an unpaid member of the museum committee. That job was solely a labor of love, and it filled all my time for a number of months. But I knew I had to find a real job, so I was interested when Elie Kirschner approached me with a business offer – my first commercial bread-and-butter job.

Elie, a Tel Aviv lawyer who was an important figure in the Africa-Israel Investment Company, offered me the presidency of the company. I hesitated, mainly because Tamar and I would eventually have to leave Jerusalem and live in the rich-man's suburb of Savyon, near Tel Aviv, one of the company's major interests. But I finally decided to accept the offer and leave the suburb problem to be faced later. One of the company's enterprises was the Tiberias Hot Springs, across the lake from

Ein Gev, and that had an appealing point for both Tamar and me. I asked Meir Sherman, who by then had moved to Israel, to negotiate my contract. The salary and benefits were high at the time. In fact, despite the rapid inflation in Israel, I reached the same amount on my mayor's salary only ten years later.

That was early in 1965, and the company was in the doldrums. It had good basic investments in real estate in and near Tel Aviv and around the Sea of Galilee, but suddenly all the shares in Israel began to fall because of the onset of a serious economic recession. Anyway, I remained president of the Africa-Israel Investment Company for eight or nine months, during which the company achieved some minor successes – though I don't think that they were much of my doing. Even though I found my presidential job a bit dull, I fully intended to stay. I wanted to leave public life – with the exception of the museum – and for the time being Tamar and I continued to live in Jerusalem, so that I could go to the museum every evening and deal with the important developments of its initial period.

In some ways, being out of government service didn't change things. I was never an active member of a political party, and I never did have a taste for politics. I had belonged to the largest Labor party, Mapai, as a matter of conviction, but I had no desire for elective office or any type of party appointment. In the thirteen years I was in the Prime Minister's Office under Ben-Gurion, I rarely attended party meetings.

Nor was I in line to be appointed a minister. In fact I was always of the opinion that party politics played too great a part in the country's affairs. The pleasant thing in the Prime Minister's Office was that I could do a variety of jobs without paying for the privilege by political hack work. I also made it clear on every occasion that I would not accept a long-term job abroad. There was occasional talk in the press about my being appointed ambassador to Washington, but I would never have wanted it. An ambassadorship is a way of life to which I do not feel particularly suited, and I know Tamar would have cared for it even less.

Then in 1965 Ben-Gurion, who was in retirement at Sdeh Boker, broke with the Mapai Party. A minority of the Mapai members went with him and created a new Labor party – Rafi. I wasn't really enthusiastic about the idea, but I cared about Ben-Gurion and some of the others who rallied to him, and I wanted to see them prevail. The principal reason for my joining Rafi was that I thought the Mapai old guard – Eshkol, Golda, Aranne, and the rest – were behaving abominably toward Ben-Gurion. Not that he hadn't given many reasons for criticism; but in my view, he was basically right. The other major reason for leaving Mapai was my feeling that it was of great importance to fight the rising influence of Pinhas Sapir and what he stood for. I was not among the first to join Rafi. Still, Dayan joined even later than I did.

Once he had come into the ranks, however, he seemed more optimistic than I. 'We'll show them,' he said. 'We'll get more than ten or twelve Knesset seats. We'll get at least twenty.' (There are 120 members in the Knesset.)

I also held others who left Mapai in high regard. Among them was Shimon Peres, even though in his deep belief in the greatness of the Jewish people, he sometimes overrates our strength and importance. He thought that we could build a super-modern industrial economy and coined a slogan about 'a car for every worker', and he believed the French had a genuine interest in a permanent alliance with Israel, beyond their temporary trouble with Algeria. Between the wars of 1967 and 1973, Peres even believed that we were the strongest country between Europe and Japan because we used more electricity per capita or more fertilizers than India or any other country on the Asian continent. This deep conviction about our strength occasionally distorted his political judgment. But I was always impressed with Peres' loyalty, especially to Ben-Gurion. Following Ben-Gurion to Rafi certainly did not advance his personal career at all. He could easily have remained deputy minister of defense under Eshkol, if he had been willing to part with Ben-Gurion. And his loyalty toward Dayan after the Yom Kippur War prevented him from doing better for the Rafi people – and for himself – when he opposed Dayan's offer to resign. The Israeli government had no more articulate spokesman of its policy than Shimon Peres. He certainly is one of the good men the country has.

During the summer of 1965, when the election campaign opened, I became politically active for the first time in my life. I wasn't seeking office for myself, but I wanted to be of use to the Rafi Party in its first national contest. In the main, I traveled to rallies all over the country, and, of course, I spoke at meetings in Jerusalem. The last day for the announcement of party candidates was at the end of the Sukkot holiday in early fall. I was driving up to Ein Gev for the holidays, and on the way I stopped in Tel Aviv and had lunch with Moshe Dayan, Shimon Peres, and Yitzhak Navon. They wanted me to run as a Rafi candidate for the Knesset, but I wasn't interested; I have never seen myself as a legislator. Even when they repeated that Rafi was having an uphill battle in its first campaign and that my name would be of value, I told them that law-making was not for me. I preferred a more active life, and all my experience had been as an executive or administrator.

Then they came up with the idea that I should run for the mayoralty of Jerusalem. They felt that I would get a substantial vote in Jerusalem and that whoever voted for me would tend to vote the Rafi national ticket as well, thus increasing our support in the Knesset. I backed away and suggested Dov Joseph. He knew Jerusalem well and had been the civilian governor during the difficult days of the siege in 1948. More recently, he served as minister of justice under Ben-Gurion and, briefly, under Eshkol. But Dov Joseph turned down the Rafi offer. In the meantime I had continued on to Ein Gev, where I was visited by Amos Manor, a very old friend whom I had first met in 1934, when I visited the youth movement in Rumania. He is years younger than I – a tall powerful man, one of the few to survive Auschwitz – and he became head of the Shin Bet (the Internal Security Service), having worked for years under Isser Har'el. Amos and I often saw things in the same light, and he pressed me to run for mayor. So did many others who happened to look me up just then.

They finally convinced me. Not that I had a deep interest in city problems. Many of us in public service believed that a good appointed official could run the cities much better than elected mayors. And except for Haifa's Abba Khoushy, the mayors didn't seem to be doing a very good job. I sometimes had meetings with Mordechai Ish Shalom, who became mayor of Jerusalem after the death of Gershon Agron. He turned to the prime minister for help because Orthodox Jews had been throwing stones at the Mandelbaum Gate on Saturdays, when buses carrying Christian pilgrims from Jordan disrupted their Sabbath, and Ish Shalom was helpless to do anything about it. There were many similar examples of poor government in the city. Ish Shalom and his associates seemed to lack any spirit whatsoever. I once tried to get them warmed up about the idea of the museum. I began to address them, and halfway through my speech I stopped. It seemed a waste of time. So it seemed ironical to me that I should end up in this municipal business myself.

At any rate, I did not believe I had the slightest chance of winning against the strong Mapai machine in Jerusalem, which had always been victorious. The real reason for running was to demonstrate my loyalty to Ben-Gurion, even if there was no chance of success. Like me, Tamar didn't believe that anything would come of the idea. My brother, Paul, who also thought it was a dead end, advised me against getting caught up in lost causes. I imagine that as a businessman, he saw a better future for me in private enterprise. My son's attitude was less enthused and more specific: 'What will happen if you win? You'll be in charge of the garbage?' That was pretty much the way I viewed the mayoralty myself. But time was running out, and I had to make a decision. When I left Ein Gev and returned to Jerusalem on the last day for announcing candidacy, I had decided to run.

I entered the shabby Rafi headquarters on a side alley in Jerusalem, signed all the papers, got together a list of running mates, and I was in the fight. I was also still with the Africa-Israel Investment Company, which made for a crowded day. Every morning at six I traveled to my business office in Tel Aviv and worked until two or three in the afternoon.

Then I would return to Jerusalem, spend an hour at the museum, and from five until late in the night I worked on my election campaign. I cannot remember when I ate or whether I ate, which is most unusual for me. We opened a special office for the municipal election campaign in the King's Hotel. Two younger men I had known over the years, Meron Benvenisti and Uzi Michaeli, worked hard and ably. Even my skeptical son, who was about to join the army, devoted a few hours a week to the general effort. But looking back I can see that we all went about it amateurishly. After all, I did not really believe I had a chance.

Eshkol was very upset when I left Mapai and joined Rafi, especially once I decided to run for office. Several times he warned me against it – for my own sake. When a book about Eshkol was published in time for the elections, he sent me a copy inscribed : 'With friendship and affection, with sorrow and anxiety.' He meant every word. Eshkol was one of the few Mapai leaders I could still talk to even after I was elected mayor. Many others, including old friends, avoided me like the plague when I joined Rafi.

Take, for instance, Abba Eban. I had known him a long time, even before he came to Palestine as a British Army officer in 1942. In 1946 I urged Moshe Sharett to bring him into the Agency; a year later I helped persuade him to remain in Palestine and work for the future Jewish state, rather than pursue a diplomatic or academic career back in England; and in 1948 I fought for Eban to become number one man at the United Nations, when Sharett thought he should be number two. I worked with Eban very closely in Washington when he was both ambassador to the United States and our top man at the U.N. We were never very close personally, but I had and continued to have high regard for his abilities, and I deeply regretted that in recent years they were not always put to the best possible national use.

In the midst of the 1965 elections, Eban attacked me personally, saying flat out that much in my campaign speeches was untrue and boastful, meaning that I had never done what I claimed to have done. When some journalist rang me up about Eban's statement, I said, 'I can prove what I said, but I would have to give away some secrets that might be embarrassing to the government. If Eban won't withdraw, though, I'll have no choice. I cannot let myself be called a liar.' Eban withdrew his statement but continued with his general attack. In a sense, he was a newcomer, unattuned to party politics, and I suppose he had to prove himself.

Election day was drawing near, and I can't honestly say that toward the end I still didn't care. Running for office inevitably becomes a very personal challenge. You don't want your family and friends to see you lose, and you cannot stay detached. I, who had always been opposed to party politics and indirect elections, increasingly felt that the race in

Jerusalem would be decided in a unique way : one man versus a party machine. The realization gave me an additional incentive to win. According to the system of municipal elections back then, the public voted for party lists, not for individual candidates. The list that received the most votes was given the opportunity to form a coalition, if necessary (and it always was), and place its leading personality in the mayor's chair. Our national elections are run the same way to this day (although the municipal elections are now direct ones), and the cities simply copied the system.

From the very start, I opposed indirect elections – a system modelled on the electoral traditions of Central and East European democracies of the post-World War One era – and favored direct constituency elections. Not that issues don't play a part in an election campaign. But the most important thing is for people to know whom they are electing and for the elected official to have direct contact with a definite constituency and represent its interests. As things work today, candidates for the Knesset are chosen by party secretaries, often on the basis of loyalty rather than ability and without any consideration for the people's wishes. When the next election comes around, if the electorate feels that any individual Knesset member was particularly good, or conspicuously poor, it has no power to ensure that the member in question is either promoted on the party list or dropped from it altogether. At the same time, Knesset members from the same party may have opposing views, and the voter has no way of knowing which policy will be implemented.

In 1948, when I talked to Ben-Gurion about direct elections – in which he believed even more strongly than I did – I failed to foresee all the dangers of the system that eventually evolved and has actually made our democracy a farce. What we have in Israel is political liberty and freedom of expression. But of democracy – in the sense that the people have an influence on the legislator – we have very little.

In the case of municipal elections, the system was even more inappropriate. In choosing a list, the voter was identifying with a party's national policies, rather than directing his attention to problems specific to his own town or city. The positions a particular list adopts in the realm of foreign policy or economic affairs have little or no relevance to municipal matters. Yet when people went out to vote for their city council, these were the issues on which they had to choose between one party and another.

The basic point is that a man should bear direct responsibility to the people who elect him. This is particularly important in city elections. I think it is essential for a mayor to run on a personal ticket, rather than a party list, and come to every street once in a while, meet with the citizens, hear their complaints, and remain accessible to his constituency. Today, as a result of public pressure, we have a sort of compromise between what the people really want and what the parties are willing to concede. Elections for mayor are direct and personal ones, but the city council is still elected by party lists – meaning that the whole city is one constituency and individual districts cannot vote for their own representatives. I believe this modification – which is still not totally satisfying – came about because public pressure had become too great (starting in Jerusalem in 1965 and subsequently reaching Tel Aviv and several smaller places). Changing the municipal election system was the Knesset's way of throwing a bone to the public. But I hope that the people will find a way to enforce a change in the national elections system as well.

In my first election, a newspaper poll predicted that I would get as many as three out of the twenty-one seats on the city council, which certainly would have precluded all possibilities for the mayoralty. Mordechai Ish Shalom, the incumbent mayor and Mapai's candidate, was positive he would win. He never doubted it. In the end, I did better than expected. I got five seats, and Mapai got five – a tie. But my total did not help Rafi in the national election as much as we had hoped. There was a sizable discrepancy between the number of votes Rafi's national slate received in Jerusalem and the number cast for our city list. The city vote was to some extent personal and a popular expression of support for the direct election of mayors.

When I say I did comparatively well, it was only in comparison to my low expectations. I hadn't come through with a smashing victory, but for the first time the Mapai party machine had been beaten. Eventually I became mayor by forming a workable coalition. From the beginning, I had stressed the need for a much broader city coalition than had been customary until then. The main lists that had taken part in the elections were Mapai, Rafi, the religious parties, and the right-wing Herut Party (which is today a part of the Likud Party). On a national level, I would have opposed cooperating with the Herut Party. They represented a radically different foreign policy and stood to the right even in social matters. All during their history, the Revisionists (later Herut) had been a party issuing doctrinaire, declamatory statements, and for a short period they espoused terrorism, which was an even more dramatic expression in the same spirit. Mr Begin had his roots not in the Russian anticlerical enlightenment (as did his mentor Jabotinsky) but in Pilsudski's Poland, a country run by an officer class that has been described as willing to die heroically for their fatherland but never to work for it. The Labor movement, in its origins at least, believed in tilling another acre, building another settlement, organizing the vast majority of young people into a popular, countrywide defense force – in short, personal achievements without panache. I have always believed that the Jewish state came about not as a result of acts of terrorism but because of the intensive settlement throughout the country, the great numbers of 'illegal' immigrants brought in by the Haganah, and the quiet diplomatic work carried out by Weizmann and Ben-Gurion.

The British did not bow out of Palestine because of a few bombings or assassinations. Terrorism is uncomfortable for any government, but its main result is suppression, wherever it occurs (this was as true then as it is today). The situation became untenable when the mandatory authorities, under Arab pressure, began deporting survivors of the Holocaust from the only land ready to receive them. The massive 'illegal' immigration organized by the Haganah – and not by the Irgun Zvai Leumi – and the continued establishment of settlements against the active intervention of British troops brought about international pressure (particularly from the United States) too strong to withstand. Jabotinsky's friends and followers belittled these actions and believed sincerely and deeply in the power of the word and political action. Nonetheless, I felt no hesitation about working with Herut in a city government, and the years have proven that they have been very constructive partners.

Since Rafi and Mapai had each won five seats on the City Council, it was up to one of us to form a coalition. Herut would have agreed to form a coalition with Mapai as easily as with us. Indeed, it would have been more prestigious for Herut to form a coalition with the great Mapai. But the Mapai people were trapped in their own slogans and never even considered it. Anyway, this was the first time that Herut had been invited to join any coalition whatsoever, so they were happy even with us.

The actual coalition negotiations were handled by Yitzhak Navon. He had connections with all the religious parties from the time he had been Ben-Gurion's secretary. The strongest religious party in Jerusalem was the most Orthodox one, Agudat Yisrael. No municipal government in Jerusalem could do without its cooperation. It had been part of every city coalition, and Rabbi Porush had been deputy mayor for years. I had to gain the confidence of the Agudat, and Yitzhak was a brilliant go-between, taking me to visit several of their great rabbis. It was an entirely new experience for me, and in some respects I was probably more acceptable to the religious parties than a semi-religious person would have been. At least they knew where they stood with me.

Another quite unexpected factor helped me gain their confidence. I had hardly known Tamar's grandfather, Rector Aryeh Adolph Schwarz, a great authoritarian figure who headed the Rabbinical Seminary in Vienna. Nor did I know Tamar's father very well, since he fell ill practically immediately after his arrival in Palestine in 1938 and passed away. When I began coalition negotiations with the religious parties, however, my antecedents were thoroughly investigated (though I didn't know that until years later). As it turned out, quite a number of outstanding rabbis in Jerusalem had been pupils of Tamar's grandfather or had maintained a correspondence with him, and many others had been contemporaries of her father. This made me 'kosher'

I should add that my own attitude toward religion has gradually changed during my tenure as mayor. I was brought up to a large extent on anti-religious feelings in both a socialist youth movement and a socialist country. We expressed our Jewishness by leaving our (mostly middle-class) homes in order to work the land in Palestine in the hope that this would lead to the creation of a healthy Jewish society living in its own country. For the members of our movement, this was a stronger expression of our Jewish identification than observing religious laws, like not using electricity or not driving a car on the Sabbath. And I still believe you can be a good Jew even if you don't adhere to all the 613 commandments. Certainly a kibbutznik living on the Syrian frontier is no less a devoted member of the Jewish people than a *yeshivah* student who throws stones at cars passing by on the Sabbath.

My first close acquaintance with religious circles in Israel developed while I worked in the Prime Minister's Office and had dealings with the religious parties in and out of government. The result of these encounters was to reinforce my basic belief that religion and politics should not be mixed. The idea of bargaining over religious principles to make a coalition possible has always impressed me as being contrary to the essence of religious faith. Today, this basic objection on political grounds still remains, and I view it as a fundamental issue for Israeli society. Defining the place of religion in a modern democratic Jewish state is by no means a simple matter, but it is hardly an appropriate subject for coalition negotiations.

On the other hand, I have come to understand that adherence to religious practice is not just a passing phase in Jewish history. It is an elemental means of preserving the Jewish people – and that, for me, is a basic value in itself. If a religious family is unable to educate its children according to its beliefs, the result is often not 'liberated' young people of strong moral fiber, but youth without roots, aimless youngsters who are unable to replace their religious beliefs with anything else and sometimes deteriorate into juvenile delinquents. I also acquired respect not only for some of the religious politicians, who are outstanding and decent people, but for the many religious people in Jerusalem who have raised large families under very difficult economic circumstances and were able to preserve their sense of values. These families represent a strength and dignity that has earned my deepest admiration. Of course we must still aim at developing greater mutual understanding and tolerance between the Orthodox and non-observant sections of our population, and I have tried to do this since becoming mayor. More

Above With Rabbi Porush, exchanging hats at the inauguration of a new fire station (courtesy Ross Photo).

Previous page A view of the Israel Museum, which was designed like a Mediterranean village set into the mountains (courtesy Keren Or).

Teddy 'next to the most famous pair of legs in the world'
(courtesy Michael Maor).

Above Toppling the wall
that divided Jerusalem
(courtesy Photo Ross).

Left With Axel
Springer on the
inaugural run of the new
bus route to the
Jewish Quarter in 1970
(courtesy H. Pinn).

Opposite At David's
Tower with potential
voters on Election Day,
1969 (courtesy
Y. Braun).

Above Catnapping next to an enthralled Yitzhak Navon.

Opposite, below With Simone de Beauvoir overlooking the Wailing Wall plaza and the Mosque of Omar on the Temple Mount (courtesy Rachamim Israeli).

Opposite, above With Ruth Ceshen (left), Mrs Dorothy de Rothschild, and architect Dan Tannai on the way to the opening of the reconstructed Ben Zakkai synagogue complex in the Jewish Quarter (courtesy Zev Radovan).

The Municipality of Jerusalem *vs* Boys' Town, Jerusalem,
in the nation's favorite sport.

Teddy and Amos Kollek in the Jewish Quarter, 1976

synagogues and religious schools were built during my term than in any other period in the city's history; more roads in religious quarters were closed to Sabbath traffic; and incidents of incitement by purposely driving through an Orthodox quarter on the Sabbath have stopped. Such accommodations can only be maintained, however, if both sides display understanding toward their fellow citizens.

The Jerusalem coalition agreement was reached at 6 A.M. on November 12, under pressure of my planned departure to the United States two hours later. My term didn't start until December 1, and I had to settle various matters in the United States, including some museum business. In New York, I had dinner with John Lindsay at Bennett Cerf's home. Lindsay had been elected mayor of New York on the same day I was elected. We joked about that and promised each other asylum in case we became refugees from our respective constituents. It was also on that trip that I obtained the first modest contributions for the city of Jerusalem. One donation in particular was designated for the first pocket park of my administration, a small garden and playground. We added a stone gazelle on which children could sit and 'ride', and it became the prototype for over eighty such parks created throughout the city, most of them in the poorest areas.

My first evening at the Municipality building was just after I returned from the States. I knew nothing about being a mayor, and the prospect frightened me. I knew that the Mapai-dominated national government and many city bodies would be against me. Even the weather was gray and grim. I dropped in on Ish Shalom (officially, he was still mayor), and he sat there looking sad. My first council meeting was to start a few moments later. We had a big majority – sixteen out of the twenty-one seats – and our only opposition was Mapai.

At the council meeting I officially took over from Ish Shalom. It was a depressing ceremony. He made a farewell speech, and I made an acceptance speech. The Chagalls were staying with us that evening, but they did not attend. When Tamar and I returned to our apartment, we found that Marc Chagall had taken all his books and albums from my library shelves and had sketched a little drawing in each of them – his way of consoling me. It was a very gracious act by that most unpredictable artist, and I cherish those books more than I can describe.

Two weeks after the elections, our son Amos joined the army, and during the following three years I saw very little of him. In fact, that was true for his childhood years as well. He was a very closed boy, and I had very little free time. Communication wasn't easy, and during his service it occurred to me that we had never really talked. So in the fall of 1968, following his release from the army, we took a trip to Europe together. We rented a car in Geneva and drove south through France, Italy, and a lot of traffic lights, stopping on the way to visit the Chagalls in their home near Nice and the Jacques Lipchitzes near Lucca, Italy. For the first time we had some time to chat. Then I returned to Israel, while he stayed in Europe.

One day when tension was rising in the area, Amos phoned from London and asked whether there would be a call-up of reserves and he should return. We told him not to worry because it did not look that way. At the end of the conversation he said, 'Incidentally, I got married yesterday.' His bride, Regina, had come to Jerusalem from Switzerland following the advice of her sister, who had spent some time here and had liked it. Regina decided to settle here, and she and Amos had met in Jerusalem and then again in Europe.

They returned to Jerusalem soon after. Regina was a Swiss Gentile and had not yet converted to Judaism. Both Amos and she were very understanding and felt that it might be an embarrassment for me, the mayor of Jerusalem, to have a *'shiksa'* as a daughter-in-law. Regina offered to convert, but I certainly did not intend to take any position on that. I explained to them on several occasions that the decision was theirs alone. Regina took lessons with a rabbi over a fairly long period of time, but the difficulties placed in the way of her conversion were so frustrating that she finally gave up.

Amos went on to writing books. His first novel, *Don't Ask Me If I Love*, was initially published in New York and then translated into Hebrew, and for a few months was number one on the local bestseller list. It was a novel with an autobiographical slant and quite critical of his parents. I particularly felt caricatured. But the book was very readable, and I was happy that Amos had found a publisher and started on his way without my help.

For a long time Amos and Regina seemed to have a very good marriage. When the Yom Kippur War broke out they were abroad, but within eighteen hours they had made it back home, having spent half that time at Heathrow Airport trying to get on a plane. At 3 A.M. the bell rang and there they were. Early the next morning, Amos was in uniform and joined his unit on the Syrian frontier. Yet the marriage did not last, and they parted company shortly thereafter. In the summer of 1974 Amos met a very attractive American law student who was studying Hebrew and challenging Jerusalem to tennis matches. He married Janet Kanarek two years later. From time to time she sends me her ideas for improving Jerusalem – sometimes outrageous but always intriguing.

Amos and I never talked about this, but I think he suffered from my involvement in a hectic public life. Osnat, thirteen years younger, adjusted with greater ease. When she was a small girl, she actually seemed to enjoy being the mayor's daughter. But over the years she gradually changed her attitude and became much less excited about the idea, particularly as life at home became more and more affected by my job.

There's no doubt that Jerusalem was a tough inheritance. My memories of this first period are blurred, but I do recall that about once a month I wanted to resign. I had made some promises – though not many — about cleanliness and helping out the recently established outlying districts. My old friend Ya'akov Yanai tried to comfort me with common sense. 'Why should you break your back over Jerusalem?' he said. 'It's been dirty for two thousand years; you can't change it in a day.' Tamar kept saying that I must not give up. She reminded me that I could not let down the people who had voted for the Rafi list because of me. If it were not for her encouragement and insistence, I might not have stuck it out.

The first days were the toughest, and the Mapai opposition was as unpleasant as it could possibly be. On the council, Ish Shalom was the only decent one among them. He held back to some extent, playing the elder statesman. But it was rough. After their long dismal administration, the Mapai councilmen quickly attacked me for the very things they had not achieved in years. That was not even good politics from their point of view! But they were terribly chagrined about having been thrown out of office. It had never happened to them before – anywhere. And beyond this, we faced complications in relations with the national government as well.

A basic misconception about city life prevailed in Israel. My own feelings were a typical example. My experience consisted of years in a kibbutz and then involvement in the national government, and I must admit to having had a cavalier attitude toward mayors and city councils. I was convinced that existing municipal problems were simply the result of a lack of administrative abilities on the part of the local authorities.

It did not take me long to realize otherwise. I suddenly became aware of the fact that eighty percent of our citizens lived in cities and it was there that we had to develop our nation's resources and renewal. But in the eyes of the government establishment, Israel was still a country characterized by kibbutzim and agricultural settlements. In fact, practically all members of the Cabinet had come from these settlements and spent weekends and holidays there. While some had additional experience in the army, none had made a political career in urban affairs. One has only to add to this the weight of foreign affairs and security problems in Israeli life to understand the emergence of such an unbalanced view, which brought about gross disregard of city problems. Jerusalem was particularly neglected. There was still a certain pride in Tel Aviv, which was the first Jewish city created out of the sand dunes of the Mediterranean shore and was situated in the demographic heartland of the country. But Jerusalem, although the nation's capital, was until 1967 situated at the end of a narrow corridor with roads leading to nowhere.

I believe that this distorted outlook on cities included a basic misunderstanding of city dwellers as well, particularly the working class. It ultimately led to a gradual alienation of the government leadership from a growing urban electorate, which viewed the socialist kibbutzim as an elitist movement and, in many cases, as not very considerate employers.

The Rafi principle had been the Ben-Gurion slogan, 'What is good for the country is good for the party.' Following that principle, I always put the city first, but it was not always easy. In our public life it is a common practice to build a cadre of people who owe you loyalty for past favors and work on your behalf within the party. I never believed in this practice and wanted nothing to do with it. I have obviously been in positions that enabled me to do many favors, but I never did a favor for anyone in order to place him in my debt. I don't like people to be 'my boys', as it were. Once or twice it happened that Meron Benvenisti, Ronny Feinstein, and one or two others who worked closely with me were called 'Teddy boys'. I don't remember when that phrase was adopted, but it disappeared quickly. The truth caught up with it.

On my very first day in office, the former mayor's assistant, Ronny Feinstein, offered me his resignation. I told him that being associated with the opposition was not in itself reason to resign. What did concern me, however, was that he did not seem to have served Ish Shalom too successfully as campaign manager, otherwise Mapai might not have lost the election. I told Ronny he was welcome to try and stay. He proved to be an outstanding and effective administrator, the best in any city I know. He also became the first, and so far only, city manager in Israel, a post we borrowed from the U.S. municipal system.

One of the first issues I faced in office was where to locate City Hall. The preceding administration had decided to move to new premises. Before 1948 the City Hall building, not far from the Jaffa Gate, had been smack in the center of Jerusalem. But after Jordan had taken half the city, our municipal building found itself right on the border facing the enemy gun positions on the Old City wall. The division of the city had by then gone on for seventeen years, and Ish Shalom may have accepted it as permanent. He and his associates wanted a new City Hall – central and safe. They acquired land in the center of the Jewish part of town and held an architectural competition, so that when I moved into my office I found elaborate drawings, blueprints, and models all prepared at considerable expense.

I decided to drop the project, write off the investment, and stay where we were. My principal reason was that to abandon the old City Hall would in a way mean accepting the division as permanent. But by staying put on the frontier, we were giving expression to our faith in the eventual unification of Jerusalem. I had, of course, no inkling that a war would bring about the unification so soon. Back then my feeling was more an 'historical' one.

There was another reason for not moving City Hall. Since 1950 many of the new immigrants – largely from Arab countries but also from Europe, particularly Rumania – had been settled in neighborhoods on the border. I felt it was immoral to leave these thousands of newcomers in such a vulnerable spot while the City Fathers moved themselves safely and expensively out of the danger zone. Besides, the cost of a new City Hall would have run into the millions, and that money could better be spent on many more urgent needs.

The situation in Jerusalem was uniquely difficult. Half the time you drove down a road or a side street, you ran into a sign reading: 'STOP! DANGER! FRONTIER AHEAD!' There was hardly a month in which somebody was not killed or wounded on the frontier, or at least struck by a stone thrown from the wall. When we complained to the Jordanians, they said, apologetically, 'A soldier went mad.' The city was divided by walls fifteen to twenty foot high wherever a through street had previously existed and by stretches of no-man's land, barbed wire fences, and mines. There was only one crossing point, the 'Mandelbaum Gate', though it wasn't actually a gate at all. The crossing was near a house that had once belonged to a Mr Mandelbaum, and the name stuck to the open roadway with a barrier across it. In the beginning of 1964, right before the Pope's visit, we put a roof over part of the crossing so that even in the rainy weather the departing Pope could step out of his car and bid goodbye to the people accompanying him. It finally gave the crossing an appearance that justified the word 'gate'.

Clergy and diplomats were allowed to go through the gate and return, as were U.N. personnel. Tourists who were neither Israelis nor Jordanians could cross too, but only in one direction; they weren't allowed to 'double cross'. After years of pressure from the Western countries, Israeli Christians were finally allowed to visit their holy places on Christmas and Easter and then cross back. We had to present short-lists of these pilgrims, and the Jordanians cut the number down even further. The permits to cross were for only thirty-six to forty-eight hours. On the first Christmas after I became mayor, I accompanied the Israeli district commissioner to the spot between the two police stations at the Mandelbaum Gate. Without our knowing it, a press photographer snapped a picture of us together with the Jordanian governor, Anwar el-Khatib. The photograph appeared in the *New York Times* and apparently created quite some difficulties for the governor, because he was meeting not only with his official counterpart but with the mayor of Jewish Jerusalem.

F.J.—7

I had contact from time to time with clergymen living in Jordan, especially the Greek and the Armenian Patriarchs, who had standing permission to cross over. Sometimes an American or a British diplomat stationed in Amman would also come through the gate, and we were, of course, interested in meeting them. But the only other contacts between the two sides were those of the health authorities in their joint fight against stray dogs and the mosquitoes breeding in no-man's land. No-man's land itself was mined. I remember one tragic incident that illustrated how difficult it was to cross it. A prominent Baptist minister, Dr Lindsey, had been living in West Jerusalem for many years and had a community on the Jordanian side of the city as well. He apparently decided to smuggle a sick boy through no-man's land in order to get him better medical care in Israel. He knew the Jordanians wouldn't let him out through Mandelbaum Gate, so he tried to cross no-man's land at night and had a foot blown off.

This half-city was the only place in Israel, except for the border kibbutzim, where you constantly sensed an atmosphere of war and the enemy close by. When a Tel Aviv resident came back from his reserve duty in the army, he could quickly become a civilian again. But in the split city of Jerusalem, you felt you were in the reserves fifty-two weeks a year. People were glad just to be alive and didn't start thinking about how badly off they were for housing and many other things until after the 1967 war. When they felt secure, they began to look around and want some of the good things of life. The government finally began to listen to their voice – and mine. But in spite of the accelerated pace of meeting needs, we haven't yet made up for the neglect of Jerusalem between 1948 and 1967.

I started trying to find ways to put Jerusalem on the international map. First I insisted that something be done for the diplomatic corps in the city, like an annual dinner for all the ambassadors and a Christmas party to let the U.N. personnel know they were welcome. I also found myself playing host to a gallery of internationally famous personalities, as I had done in the Prime Minister's Office. Now, however, as mayor of Jerusalem, the effect of my role sometimes had an unexpected or ironic twist. For example, early in 1966, Marlene Dietrich came to Jerusalem in preparation for an Israel Bond tour in the United States. She gave a magnificent concert, filled with sentiment, and attracted the older generation of German-speaking people to hear songs from the days when they and she were young. The next afternoon Marlene was in our living room for tea. The room was crowded and there weren't enough chairs, so as host I sat on the floor. A photographer was on hand to take pictures, and somehow one of these photographs – showing me next to Marlene's legs – found its way onto the cover of the *Ha'aretz* newspaper's weekend supplement.

The next thing I knew, one of the religious city councilors stood up at a council meeting called to discuss the annual budget and made an indignant speech : 'Here is the mayor of Jerusalem, a man who should represent the city's dignity, all its elements – including the religious ones – and morality in general. And look at him, sitting at the feet of an actress notorious for her legs!' He waved the picture around, showing it to the other councilors. 'Take another look at the picture and see the expression on my face,' I said. 'There I sit, next to the most famous pair of legs in the world, and do I seem happy? Am I enjoying the privilege? I'm not even looking. And why not? Why is my face so serious? Because I couldn't think of anything but our annual budget. And I wish you would do the same and not waste any more of our time looking at those legs!' With that, the subject was dismissed.

In 1966, shortly after I was elected mayor, the German publisher Axel Springer made his first trip to Israel. I had never met him, but the Israeli Ambassador in Bonn had described Springer to me as a man of character and public spirit and as a friend of Israel. Springer's anti-Nazi record was beyond doubt. Before the rise of Hitler, he and his family had been publishers, and after the war he resumed his career in this field. He once told me an anecdote about that period. The Allies were looking for a man to publish the first German paper after the war, and the candidates were being interviewed by a British officer in Berlin. Naturally, all the hopefuls were trying to win the officer's confidence by telling him how they had resisted the Nazis and suffered under their regime. The British officer was apparently weary of these stories, and when young Springer walked into his office, he asked him : 'And whom did you suffer from? Who was after you?' Springer said : 'Only the girls.' He was given the permit to publish the paper and thus started building an empire whose great success is well known. Springer owns the Ullstein Verlag, which the Nazis had wiped out together with most of the Jewish family that had owned it. The remaining members of the family eventually transferred the property to him. I remembered reading that he was going to revive the famous *Propylaean Kunstgeschichte*, the great history of ancient and contemporary art and archaeology originally published by Ullstein, which had been burned by the Nazis.

I liked Springer immediately. We went up to the roof of City Hall, and I pointed out the dividing wall twenty yards away and the nearest Jordanian gun position about a hundred yards away. I also expressed my belief in the eventual unification of Jerusalem and explained why I had decided to keep the Municipality in the center of the entire city. I did not know then that Springer, for similar motives, had decided to construct his own office building next to the Berlin Wall. Perhaps it was this comparison that moved him to offer a gift to Jerusalem. Since I was deeply involved with our fledgling museum, I suggested that he endow it with a library for art and archaeology. He asked to have time to consider my suggestion. That night he phoned me from Tel Aviv and asked me to meet him. By the next day, we had settled on a gift of about $1 million for a library and auditorium wing of the museum. There were no strings attached. Springer did not donate the money to immortalize his name. He did it because he cared about Jerusalem, cared about art and about books, and thought it was a fitting idea.

When I reported the donation to the museum board, to my astonishment two members indicated their readiness to accept the gift but demanded that Springer's name not be mentioned. They wanted it to be considered an anonymous contribution because Springer was a German – as if the money had come from the Nazis! Moreover, because of local political rivalries, they wanted to exploit the occasion to brand me as a man without principles who was just out for the money. I was shocked at their narrow-mindedness, and I refused to accept the gift on these conditions. Then came the great fuss. Ziama Aranne, the minister of education, was called in to mediate, and he agreed with them (perhaps because he also shared their political feelings toward me). The storm even reached the newspapers. On the whole, the press was on my side, as was a majority of the museum board, including Yigael Yadin.

Finally we announced publicly and officially that the library was a gift from Springer. The library has no special name; it's just called the Museum Library. But at its entrance is a small plaque – exactly like the others designating the wing donated by the Bronfmans or the period room contributed by Baron Edmond de Rothschild – stating that it was presented by Axel Springer. Springer himself, who had more understanding for this anti-German feeling than I, sent a very gracious cable from Berlin : 'I never intended having the building named in my honor. All I wanted was to have a share in building Jerusalem.'

13 Jerusalem United

THE 14th of May, according to the Julian calendar, is the date on which Israel proclaimed its independence in 1948. But we hold our annual Independence Day celebration according to the Hebrew date, and that falls on May 14 only once every nineteen years. Since the two dates coincided in 1967, we wanted the official national celebration to be held in Jerusalem. That was no simple matter because of the traditional military parade. The United Nations had passed a resolution that arms – and all other military equipment – should not be permitted in Jerusalem, and our Foreign Ministry was unhappy about any act that might provoke U.N. criticism. But we overcame all opposition, and Independence Day 1967 was celebrated in Jerusalem.

Years earlier, when I was still in the Prime Minister's Office, a group of us had decided to add a national song festival to the annual Independence Day celebrations. It was organized by Kol Yisrael, the Israel Broadcasting Authority, and in 1967, the director of Kol Yisrael came to discuss that year's festival with me. Since Independence Day was to be celebrated in Jerusalem, I suggested that we sponsor a song about the city in addition to the general competition. Naomi Shemer, a well-known songwriter, was commissioned to write it, and on May 15, 1967, three weeks before the Six Day War, 'Jerusalem of Gold' was sung for the first time. It was a beautiful song – telling of Jerusalem, the Old City, the Temple Mount, and our longings – and it became an instant hit. Three weeks later it was to become the hymn of the Six Day War.

But war was the furthest thought from our minds while we prepared for that special Independence Day. On the program for the opening ceremony was the recital of a well-known piece by Natan Alterman, probably the country's most popular poet. It was a poem of spirit and independence, but it also contained a warning to the Arabs that if they ever started anything, we would be quick to retaliate. While the program was being rehearsed in the Hebrew University stadium, Yitzhak Rabin, then chief of staff, was summoned by Prime Minister Eshkol, who was worried lest the poem might antagonize our neighbors

and even trigger actual fighting! After a long discussion, it was decided
to delete the verse of the poem containing that warning. Ironically
enough, in that period before Independence Day, we had no idea that
President Nasser of Egypt was actually cooking up a war while we were
rehearsing parades and poetry. We dropped the stanza in the poem
because we didn't want the Arabs to think we were trying to pick a fight.
Yet on Independence Day itself, after the poem had been recited – minus
that sensitive stanza – the chief of staff received the first information that
Egyptian troops were massing in Sinai, clearly Nasser's opening act of
belligerency. In retrospect, I suppose we should have left that stanza in.

In the days following May 15, as the tensions with Egypt continued
to rise and Nasser closed the Straits of Tiran at the tip of the Sinai
peninsula, we turned to digging trenches and building shelters. The
people living near the border were particularly vulnerable, and evacuation from some quarters might have to be our first move if we were
attacked. The Municipality staff knew basically what to do and got some
good advice from Moshe Dayan, who had asked Eshkol and Rabin to
reactivate him in the army and went up and down the country inspecting
preparedness. (This was, of course, before he was appointed defense
minister.) We were also worried about supplies of basic food staples and
brought up stacks of supplies from the center of the country, mainly by
rail. Then we organized porters, volunteers, foreign students at the
university, and middle-aged and elderly men who had not been called up
for service to distribute these supplies to stores throughout the city.
There had been some nervous hoarding early on, and only a steady
supply of staples could alleviate these jitters. Night after night I passed
the warehouses and distribution points to ensure that everything was
running smoothly.

Throughout the preparations, the people of Jerusalem had shown
remarkable spirit. Everybody helped – even the very religious boys
studying at the anti-Zionist *yeshivot*. One evening I went to Yeshivat
Mir (which was hit during the war) and was received with enthusiasm.
It was a place where I normally would have been ignored, but now the
yeshivah boys were busy filling sandbags. Not that it was easy to get the
sand from the quarries. All commercial trucks and drivers in the city had
already been called up for duty. In fact, in any kind of emergency
practically our entire army supply depended on civilian vehicles. But we
did our best with what was available. At the same time, we held
maneuvers for civil defense and the Red Magen David (or local Red
Cross), a particularly efficient organization in Jerusalem. Tens of
thousands of people donated blood for possible emergencies. We provided evacuation centers for the people living on the border and laid in a
supply of blankets and food for them. We even foresaw a water shortage,
instructing people to collect water in all cisterns and filling all the city

reservoirs. Naturally, there were scores of details to attend to. Instructions were issued for all automobile lights to be painted blue and all windows to be taped so that they would not shatter in a blast. On Sunday, June 4, we ordered the Israel Museum curators to put all the museum's treasures in the cellar. And, of course, I held regular meetings with the local army commanders and General Uzi Narkiss, who headed the army's Central Command but was in Jerusalem most of the time.

By June 1, when we had done everything any and all of us could think of, I called on Dov Joseph, who had been the civilian in charge of Jerusalem during the siege of 1948. I took him through the city and showed him the trenches, shelters, and everything else. His comment: 'All this is no good.' He cautioned that we were not prepared against gas and this, that, and the other. He found almost all our work to be pointless and defective. It was not a very encouraging hour. But it was too late for us to revise our arrangements. Fortunately, when war broke out a few days later, we found that our preparations were, on the whole, satisfactory.

I must confess that for all our work and worry, deep down we believed that Jerusalem would remain as quiet as it had been during the Sinai Campaign. After all, we thought, Jerusalem is a holy city. Nobody wants to offend the international community. And besides, the side that attacks will suffer as much as the defending side. We were never sure when – or even if war would break out. But if it did, we were pretty confident Jerusalem would be spared. Yet we prepared, especially for evacuation of the crowded areas along the frontier.

On Saturday, June 3 (two days before the war), a small group of American friends had come to Jerusalem to encourage us and to collect impressions for the purpose of raising money and rousing public opinion in America. Among them were two men who were always around when we were in trouble: Sam Rothberg and Lou Boyar, successful businessmen, who had always been generous with their time and their money. In the afternoon we went to the frontier district of Abu Tor. People were living next to the forward outposts, and children were at play across the street from enemy positions. It was clear that we would have to evacuate these people if it came down to a war. We had already dug trenches and packed thousands of sandbags into their windows, but we knew that would not be enough. Still, the question remained: would there be battle again in Jerusalem?

On the same Saturday, Chief of Staff Rabin came to the city for a few hours, and some of my staff and I joined him at Jerusalem's local army base to discuss the situation. Rabin did not tell us that the war would start on Monday, and that was only proper: we were civilians. But we all sensed it was bound to happen. In fact, most of us thought it should have happened a few weeks earlier. We feared that Nasser's creeping aggression would paralyze us to the point where we would have to raise our hands and surrender. The whole country had been mobilizing and preparing – and waiting tensely – for almost three weeks, and many of us felt that by waiting we had let ourselves in for a more difficult war.

We civilians were not as optimistic as the army. It seemed to us that Eshkol's hesitation about attacking derived from weakness, not wisdom. Later, his supporters gave statesmanlike reasons for the endless delay: we had to let the world see how peaceful our intentions were; we were willing to take the greatest risks and give the Americans and British every chance to send a naval unit through the Tiran Straits, and so forth. Much of this was nonsense (even after the American or British ships would have gone through, the Straits could have been closed again). It was good for some favorable editorials in newspapers and a few kind words on American television, yet it made no more difference in the United Nations than if we had attacked on May 15. Admittedly, a decision to carry out a pre-emptive attack is not easy. But Eshkol seemed to be waiting forever. The fact that all turned out well was his good fortune and a result of Moshe Dayan's leadership and the army's state of preparedness.

On Friday, June 2, the Defense Ministry was handed over to Moshe Dayan after weeks of public uproar that culminated in a demonstration in Tel Aviv by the wives and mothers of our soldiers. Up until then, Eshkol had been both prime minister and minister of defense, a holdover from the days when Ben-Gurion had held both portfolios. By the beginning of June, however, Eshkol and Golda, who had desperately maneuvered to keep the defense post from Dayan, could no longer hold out. They didn't like it, but they agreed – and on Dayan's terms. His appointment restored the country's self-confidence.

Monday, June 5, 1967, started like any other day. As usual, I came to my office early. The only difference for me was that my driver had been called up, so I was now driven by an elderly man with an ulcer. We drove around the city for a while and saw that everyone was still laboring at safety and defense preparations. I realized that war was actually on its way, but I thought in terms of days, not hours. When we returned to the Municipality, I got the news: we were at war with Egypt. For a few moments I just sat in my chair without doing a thing. The war was far off, somewhere in the Sinai desert. But I certainly could not attend to my routine work. I started doing a little here, a little there. People started to show up, and journalists came (there were carloads, hundreds of foreign journalists in the country, and they drove in and out of Jerusalem all the time).

Then suddenly, while it was still morning, the shelling started in Jerusalem. We could hear it and see it. There was no other fighting, no soldiers shooting rifles; just shelling from the Arab side. I ordered my own staff to begin telephoning the schools and instructing the principals to speed the children home wherever possible. Where it was not possible, other arrangements were made to protect the children and keep up morale. I immediately left to tour the shelters and the outlying districts of the city. On the way I passed the Israel Museum. One of the first shells had scored a hit there (it was probably aimed at the nearby Knesset), and some of the museum's windows had been broken and a roof had caved in. But most of the art objects were already in the basement, and nothing valuable was damaged. Some shells also fell around our house (they may have been aimed at Prime Minister Eshkol's home nearby). I dashed into the house for a moment to check that the tenants, including Tamar and Osnat (then seven) had moved into the small shelter in the cellar. Amos, our nineteen-year-old, was with his army unit.

The immediate need in Jerusalem was to maintain morale in the shelters, homes, and schools and counteract the effect of the shelling. Ordinarily I would have gone on the radio, but the army had ordered radio silence to prevent the enemy from gleaning any vital information that might be a by-product of almost any communiqué. Our silence gave the Arabs a temporary advantage because they dominated the air-waves with the most extraordinary accounts of one sensational victory after another – all pure fiction. I had to counteract that by going from shelter to shelter and telling the occupants that the Egyptians were lying and that our situation was very promising. Actually, the whole Egyptian air force had been wiped out on the ground by our bombers that very morning, but I didn't know that yet. All I could do was hope that the enemy radio broadcasts were the lies I claimed they were.

The people of Jerusalem behaved extremely well and were very disciplined. Hardly anybody was out on the streets. Everyone quietly did his or her job or what they were told to do. The discipline held through all levels, ranks, and ages. In my visits around the city, I saw a few grim pictures : children who had not managed to get home in time crowded in special shelters in their schools; barricaded windows and doors everywhere; empty streets (all able-bodied men from seventeen to fifty had been called up). The shelling had become heavy. In fact, during the three days of fighting in Jerusalem, about 1,000 apartments were hit.

Just before noon, I went home briefly to change my white shirt for something darker, so that I wouldn't be too easy a target. When I returned to the office, I heard the enemy air forces had been destroyed. But we had no time or spirit for jubilation. Heavy fighting had broken out next to City Hall, and we were right on the front line. Across the road from the Municipality was an old building that had gradually deteriorated into a slum. The seventeen or eighteen Jewish families that lived there had been evacuated hours before. Next door to it was the ruined and deserted shell of an old French convent, St Mary Reparatrix. The convent and the old building provided our machine guns with a good view of the Jordanian position favorably placed on top of the Old City wall about twenty yards away. But soon the Jordanians were moving to another position on the roof of the College de Frères, a little higher and right behind the wall. I wanted to see what was happening, so I walked fairly safely to the corner, shielded by the Municipality building. But then I had to cross the street, which was riddled by sporadic machine-gun fire from the Jordanians. I waited for the next break and ran across the street, where I spent fifteen or twenty minutes in the Israeli position looking across at the other side. To my surprise, I found some of the families in that old building had stayed in their apartments. Under the circumstances, evacuation now would be too dangerous, and they were safer staying put with the sandbag-and-trench protection and our return fire power.

Praying that our decision not to evacuate them was right, I maneuvered back through the fire and visited the headquarters of the Central Command, where I learned that the Jordanians had taken Government House, the seat of the United Nations in Jerusalem since 1948. Then I went on to a school that had been unable to send the children home in time and followed up by driving to inform some of the parents that all was well. I had some journalists in the car, so we drove over to a spot where we could catch a glimpse of the battle going on around Government House. I sat in front with the driver. In the back were Arthur Veysey of the *Chicago Tribune*, Dalia Shchori (an Israeli newspaperwoman), and an Australian journalist whose name I cannot remember. As we drove up an exposed hill, three bullets hit the car, one of them about an inch from Mr Veysey. I never saw a driver maneuver so quickly before – or since.

We hurried back to a nearby residential area to report to some parents who were very anxious about their children. A shell had fallen on a garden in the neighborhood and another had dropped on one of the small houses. There was no loss of life, but the residents were in danger, and they naturally assumed their children were in danger too. The telephones in their neighborhood were not working, and they had had no word until I arrived. I reassured the parents and then hurried back to the school to reassure the children that their parents were unharmed. In the rush and excitement of those first hours of war, it never occurred to me how absurd it might later sound that the mayor of a city under attack was dashing around carrying messages between parents and their children because the phones were out. But the truth of the matter is that I really had nothing better to do, and it still seems to me that personally helping to promote calm in the city was far more constructive work than sitting in the mayor's chair pretending to do something important.

Despite the shooting and the general hardship in Jerusalem, the overall war news, as it came in during the day over the phone, was overwhelmingly triumphant. Moshe Dayan and other leading figures, including Ben-Gurion, began converging on Jerusalem and on the Knesset. During the afternoon of June 5, Dayan was scheduled to be sworn in as defense minister, and great decisions had to be made. At about 3 P.M., Ruth Dayan phoned to say that her car was stuck and asked me to pick her up at the gas station near the King David Hotel. I found her in La Regence restaurant, the safest place in the hotel. It is two floors below the lobby, and its few small windows were all sandbagged. Despite the mounting tension since Independence Day, the restaurant had maintained the pleasant atmosphere of a luxury hotel. The few tourists who had remained in Israel, together with a miscellany of journalists and foreign emissaries, filled the room.

Ruth and I reached the Knesset building about five in the afternoon. The mood was momentous and exciting. Cabinet ministers, Knesset members, party leaders, and journalists were milling around the halls, and a Cabinet meeting was expected to take place at any moment. The one question discussed everywhere was whether our army should counter-attack and take East Jerusalem. To advance on the Jordanian-held sector of Jerusalem was, of course, more of a political risk than a military one. Each of us knew in his heart that once we took the Old City, we could never give it up. Thus it was truly an historic decision that had to be taken that day. People were standing in line in the Knesset lobby to ask Ben-Gurion his opinion on the question. He was clearly in favor of taking the Old City.

Oddly enough for the mayor of the city in question, my main feeling that afternoon was fatigue bordering on exhaustion. I had been up nights visiting each and every installation, military and civilian, and had been racing around all day. I just did not feel up to having an opinion on this complex international subject. Of course, I had always been in favor of a united Jerusalem. But at that moment I did not want to be the one to say anything, push anything, or do anything.

Although Eshkol did not arrive and Dayan left for his headquarters (he was not sworn in until ten days later), one thing and another kept many of us at the Knesset building until after dark, and we watched the fluorescent bullets and the explosions of battle in the distance. Just as night fell and the city was fully blacked out, there was a moment when it looked as if the Knesset building would become a target too. Suddenly, right below us, a light went on. It was the powerful spotlight we had installed to illuminate the Monastery of the Cross. Shining brilliantly just across the road, it made the Knesset a perfect target. Why it had not been switched off, nobody knew. It was probably on a different circuit. Someone finally gave an order to shoot out the light. Then we turned our attention back to the battle in the distance until we learned that the Arabs had retreated.

That night and the next day and a half, up until Wednesday noon, were essentially more of the same. There was a point at which I was so tired I just couldn't rest – like a long second wind of the nervous system. In between periodically checking in at the Municipality, I spent time visiting the Central Command headquarters and climbing up to observation posts to watch the shelling. I saw our paratroopers break through to the Jordanian half of the city and later witnessed the sad scene of bodies being returned to our lines. I just kept on going and going : more shelters, more evacuation centers. I hardly went home. A few times I passed our apartment building, where Tamar and Osnat were waiting in the shelter, but I only came home in the morning to shave and eat. At one point I had not slept for sixty hours, and toward the end of the war I dozed off a few times in the office. Those days were so crowded that I can only say I remember them impressionistically. But I do remember that nowhere in Jerusalem did I encounter panic.

On Tuesday, June 6, an armored brigade reached Jerusalem and went into action with air cover. Their orders were not to harm any place within the Old City and to be sure that all the Holy Places were left intact. That night our paratroopers broke through and began their advance. By Wednesday noon things had reached the point where I had to call a special meeting of city officials to deal with the task of providing for the greatly increased population of which I was rapidly becoming mayor. The same day, Chaim Herzog, a reserve general who made a remarkable impression with his radio comments during that period, was appointed military governor of the West Bank and established himself in the Ambassador Hotel in East Jerusalem. I went to see him, and in the Ambassador lobby I was stopped by the American consul, who introduced me to Ruhi el-Khatib, the mayor of Jordanian Jerusalem. He looked extremely bewildered. Later we were told by several local Arabs that a few days before the war they had made a date to meet for a drink at the Tel Aviv Hilton forty-eight hours after the fighting would start. That had apparently been the general mood in Arab Jerusalem, though one would have thought that looking at Israeli Jerusalem from the Mount of Olives or from the crenellations of the Old City wall would have made Jerusalemites, more than other Arabs, aware of Israel's potential and its attachment to this city in particular.

Such a reversal of fortune – defeat replacing the expectation of a great victory – would have disconcerted anyone, and el-Khatib was certainly very shaken. As we saw later, his administration of the city, though hardly progressive, was in many ways perfectly satisfactory. Nevertheless, he had not been admired as mayor. The fact that he had come in fifth in the elections for the City Council and that he owed his position to an appointment by King Hussein was only partly the reason. Arab Jerusalemites felt that their city had been neglected by the Hashemite rulers and that the city administration shared the blame with the Jordanian government.

Only on the way back from the Ambassador Hotel, when I reached Mandelbaum Gate again, did I become fully aware of the fact that for the first time since 1948 I had been on the forbidden 'other side'. Suddenly I was filled with excitement. When I became mayor I had made certain practical decisions concerning roads, buildings, and so forth that took into account the possibility that the city would one day be reunited. It was a dream – perhaps for the next generation. Now here I was witnessing that day. The elation I felt at that moment dispersed any thoughts of the problems I knew lay ahead.

Later that day Dayan rang and invited me to join him. We drove in command cars from Central Command headquarters to the Lions' Gate, where the famous picture was taken of Dayan, Yitzhak Rabin, and Uzi Narkiss walking into the Old City. In a gate leading to the Temple Mount there was a niche piled up with Jordanian arms that had been found in the area of the Temple Mount, with total disregard for the danger this entailed for the nearby mosques. Stacked boxes of ammunition, machine guns, and cartridge belts were all over the sidewalks. An Israeli flag flew from the top of the Mosque of Omar, but fortunately somebody gave an order and it was immediately taken down. A photograph of the mosque with that flag, which was raised by an over-enthusiastic soldier, has served Arab propaganda for years. Then we walked through the Moghrabi Gate (the Moor's Gate) and climbed down the stairs (which no longer exist) right into the narrow alleyway of the Western Wall. Following a centuries-old custom, Dayan jotted something on a piece of paper and stuck it in a crevice of the Wall. It was a prayer for peace.

That night, I attended a meeting of officials at Herzog's headquarters, where we divided up responsibilities between the civilian authorities and the army, and Thursday morning we went to work, which included burying the dead, Arab as well as Jew (there were many of both in the streets). By the time I set foot on Mount Scopus on Thursday, I was more exhausted than exhilarated. But then the press conferences began : thirty or forty journalists, mostly foreign, followed me around and met me at my office as frequently as every few hours while we still heard bullets and shells exploding. The details of the hectic work are no longer clear in my memory. My staff was in constant touch with the military, and I was informed of any move that would affect safety, water supply, power lines, food supply, or civilian medical resources. I convened my entire staff at least once a day and planned the day's program and the means of keeping in touch. Where the damage was heavy, we had to improvise at a feverish pitch, especially in evacuating people. But on the whole, our preparations, as well as our improvisations, worked out pretty well.

All this emergency activity was mixed with the never-ending press conferences and extending hospitality to the well-wishers who began to arrive. Edmond de Rothschild and a French delegation wanted to express solidarity by flying to Israel on Monday, at the beginning of the war, but they had difficulties in arranging a flight, so they reached Jerusalem only on Thursday morning. Axel Springer came accompanied by Ernst Cramer. Axel walked around the newly united city for a day or two – morning, noon, and night – and before leaving he handed me a large check, saying, 'You'll need this for many immediate expenses.' He was right – and his gift was of invaluable help in dealing with emergencies that could not await discussion and committee approval. The streets were still not safe: there was sniping and even an occasional grenade was tossed. Nothing functioned in the Old City, shops were closed, and there was a curfew. The military ruled with great care.

Despite the clamor of thousands of Jews, you could not yet visit the Western Wall without a permit. On Thursday morning, however, Tamar and I, the Rothschild guests from France, and a group from England went to the Wall with Ben-Gurion, and everyone came to our apartment afterward for an impromptu lunch. Ben-Gurion was deeply moved. Of course, everyone was excited, especially the old Jerusalemites among us. But Ben-Gurion's reaction was special and hard to describe. 'What now?' somebody asked him. The consensus was that peace would come. It may be hard to believe today, but back then we all thought: 'Now, at last, we will have peace. The Arabs will have learned that they cannot fight us and win.' Yet Ben-Gurion's reply was, 'This is not the end of the war. The Arabs cannot take such a defeat and such humiliation. They will never accept it!' We were all taken aback.

Immediately after the Israeli victory became obvious, Arabs started fleeing Jerusalem in droves. They apparently expected us to behave as they had planned to. (Among the documents in various Arab Legion posts, we found detailed orders on how to liquidate the Jewish population.) But after a day or two, when the Arabs saw that no one was being harmed – on the contrary, everybody was treated in an exemplary way – they started to return. In fact, I do not think anybody failed to return; at least we did not find any empty houses (with the exception of the consulates of the various Arab countries). I also think the Arabs had learned a bitter lesson since 1948: it is better to stay put under Jewish rule than to become a refugee in an Arab country. We were also eager to show our good will and put the city on the proper footing as quickly as possible. On Thursday we started distributing fresh milk and water in the Arab part of town. The next day we entered the Old City with supplies and began to connect its water mains to ours. I visited East Jerusalem's City Hall and called on Ruhi el-Khatib. Seven or eight of his ten councilors were there, and we discussed means of cooperation. They were greatly troubled and in a state of shock. When we arrived we found our city flag flying outside their building.

The day after the Old City fell, it also became clear to me that something had to be done about the small slum houses that crowded close to the Western Wall – the Moghrabi Quarter. The one area that should have been spacious and bright was cramped and dark. In Jewish homes throughout the world, a picture of the Western Wall held a prominent place. As the only remnant of the Temple compound that Titus destroyed almost two thousand years ago, the Wall symbolized the continuity of a people, a focal point of hope throughout the centuries. One of the points of the Armistice Agreement with Jordan signed in 1949 had been that Jews would have free access to the Wall. But the agreement was not kept by the Jordanians, and for nineteen years Jews had been denied access to their only Holy Place. A wall of an apartment in one of West Jerusalem's central residential areas had been hit by a shell and collapsed. It bore a large sign: 'We lost a wall, but we gained a Wall.' This was the general mood of excitement about having access to the Wall again.

On June 7, soon after our troops reached the Wall, people from throughout the city rushed there, and it was difficult for the soldiers to convince them to wait until a cease-fire went into effect. When we decided to allow the first pilgrimage in nineteen years on the following Wednesday, the holiday of Shavuot, we expected hundreds of thousands of people to take part. The pent-up feelings of a generation would express themselves in the chance to touch the stones of the Wall once more, to pray at this holiest of Holy Places. But how would these hundreds of thousands reach the Wall through the dangerous narrow alleyways?

The only answer was to do away with the slum hovels of the Moghrabi Quarter. I received the go-ahead from Herzog, Narkiss, and Dayan and called a meeting of Ya'acov Yanai, Yigael Yadin, the architect Arieh Sharon, and several others. My overpowering feeling was: do it now; it may be impossible to do it later, and it *must* be done. To make the decision formal, I turned to my own Municipality group, and they approved the move as well. Then the archaeologists and other experts went to the Wall and drew a map of exactly what should be torn down and what should not and we found proper accommodations for the families that were living in those hovels. On the night of Saturday, June 10, the work of clearing the Moghrabi Quarter began. In two days it was done – finished, clean.

Once the Wall was made accessible, an endless stream of people surged toward it. After the Moghrabi area had been cleared, the next obvious need was a road from West Jerusalem to the Wall. We had built a temporary route across Mount Zion so that people could reach the Wall without crossing the Arab part of the city, where some sniping was still going on. On Sunday, June 11, I arranged for this road to be completed by the Shavuot holiday three days later. It took some hustling to get the road finished. But beginning at dawn, on Shavuot, in spite of an unbearably hot desert wind (*hamsin*), more than 200,000 people visited the Wall.

Sometime during that first week, Ben-Gurion suggested that the walls of the Old City be torn down. I never discussed this with him, but I imagine that he was motivated by the thought that if the walls remained the city would never really be united. The idea seemed outlandish to me for historical, cultural, and aesthetic reasons. But these were not considerations for Ben-Gurion. He was a man of vision and uncanny judgment, and I believe he foresaw that one of the arguments would center around the holy and historical places. I suppose he felt that as long as they stayed separate from the western part of the city, it would be impossible to unite Jerusalem. But I could not accept his view. We kept the walls and went on with the task of uniting the city. That was now my direct responsibility, and one I had never expected to come my way. The unification of Jerusalem marked the beginning of the most exciting period of my life.

14 Bringing Down the Walls

As the war was drawing to a close, we were all filled with the sensation that a new era was dawning, and we decided to usher it in with music. In fact, the first major cultural event after the war was a concert on Mount Scopus. We wanted to present our true image to the world and not be branded as militarists simply because we had done well in battle. And we wanted Jerusalem, in particular, to stand for peaceful and civilized life.

Oddly enough, we had been thinking of concerts even during the tense days before the war. With all the effort expended in filling and placing sandbags, building shelters, and keeping track of the thousand details involving food, blankets, hospital care, schools, water and electricity, we had scheduled a matinee concert for Friday, June 2. Nobody knew then that war would break out three days later, but it would not have made any difference. The concert featured the pianist Daniel Barenboim and the cellist Jacqueline du Pré, who were married soon after, and the proceeds from the full house went to the Soldiers' Welfare Fund. During the weeks before the war, our troops were also entertained by Barenboim, Roberta Peters, Jan Peerce, Richard Tucker, and others who came to Israel for this purpose.

Another concert was to be conducted by Erich Leinsdorf a few days later. But the various foreign consulates had been issuing warnings to their countrymen to leave, and Leinsdorf had returned to the States. In the meantime, however, Zubin Mehta, who had always had a special relationship with Israel, cancelled all his commitments and rushed here. He arrived shortly after the war broke out and took over the concert, which was held on Saturday night, June 10, the last day of the war. It was a moving event, expressing the sense of victory and relief that pervaded the country.

By the time we were ready for the grand affair on Mount Scopus, Zubin Mehta had returned home. But Leonard Bernstein, Isaac Stern, and Jennie Tourel came specially for the event and were joined by Israeli singer Netanya Dovrat. The amphitheater of the Hebrew University on

Mount Scopus was still unrestored, but there was not an empty space that afternoon. It seemed like everyone was there – Ben-Gurion and Paula, Eshkol, Golda, Dayan; it was truly an historic event. The concert, 'Hatikva on Mount Scopus' and a Mahler symphony, was recorded; and to indicate our intentions, the proceeds (which amounted to more than $25,000) were donated to promote Arab-Jewish youth activities. The same program was repeated that evening in the National Convention Center, again to a packed house. It was also taped in the evening, because the amphitheater acoustics and the barking of stray dogs from what used to be no-man's land had marred the first recording. But the version of Hatikva on the recording, in all its fervor, was the one played at the Mount Scopus concert.

On June 28, attention was again focused on Mount Scopus, as the Hebrew University awarded its honorary degrees in a ceremony there. But I witnessed only a brief part of that occasion, because June 28 was a very busy day for me. It had been decided that on the next day Jerusalem would be formally united, and my greatest concern was that this act would be consummated harmoniously, peacefully, and under the most careful supervision. Throughout June there had been no free movement between the two sectors of the city. The military was in control, the dividing barricades were still standing, there were check posts everywhere, and permits were required to cross from one sector to the other. I feared that the sudden removal of all restraints could be dangerous. Who knew what smoldering hatreds might flare up if you suddenly gave Jews access to the Old City and allowed Arabs to move freely in West Jerusalem? But that was just what Dayan had proposed to do: open the entire city to all its inhabitants at the crack of dawn. The idea worried me – and several of my colleagues, as well – and we wandered around Mount Scopus among caps and gowns looking for the minister of the interior. I wanted to get him together with Dayan, the inspector general of police, and the district police commander and work out a practical, 'sane', step-by-step plan. 'Do it gradually,' I thought. 'Perhaps allow limited freedom on the first day for a short time – say, two hours – and see how it works. Then accustom the people to it.' Any other way seemed a wild risk.

I finally got Dayan and several others together on the terrace of the King David Hotel. As minister of defense, Dayan had absolute administrative responsibility for all the occupied territory, and he was going right ahead with his audacious action. We argued strongly for taking things slowly, but Dayan just sat back with his feet on the table and would not be moved one inch. Gradually we saw that his behavior was not stubbornness; it was borne of conviction based on an entirely different concept how the Arabs would act when faced with a *fait accompli*. When he explained why he thought there was little likelihood of vengeance on the part of the Arabs and retaliation by the Jews, his theory had considerable substance, and we were eventually convinced to take the risk. I recall seeing some bright young men on Bobby Kennedy's staff at the King David after the meeting with Dayan. When I told those liberal American Democrats that on the following day Jerusalem would be united all at once, they did not believe we would dare to do it. 'Impossible,' they said.

Nonetheless, from the moment the decision was made, I took care that it would be carried out properly and thoroughly. The basic decision was a political one. The physical consequences were the tearing down of walls and fences and barriers. I remembered *The Jerusalem Plan* by the British townplanner Kendall that was published during the Mandate. It had impressed me by its common sense and simplicity, and I was told that the British had wholeheartedly agreed with the plan but never had the courage or the money to implement it. It now struck me that June 29 was the perfect time to carry out some of the recommendations of that plan, and more. Apart from blowing up each and every wall and fence that divided the city, we decided to clean up areas that had disfigured Jerusalem for a long, long time.

Dawn came and we did it. We removed all the fences, dismantled all the check posts, and started blowing up dividing walls — first the two big walls near the Municipality that closed off Jaffa Road and Suleiman Street. And along with those walls came all those structures built up against the ancient city walls over the last century and buildings that had deteriorated into slums. Eventually it cost us a lot of money to compensate the owners for those torn-down buildings, but the results were well worth it: the beautiful Old City walls were visible again and a green belt could be laid out around them. We did almost too good a job. I remember the army engineers saying, 'Here you need so-and-so many pounds of explosive, but to make sure add fifty percent,' and the individual sappers added even more. The results were a few broken windows in a fairly wide circle, which we had to repair.

All these were purely municipal decisions. I discussed them with my municipal colleagues and the proper councilors, of course, but I did not consult any outsiders. It was clear to me that some damage was inevitable if we did the job at lightning speed, and I accepted the risk. I also decided to eliminate many of the derelict houses in no-man's land in the valley near Jaffa Gate and the abandoned buildings in what had previously been a 'frontier' neighborhood to prevent squatters occupying them.

While we were working, benign miracles were occurring everywhere in the two sectors. It was a great day, not only in our history, but in the history of mankind. The world knows that June 29, 1967, was a day of euphoria in Jerusalem as Arabs and Jews moved about with freedom and more curiosity than rancor. At first a few crossed the frontier lines, watchful and timid. There were police and soldiers around, but they just looked on. Then, in the afternoon, there was a tremendous flow of people. It was contrary to all predictions – except Dayan's. Many Jews were scared. Some people said that families with teenage daughters would not go on living in Jerusalem for fear of the Arabs. Others made all sorts of dire predictions. None of these came true.

In one radiant day, Dayan was proved right. The Arabs were astonished at what they saw and heard as they walked around and looked at houses they had lived in. They knocked on the door, were invited in for a cup of tea, and sat down to discuss with their Jewish hosts whether they would have their property returned or what compensation would satisfy them. Jews did the same in the Jewish Quarter. Both sides believed that all problems would be solved easily. I gave an interview for foreign television networks. As I stood with the Wall in the background, the United Nations was meeting to express loud disapproval. My only comment on that was : 'If the U.N. delegates could see how this is working, they would talk differently. If they left us alone, this is how we would live together in Jerusalem.'

It took the U.N. a few months to do anything but noisily disapprove, but in the fall Ambassador Ernest Talman was sent by the secretary-general to observe the situation. We prepared rather carefully for his visit, and it was an intensive one. In a sense, it was the first international test of the unification. He checked on everything from sewage to education, freedom of religion to street cleaning. By then we had already done a lot to improve roads, water supply, and schools and had proposed legislation to enable the eastern part of the city to continue life much as before. These efforts were the basis for Ambassador Talman's fairly favorable report. We were pleased, and in a sense it launched us on our way in presenting our case to the world.

By the time Talman arrived, we had accomplished a lot of concrete work. But our most important task was still to develop a viable relationship with our Arab neighbors in Jerusalem. Everyone knew that building such relationships would take a long time. We started by taking into consideration everyday problems – real and psychological, big and small – like having Hebrew and Arabic used equally in all official matters (we were fortunate that through the nineteen years of division, we had used Hebrew, English, and Arabic on our street signs) or clarifying for the Arabs the procedure for registering for identity cards so that the queues would not be intolerably long. We also tried to simplify the procedures used in applying for permits to cross the bridges to Jordan.

Our efforts were not confined to helping the Arabs with bureaucratic matters, however. We wanted to broaden the sense and scope of cooperation from the outset. The majority of the Arab former city councilors had remained in Jerusalem, so we suggested that they be invited to function as an advisory board in the new Municipality. Our Ministry of the Interior had a different approach. It wanted the Arabs to accept appointments as full councilors and to enlarge the council accordingly. In this way the Arabs of the city would officially recognize the new unified Israeli Jerusalem. The Arabs could not and would not accept this plan or what it stood for, and we in the Municipality knew it without asking them. Our plan, on the other hand, would allow the Arab councilors to remain a nominally independent group, yet the city would receive the benefit of their experience and goodwill. But the Ministry of the Interior wanted to enforce Arab cooperation, and as a result we failed to create any relationship at all on the level of elected representatives. There were results on other levels, however. We united the Municipality by incorporating the many hundreds of Jordanian municipal officials, and the Police Ministry assumed responsibility for all the East Jerusalem policemen, retained them, and incorporated them into the Jerusalem Police District.

Immediately after the war, we also had to deal with the opening of the school year in the Arab part of town. Admittedly, we knew little about the situation in the Arab schools, other than the fact that about twelve or thirteen thousand children had been enrolled in municipal primary schools and the city's two major high schools – one for boys and one for girls. It soon became obvious that some of the veteran Arab teachers had decided not to work with us, partly for nationalistic reasons but mainly because they were afraid of losing their pensions from Jordan. On the other hand, we were determined to reopen the schools, and we did so by employing many young undergraduates. They lacked teaching experience, but they were certainly intellectually capable of replacing the experienced teachers.

Although some problems were not solved for weeks – even months – the Arab schools opened on the same day as the Jewish schools. We were very dissatisfied with the physical conditions we found in the Arab schools. Hundreds of classes were held in small rooms in rented apartments, and there were no kindergartens at all (under Israeli law there is a compulsory preschool year for children aged five to six). On the other hand, their system was the same as our school reform had recently introduced : six years of primary school, three years of junior high, and three years of senior high school. The one difference was that under Jordanian rule all schooling was free, while in West Jerusalem we had free education only through grades nine or ten. We therefore decided to preserve free education in the Arab schools, so as not to downgrade conditions, and add kindergartens over a three or four year period.

The most difficult problem was the curriculum. We began discussing it in June 1967, while East Jerusalem was still occupied by the army.

Then a meeting was held with Dayan, representatives of the Ministry of Education, several others, and myself. I favored maintaining the same curriculum that was accepted for the administered territories – that is, basically the Jordanian curriculum with the elimination of material we viewed as incitement and anti-Israel propaganda. The Ministry of Education, however, decided to introduce the curriculum long established in the Arab schools in Israel. Never mind that for years it had been criticized in Israel as being too Jewish in content. Too many hours were devoted to Hebrew poets and Israeli history and not to Arab history and culture. I, for one, agreed with that criticism and certainly felt the system was unsuitable for Jerusalem. But Dayan strongly supported the ministry on this point, and I was outvoted.

I regarded this decision as very negative. After all, the Arab educational system in Israel had not prevented Arab nationalism from taking strong root, even though – or possibly because – it failed to instill pride in Islamic civilization and history. One result of the curriculum was that many Israeli Arabs had come out of the schools suffering from a sense of inferiority, which may easily turn into hostility. The ministry, however, had made its decision, and the Arabs of East Jerusalem were quick in their response : our Arab municipal high schools lost practically all their pupils. They registered for schools in neighboring towns in the occupied territories, like Ramallah and Bethlehem, and the reason why was obvious. A boy or girl who goes to high school often intends to continue his or her studies at the university level, and the pupils in East Jerusalem clearly wanted to attend Arab universities in Amman, Alexandria, Damascus, Cairo, or Beirut. But they could do so only if they passed final exams recognized by the Arab League and based on the Arab curriculum. Our system therefore cut them off from the higher studies that would subsequently make it possible for them to find jobs in the developing oil economies, which need their skills and are a traditional place of employment for Palestinian Arabs. The anomaly was painfully obvious. The system allowed them to take an admission examination in English or French for a European school but not an Arab exam in Jerusalem. It nevertheless took several years to convince the minister of education and eventually the members of the Ministerial Committee for Jerusalem to do what we suggested in 1967.

With the agreement of the Ministry of Education, we finally appointed a municipal education committee to work out a curriculum that would be agreeable to all sides. The committee consisted of some Arab school principals, an Arab journalist who was also a teacher, several Jewish educators, and representatives of the Ministry of Education and the Municipality. The chairman of the committee was Matti Peled, a former Israeli Army general who, upon retirement, had written his doctorate on the modern Egyptian poet Mahfus. The Arabs were impressed that an Israeli general, especially one who took part in the Six Day War, respected them and their culture so highly. One aspect of forming the committee, however, was characteristic of the complex feelings and fears that lie beneath the surface of Arab life. The Arabs on the committee – all educated men who are esteemed among their own people – demanded that their names not be published or otherwise made known, even though their cooperation with us was an expression of caring about their own children's education.

The idea worked out by the committee was to institute a double curriculum that would prepare pupils for both an Arab university and an institution of higher learning in Israel. This meant adding several hours of instruction a week, but after a very short time it was evident that the students could not possibly cope with the burden. So in 1975 it was decided to offer two entirely different courses in the high schools. One would be the 'Jerusalem plan', consisting of the curriculum I had suggested immediately after the unification of the city (namely the system that existed on the West Bank) plus instruction in Hebrew and Israeli civics. The other option would be the regular Israeli-Arab curriculum. Three years before finishing high school, a youngster would have to decide where he wants to pursue his higher education. Not unexpectedly, the parallel course leading toward attendance at an Israeli university has attracted only a small number of pupils, mainly youngsters from families that have lived in and around Israeli Jerusalem since 1948. (These Arabs held Israel citizenship, so they had no chance of being accepted at a university in an Arab country.) To this day I believe it was unfortunate that instead of offering a sensible solution at the beginning, our government insisted on an impractical, dogmatic line, only to give in to Arab pressure in the end. It is unimportant that some of us agreed with the Arabs from the start. The internal differences between Israelis are irrelevant; in the Arab view, it is on the whole 'them' and 'us'.

Another problem we faced immediately after the Six Day War was the stagnation of the Arab economy. We wanted to start business rolling in East Jerusalem, but the Arab banks had all closed (their central offices were in Amman) and merchants remained without credit. Often all their money was in Amman as well, and they could not get it released. To deal with this situation, we established a credit corporation, a combined effort of the Finance Ministry, the Municipality, and some of the Israeli banks. In addition, many of these merchants had partners who were residents in enemy territory. According to the letter of the law, a part of their property should therefore have been taken over by our custodian of alien property. But this very complicated legal situation was eased by the quick and decisive action of the minister of justice, who published a legal decision that enabled Arabs to continue their businesses and doctors, lawyers, and pharmacists to practice under their Jordanian licenses. It

was not always easy to justify this move to Israelis. A Jewish lawyer
who immigrates from England or America must pass the Israeli bar
exams, but an Arab lawyer – equally ignorant of Israeli law – can simply
continue his practice. An immigrant dentist from Russia must go
through a retraining course before he receives a license, but an Arab
dentist trained in Cairo can legally hang out his shingle and he's in
business (mainly, of course, for his own community).

   We could not enforce any automatic, mechanical equalization of conditions. For example, we found only seventy-eight recipients of social
welfare in the Arab part of Jerusalem, and they were mostly members of
important families who had fallen on hard times and used their connections to get the few Jordanian *dinars* per month allocated for such cases.
We based our allocation of welfare funds on objective information –
income, number of dependents, physical disabilities, and other factors –
and finally reached a list of about two thousand eligible recipients. But
we didn't automatically apply the same standards to East Jerusalem as to
the western half of the city. In Israel there are two measures of welfare
distribution : the urban basket and the rural basket. We decided that in
East Jerusalem we would distribute social welfare according to the rural
basket, which was a lower rate, for had we introduced the urban basket
our social welfare payments would in many cases have been higher than
the average wages paid by an Arab employer! The net result might well
have been that many people would have stopped working and spent their
days in cafés living on the dole, a most undesirable situation.

   Anyone tempted to read this decision as discrimination against East
Jerusalem's population – in pure monetary terms – could not be more
wrong. The full sum of the city basket was spent, but instead of allocating it individually through direct social-welfare payments, we invested the difference between the two rates on general welfare programs
in the city : health clinics, youth programs, sanitation, and the like. We
did not try to save money on the Arab population, but we applied
different standards to their specific situation.

   Another example of differentiation due to the local situation has to do
with taxation. For a variety of reasons, we sometimes spend more in
East Jerusalem than in the rest of the city. For example, boys and girls
in East Jerusalem study at separate schools, and as a result we have to
build comparatively more schools for the Arabs than for the Jewish
population. On the other hand, although in principle the Arabs should
pay the same taxes as Israelis, they often pay somewhat less. Eventually
this rate will be equalized, but the Arabs resent even this reduced level
of taxation, which is much higher than the former Jordanian rate. (Of
course, the lower taxes in Jordanian Jerusalem went hand in hand with a
lower standard of services.) They also argue that a portion of the taxes
they must pay (to the state, not the city) goes for defense, which they

have no desire to support. What is important in the end, however, is that Arab society in East Jerusalem continued to function normally; a possible source of tension in the city was avoided; and so far these inequities, and we and our Ministry of Justice, have survived the criticism.

Not that there weren't times when criticism was razor sharp – much of it directed against one of my chief aides, Meron Benvenisti. I had known Meron for a long time. In fact, we had worked together in the Tourist Corporation (before the Ministry of Tourism was founded) and then Meron helped me very effectively during my first election campaign. Afterward he became sporadically involved in affairs around City Hall, but he really came into his own immediately after the Six Day War, when he took responsibility for problems concerning the Arab sector of Jerusalem. His ideas were always original and often controversial. Since he had no particular ambition to be popular and was sometimes even abrasive, Meron was often involved in serious strife and argument. His brilliance, well-conceived ideas, and his basic fairness, however, were well worth all these complications.

Meron's quick action in initiating the process of creating equal conditions for the Arabs was mistakenly – or deliberately – portrayed by his critics as 'pro-Arab', though this is obviously the most intelligent pro-Israel and pro-Jewish attitude one can take. He came under sharp attack as a protector of the Arabs, even a would-be 'seller of Jerusalem', and people who hesitated to attack me turned on him instead. Fortunately, Meron's skin is thick enough to prevail against such attacks. Today he is deputy mayor in charge of city planning, another crucial area of responsibility equally open to dispute.

The Arabs of Jerusalem are likewise plagued by their own internal conflicts. Revealing insight into the ambivalence of their situation has come to me in the course of a friendship with Musa Alami. He is a man of high distinction from an old, established Jerusalem family, and during the British Mandate he was advocate general, the highest ranking local official (Arab or Jew) in Palestine. Although Alami is an ardent Arab nationalist, he has always sought to create reasonable relations between his people and ours. For years he tried to find a common language between Ben-Gurion and the mufti of Jerusalem, and he was the one Arab who followed a constructive path after 1948: he established an argicultural school in Jericho for Arab orphans of the 1948 war. It gradually became a first-class school, and its graduates have improved farming methods all over the Arab world. Experts from Beirut University and from the Ford Foundation predicted that what Alami's farm eventually achieved could never be done in this particular area because the soil was too salty and other factors would prevent success. But he wanted to give his people pride, to prove that they could farm as well as any kibbutz in Israel or any modern agricultural enterprise in Europe, and he succeeded.

My first direct contact with Alami was at long distance during the Six Day War. We had met only briefly before 1948, but I knew all about him from his admirers, particularly two Arab brothers I had known since World War Two – Albert and Cecil Hourani – one an Oxford don whom I met from time to time between 1948 and 1967. On one of the tense days of the 1967 war, I received a cable from Alami in London. As all communication had been cut off with his farm near Jericho, which was in territory that had been overrun, he asked if I would look after his farm and see that no senseless damage was done. I found that the farm had been cut off from its source of electric power, its fuel was gone, and its trucks had been confiscated by the army. The milking machine could not work without electricity, and there were not enough experienced people to handle the large dairy herd without machinery. As a result, some of the cows had died and others were sick. I had the electric power hooked up, fuel was supplied, and the trucks returned, as our army no longer needed them. I was happy to do it, since I was well aware of Alami's earlier relationship with Ben-Gurion. I remembered the story of how they once met by chance in a London hotel, embraced each other, and sat and talked for hours, and I was eager to meet this man and to know him better.

That did not happen until much later, however, because of a psychological mistake Ben-Gurion made right after Jerusalem was united. He phoned Alami in London and invited him to Jerusalem. To return at the invitation of a prominent Israeli, even though Ben-Gurion was then out of office, would have been a fatal step as long as other Palestinian refugees were not allowed to return. It was two years before Alami and I met, first in New York in 1969 and then on his farm in Jericho, when he finally did return.

When I met him in New York, he suggested the initiation of political talks. His basic idea was that our army should be withdrawn from the West Bank and the area should be placed under a U.N. Mandate for five or ten years. Then the Arabs of the West Bank would decide their future in a plebiscite. One of his arguments against freezing the situation was: 'Our generation knows you with your faults and your assets, as you know us from previous times. It would be easier for us to get together than for the next generation, which will be more extreme on both sides.' History will decide whether or not he was right. In any case, Musa Alami did not represent anyone but himself, and our Foreign Ministry and other government leaders did not feel it was worth making a great effort to meet him. A meeting with Abba Eban was arranged in New York on 'neutral' ground, but in the end our security men decided that it might be a trap of some kind, and it never materialized. A pity.

Soon after Alami's return to Jericho, he came to see me about supplying water and electricity to a new poultry farm he intended developing for an Arab orphanage within the boundaries of Jerusalem. I was slightly worried about his visit. 'Your people will think you came to make a secret political deal with me,' I cautioned him. So to play safe, he placed an item in a local paper saying he had come to discuss water and electricity for the orphanage. A few days later he returned to complete our business and told me : 'For my fellow Arabs, I am now a collaborator.' 'Why?' I asked. 'Because I am using your water and electricity.' I asked him what he had replied to the charge. 'I inquired what water they were using, and they said they were using the same, but "our situation is not written up in the papers." '

That episode is indicative of how business is conducted between the Municipality and the Arabs of Jerusalem. They are eagerly cooperating and, I believe, find in us reasonable counterparts; but they are not willing to accept responsibility, certainly not publicly. It will take a generation of complicated psychological adjustments and endless patience to break down this attitude. The Arabs had been victorious for hundreds of years and conquered a major part of the world. Then one shock followed another – an accumulated shock. They were defeated by the Turks, Napoleon, and the French, the British, and finally by us. There is a difference, however. The British, for example, were here under a mandate for a limited period; we are here for good.

If the truth be told, some of us are susceptible to a strain of arrogance that goes along with the confidence that we have come home again and 'we shall not be moved.' The incident of the monuments to the war dead is a case in point. On the first anniversary of the 1967 war, we commemorated our war dead by placing stone tablets at various spots in the city where severe fighting had taken place. Altogether, we put up ten or twelve tablets, each containing a one-sentence account of the action and the names of those who were killed on that particular spot. In the following months, many similar Arab monuments began to make their appearance. One difference between theirs and ours was that it turned out that many Arabs had been buried – according to Arab tradition but unknown to us – in the nearest garden or empty plot, wherever they had fallen. We did not know where these graves were, but the people who had dug them did. Gradually little heaps of stones appeared here and there, dozens of them in the most unlikely places, each with a tablet and a sentence from the Koran. It was a real problem. Suppose in a few years we wanted to build a road; graves were scattered everywhere. We negotiated with the *wakf* (the Moslem religious foundation) and worked out a plan by which it would bury all the scattered dead in a mass grave and we would agree to have an appropriate monument erected. This solution was possible because the Arabs do not regard a cemetery or

burial place as inviolably sacred ground. But none of it was simple. For
instance, the *wakf* had no authority to act in cases where a family was
willing to be responsible for the grave. But in many instances the
families did not live in Jerusalem, any part of Israel, or the occupied
territories. Even if their addresses in the Arab countries were known, it
would be difficult to reach them. Yet the nature of the problem called for
quick and decisive action if we were to save the city from what was
likely to become a serious problem, from an urban standpoint.

Before taking any action, however, we wanted the fullest possible
authorization from our own government, for dealing with the Arab
soldiers and civilians who had died fighting against us was no light
matter. We received a favorable response from the Security Committee,
which represented all ministries and branches of government concerned,
and sent copies of the committee's minutes to all the Cabinet ministers,
who responded with a show of great understanding. I don't recall any of
them opposing our plan of action, and the special Jerusalem Committee
of the Cabinet promised its support. On this basis, we went ahead and
had the *wakf* rebury the Arab dead, over two hundred of them. They
worked quietly, at night, with no public demonstrations. A few months
later, when plans for the monument were ready, I gave permission for it
to be erected. It was close to an Arab cemetery and in a very visible
position at the corner of the Old City wall, where it could be seen
from afar.

In the months between the decision and its implementation, however,
acts of terrorism had begun to take place, and the feeling of many Jews
toward the Arabs had hardened considerably. Many began to view the
Arabs not only as soldiers who fought us in 1967, but as terrorists and
murderers. Suddenly there was widespread opposition to the monument,
starting in the City Council. Of course, it is perfectly legitimate for
political parties to exploit such issues to strengthen their image, even at
the cost of exciting public feelings. The arguments they presented were
ingenious. Where, I was asked, was there a monument for the Germans
in France or in England? I explained that the situation was not
comparable. The Arabs were living in Jerusalem.

The sessions in the City Council devoted to this issue were probably
the most violent I experienced during my twelve years as mayor. All
those who had originally supported the idea suddenly vanished. The
Cabinet ministers were either silent, non-committal, or couldn't be
reached at all. The only leaders of note who publicly stood behind me in
this situation were Ben-Gurion and Dayan, who openly stated that the
monument was not only promised but justified. Over the years it has
turned out that the fears, genuine or not, that this monument would
become a place for demonstrations, the spot from which the revolt
against Israeli authority would begin, a symbol of insurrection, were all

groundless. From time to time you can see a mourner dressed in black coming to lay a wreath there, but that is all. I don't know whether the erection of the monument did much good in the long run. It certainly did not do any harm. But years later I am still proud that we had the courage and the sensitivity to carry out our decision. It has not brought us any major, permanent support from the Arabs, but it has resulted in an atmosphere of mutual understanding on at least one point: our own memorial tablets, many in Arab neighborhoods, are respected.

It was while we were planning the design for the monument that events in the city took an alarming turn. The first case of terrorism occurred one evening in the summer of 1968, when bombs went off in several places around the city and a number of people were wounded. That same evening some young Israelis went on a rampage, turned over an Arab car, and broke an Arab store window. The terrorists almost accomplished what they set out to achieve: tension between the city's two communities. The next morning Arabs were afraid to come to work and Jews were reluctant to go shopping in Arab stores. That day, Minister of Police Eliahu Sasson and I spent the day walking around from shop to shop, and one café to another to demonstrate that there was nothing to fear. Our appearances helped to diminish the impact of the bombing and stress the theme of cooperation in our city. We also did everything possible to explain to the Jews that violent reaction was just what the terrorists were hoping for.

The next incident was a bomb placed in the Zion Cinema, but fortunately it was discovered in time. The following day, Uri Zohar, the star of the hit film running at the Zion, came up from Tel Aviv with other celebrities to give a midnight show at the theater. We made a gala occasion of it; in fact, so many thousands came that we had to move the show from the movie house to the square outside. Large crowds stayed until two in the morning as a communal gesture of defiance: we would not be frightened out of going to a movie!

Toward the end of November came the tragic explosion in Mahaneh Yehudah, the crowded open-air market in West Jerusalem. I was in New York at the time, but when I received a call at 4 A.M. I took the next plane home. Eleven people had been killed, including two Arabs, and Jerusalem had changed overnight. The right-wing parties and all the other nationalists were in full cry, and the city was faced with an understandable but nevertheless dangerous stirring of anti-Arab feeling that had to be dealt with firmly and patiently.

Since 1968 sporadic terrorist incidents have occurred in Jerusalem, but they are not supported by the vast majority of the local Arab population. The reason is not that the Arabs of Jerusalem love us or that they would like us to continue to rule the city, but simply because they lead a reasonably tolerable life now. Their slogan is '*Sumud*'

('Attachment'), meaning that they intend to remain attached to Jerusalem in order to preserve the Arab character of their section of the city. The primary requirement for doing so is simply to remain in Jerusalem, and to remain here they need a flourishing economy. Terrorism would destroy that economy. Tourists won't come here if the city is riddled with bombs. Jews would shun the Arab shops and markets and would stop employing Arab labor. The result would be an inevitable mass exodus, and Jerusalem would lose its Arab population. For these very pragmatic reasons, Arabs in Jerusalem are inhospitable to terrorism.

As for their attitude toward political cooperation, that is another matter entirely. Two years after the city was united, we were again preparing for municipal elections, which were scheduled to be held in November 1969. We would have liked to see Arabs running for office; but as far as they were concerned this was as taboo as any other public sign of accepting Israeli rule. Nevertheless, we almost succeeded in getting one or two serious men to run for the City Council. We wanted public-spirited individuals, truly and proudly representing the Arabs. Sometimes politics in Israel is pursued with an eye to foreign, particularly American, reaction; but our motives were genuinely civic. We were not seeking some photogenic person wearing a picturesque Arab *keffiyeh*. That could have been accomplished. We could easily have found two or three people in the rural part of Jerusalem who had no political experience but would have been very honored to become city councilors. Then in all the news photographs or television clips of City Council meetings, the Arabs would be visibly represented. But we really wouldn't be fooling anyone – least of all our Arab constituents. We wanted educated men of commitment, and in return we were prepared to give them full respect and consideration. One or two such men were talking the matter over, and I believe they would have put themselves up as candidates if not for the wretched fire at the El-Aksa Mosque on August 29, 1969.

The fire happened two and a half months before the election, and emotions ran high. Logically, the Arabs in Jerusalem knew we were in no way responsible. But deep in their hearts they wanted to believe we were. Ultimately they interpreted the El-Aksa incident as divine punishment because the Holy Places were under the control of infidels. The infidels in question happen to be Jews, but it would have been just the same if the British, the U.N., or the Pope were ruling Jerusalem. As it happened, the fire was started by an unbalanced Christian from Australia by the name of Rohan, who in his distorted thinking believed that if the mosque burned down the Jews would rebuild the Temple and the Messiah would return.

I was at a meeting when news reached me that El-Aksa was ablaze. By the time I reached the site, the fire brigade was at work (though stories quickly circulated that the fire brigade was deliberately slow in arriving). The Arabs were trying to put out the blaze with buckets and sentiment, and the scene of the flames, with thousands of Moslems weeping, was heartbreaking. In the afternoon I returned to the mosque with Golda (who was then prime minister) and Dayan. Both of them promised help, but their offer was never officially accepted by the Arabs. Nevertheless, all the gifts that came in – marble from Italy and similar donations – were allowed into the country without customs levies and import licenses. We also provided cement at a time when there was a severe shortage. The repairs of the mosque have been expertly done. Even ancient crafts have been revived for the purpose, particularly the cutting of gypsum windows at a special angle so that when the sun shines through the colored Hebron glass at various hours, it creates different color combinations that are of particular beauty. The old man who knew this special craft trained several younger people to work with him, and thus the art is being preserved. However, the occasion was also used to replace Crusader capitals at the mosque by modern copies of Moslem-style capitals, so that any indication of Christian influence would disappear.

The frenzy over the fire cooled, but when election day came we still had no idea whether or not the Arabs would actually come to the polls and vote. Like all residents of Israel who are not Israeli citizens, the Arabs of Jerusalem could vote in municipal but not in national elections. Even though recruiting candidates from the Arab population was out of the question in that disturbed atmosphere, we did very much want a substantial Arab vote. Many Arabs feared that voting would in itself be considered an act of treason in the eyes of others. So the polling booths along the line between Jewish and Arab areas were all organized as mixed booths, in the hope that Arabs would come and vote and, if not, one could not quite tell how many Jews and how many Arabs had voted. In the end the Arabs came in numbers that exceeded our most optimistic expectations. More than eleven thousand Arabs voted, though only eight thousand of the votes were valid. (There were still difficulties with names and identity cards that had not been properly ironed out.)

The Arab vote should not be interpreted either as approval of the unification of the city or as a sign of confidence in Israeli politics. It was an expression of support for an administration that had helped generously, behaved toward the Arab populace in a reasonable and responsible way, and provided many previously non-existent services. The vote was a signal of response to an administration that had created more work opportunities and developed a proper personal approach. Most of the Arab residents of Jerusalem had never laid eyes on the mayor, or even a city councilor, in Jordanian times. We went out to visit them and learned their problems first hand, and they appreciated both the care and the

practical achievements. But one must not read too much into this relationship. It had little bearing on basic political issues. These would still
be with us for a long, long time.

Life in united Jerusalem often leads to partly funny, partly embarrassing situations. A year after the Six Day War, a well-known lord and
lady were visiting from London, and I invited them to dinner with
several other guests. The English lady, who had spent the morning
touring Jerusalem and Bethlehem, sat through most of the meal extoll-
ing the accomplishments of the Israelis to her dinner partner, whose
name she apparently hadn't caught. 'How were you able to fight against
such odds? How have you managed to build up the city as you have
done?' Toward the end of the meal, her dinner partner mentioned
something about London, prompting the query, 'What did you do in
London?' Anwar Nusseibeh's reply was simple: 'I was Jordanian
Ambassador to the Court of St James.'

Among the many visitors who came after the Six Day War, I particularly remember John Kenneth Galbraith. Years earlier I had been introduced to Professor Galbraith and had met him on subsequent occasions
both in Jerusalem and in the United States. One afternoon in the fall of
1967, Galbraith phoned me from Lod Airport. He had just arrived, had
only a few hours, and wanted to see the Old City. During our very quick
tour, using the last hours of daylight, we came to the Church of the Holy
Sepulchre. I took him to all the important spots in the church, and we
finally went into the crypt. There, bowing deeply over the great
sarcophagus, was a young man obviously immersed in devout prayer.
Ken, who is very tall and could hardly stand erect in the crypt, entered
just as the young man turned his head, looked up, and exclaimed: 'Jesus
Christ, it's Professor Galbraith!' I never heard the exclamation used in
a more appropriate context.

Teddy Kennedy was also a regular visitor with a deep interest in the
refugee problem, as well as the health problems of the area. On one or
two occasions he came with members of his family. I particularly
remember one evening, after dinner, he expressed a desire to visit the
Western Wall, which he had never seen. My son, Amos, was present,
and we drove through the Old City to the Wall. It was close to midnight, but one always finds a few people praying. Ted accepted a
yarmulka to cover his head and went up to the Wall, looked at it, and
asked if he could pray. Having finished his quiet prayer, he took a step
back and crossed himself, as every good Catholic would naturally do. I
thought to myself: 'Only in Jerusalem.'

In fact, the juxtaposition of different faiths in such close proximity is
one of the most appealing features of this city. I suppose it's only
natural that most people turn the spotlight on the complex set of
relations between the Jewish and Moslem communities here. But there

is also a substantial Christian community residing in Jerusalem – Arab and non-Arab – and our encounters with it and its leaders have been one of the most interesting and positive changes that has taken place in Jerusalem as a result of the war.

My early upbringing in Vienna – in a city that was said to have more Czechs than Prague and more Hungarians than Budapest, apart from Poles and Croats and Jews – may have conditioned me to living in a polyglot heterogeneous city. And Vienna, even after the revolution of 1918, was a very religious Catholic city. Thus when Jerusalem was united in 1967 and we suddenly had to deal with many church dignitaries, I had a certain edge over my colleagues, having at least some familiarity with church problems and clerical thinking. This certainly helped to establish a friendly relationship with Benedictos, the aged Greek Orthodox patriarch who is the senior patriarch in Jerusalem; Elisha ii, the Armenian patriarch; many of their archbishops and bishops; heads of the various Catholic churches and monasteries; and heads of some of the minor Oriental churches. I had also read extensively about these churches even before the city was united because of my interest in Jerusalem's history. To help them was only sensible. Moreover, it was crucial to prove that we could administer the city more tolerantly than any ruler or administration before us. To work with the Christian community meant first of all learning the rules that applied in the Holy Places.

Traditions in this city are very strong, especially those concerning the Christian denominations – and there are over thirty of them. The respective rights of the major churches in the Holy Places were last regulated in 1852 and 1853 in a *firman* issued by the sultan of the Ottoman Empire. The contents of this proclamation were recognized at the time by Queen Victoria, Emperor Franz Josef, the king of Savoy, Napoleon iii, the king of Prussia, and the czar of Russia. Their empires have long disappeared, and all their countries have changed. But the *status quo* as defined in that *firman* over 120 years ago is still meticulously observed – so much so that even the slightest deviation from it is grounds for conflict.

We had to do everything possible to prevent the inter-church strife that had become almost traditional. In fact, I have to spend an extraordinary amount of time on Christian affairs, especially as church ceremonials are often lengthy and far outweigh the time needed to discuss, analyze, and solve problems. Yet it's impossible to weigh the benefits of good relations in minutes, and there are rewarding by-products to contacts with the clergy. One is excellent food (particularly with the Armenians and Greek Orthodox) served in beautiful settings. To have dinner in summer with the Greek Orthodox patriarch in the garden of Akeldema (the little monastery on the site Judas Iscariot bought for his thirty silver pieces) and look down on Silwan in the moonlight is an unforgettable experience. Most important, however, some of these eminent church leaders have testified to the true situation in Jerusalem on occasions when we have been criticized abroad (for instance by the Pope in an occasional epistle at Easter).

The relative standing of the various churches in the world does not always hold in Jerusalem because certain churches have the historic advantage of having been established here earlier than others. The Greek Orthodox Church, for example, constitutes only a fraction of the world Christian population and geographically is almost wholly confined to Greece and the Slavic countries. It exists as a dim image in the Western world's centers of power, where the Catholic Church stands out in visible splendor. But in Jerusalem the Greek Orthodox own more than half of the Church of the Holy Sepulchre and more than any other religious body at Gethsemane, on the Mount of Olives, and in the Church of the Nativity in Bethlehem. Its Patriarchate also clearly has seniority here. The Armenian Church, established here in the fifth century, totals only six million worshippers in the entire world, but it owns a third of Jerusalem's Holy Places. The Copts and the Assyrians, obscure in the church councils of the world, are visibly on the scene in Jerusalem. Yet the Roman Catholic Church, which owns only seventeen percent of the Holy Places, established itself here during the Crusades and is therefore a relative latecomer. And the Protestants are restricted to singing their Christmas carols in the courtyard of the Church of the Nativity because they do not own any part of the church. They are real Johnnies-come-lately as Holy Land church history goes. Whenever the question of internationalization for Jerusalem comes up, I ask myself what would an international government do with a city where the Armenians outvote the Catholics and even the Assyrians outrank the Protestants? And this does not even begin to touch on the relative weight of the Moslems.

Probably the best example I could choose to illustrate the nature of our relations with the Christian churches is our experience with the Armenians. They are a very old, established community in Jerusalem. Like the Jews, their people have suffered oppression and persecution (especially at the beginning of this century), they have a Diaspora, and they have been fighting the tendency toward assimilation. As we became acquainted with the Armenians of Jerusalem, we began to discover the richness of their cultural heritage. The community has a fabulous collection of treasures, many of them gifts brought by pilgrims over the centuries, including the most beautiful chalices, church vestments, garments, miters, and bishops' staffs. Their library contains hundreds of illuminated manuscripts comparable to the best in the world. These treasures had never been described, and were hardly known to exist outside the Jerusalem Armenian community. We felt that they should be shown and published, that the Armenians should call the world's attention – and especially that of Armenians everywhere – to their treasures. Our enthusiasm about the glories of their cultural heritage have, I think, convinced the Armenians of our genuine belief in developing all the different cultural traditions of Jerusalem while trying to diminish the political differences.

To prove the point beyond question, the Municipality and the Israel Museum helped to mount an exhibition of the Armenians' magnificent heritage, and it attracted widespread interest throughout the Armenian Diaspora. We also convinced the Jerusalem community that much could and should be done to maintain contact with their dispersed people; that Armenians here could do for their brethren in the Western world what could not be accomplished from the center in Soviet Armenia. Perhaps this notion wasn't new, but now they began to act upon it. They even obtained approval from the community in Soviet Armenia and went out to their Diaspora, mainly in the United States, to collect funds. One of the results was the dedication in June 1975 of an impressive seminary on Mount Zion, which will train teachers and priests for the entire Armenian world. Armenians from all over came for the dedication, including the head of the Armenian Church (the *Catholicos* from Soviet Armenia), who blessed the project. During the week he spent in Jerusalem, the city seemed to turn into an Armenian capital, with theater performances, concerts, dance programs, and receptions on the part of the community and the Municipality. It could not have happened anywhere else but in Jerusalem.

We have as close an understanding with the Greek Orthodox Patriarchate, and our relationship with the Roman Catholics is excellent on the local level, although we are not always happy with pronouncements from Rome. One major step our government took since 1967 has been to revoke the Jordanian laws that prevented Christian institutions from buying land and building churches. But perhaps most important, we are not interfering with the curricula of the various Christian schools. A few years before the Six Day War, the Jordanians insisted on a controlled curriculum that entailed compulsory instruction in the Koran and other Moslem subjects. Our government has abolished this curriculum and does not interfere at all in the teaching of the missionary schools. Furthermore, this position distinguishes us from almost all the other governments in the Middle East. With the exception of the few schools still left in Lebanon, Christian institutions established in the nineteenth and twentieth centuries all over the Middle East – from Turkey to Egypt and Sudan and from North Africa to Iraq and Persia – have all been nationalized.

Yet protecting the curriculum of the schools is only a partial answer to helping the Christian community thrive in this city. Since about the turn of the century, there has been a major exodus of Christian Arabs from Jerusalem – and, indeed, the entire Middle East – mainly to South America and later to the United States and to Canada. The move was actively facilitated by the high level of education provided by the missionary schools, which were designed to provide the colonial regimes in Palestine, Lebanon, and Syria with local officials. Many of the graduates of these high schools went on to universities in France and England and never returned to their native countries. (This is a common phenomenon today for many new and developing countries.) At any rate, after the unification of the city, we learned that the churches were concerned about the gradually shrinking size of the Christian community. During the years of Jordanian rule, it had diminished much more quickly than ever before, a decrease from twenty-five thousand to about ten thousand in nineteen years. This period was marked by few economic opportunities in Jerusalem, and the young people with their fine education had a chance to join their relatives abroad. So why stay?

One of our suggestions was to provide institutes of education beyond the high school level. Following deliberations that were based in part on memoranda we submitted in 1968 and 1969 to the Anglican archbishop and to the Apostolic Delegate, the curriculum of the Anglican School, St George's, was extended for another few years, and the Catholic Church inaugurated a College in Bethlehem (it began operating in the midst of the Yom Kippur War). The first university-level institution on the West Bank (other than teachers' colleges), it has become a successful college that may one day have as many as a thousand students, Christian and Moslem.

All this is not to say that we have not encountered complications in dealing with the Christian community. A good example of a problem we faced and solved was the case of Notre Dame de France, an imposing century-old monastery opposite the New Gate of the Old City. Notre Dame was owned by the Assumptionists, a Roman Catholic order, and rumor had it that they wanted to sell the huge, antiquated building. It no longer seemed to serve any visible purpose and had in any case suffered a good deal of damage in various wars. Nevertheless, it was a powerful symbol, and I doubted that the Vatican would permit the sale. Yet one day in 1969, someone connected with the Hebrew University told me, 'We have acquired it. The University is buying it through a New York intermediary, and we'll use it as a student hostel for a few years. Then we'll tear it down and build something else.'

Shortly afterward, the Apostolic Delegate, the intelligent and attractive Monsignor Pio Laghi, brought a visitor from Rome to see me. We spent a pleasant social Saturday afternoon together, but I realized that a serious matter was at hand. It turned out to be Notre Dame. The

Church felt hurt for a variety of reasons. First of all, it was losing this symbolic building. Secondly, under canonic law any order must have the approval of the Holy See to sell a major property, and the Assumptionists had not received such approval. Thirdly, there was a rumor abroad that some of the individuals connected with the order had made a private profit on the deal. 'We have many interests in the Arab world,' Monsignor Laghi told me. ' Today the Church is not only the Church Militant, it is also the Church Social. To carry out our tasks we have to provide welfare services. Nuns have to work as nurses in hospitals, for instance. With your Hadassah Hospital you have no need of Catholic nurses. But in our relations with the Arabs, this is the truest way we can express the Christian spirit in this environment. The sale of Notre Dame might lead the Arabs to believe that the Church supports Zionism and could, therefore, prejudice such activity.'

In order to prove that the sale came about without Rome's approval, the Church would have to take legal action. Meanwhile, the situation became aggravated when somebody announced to the press that the Jewish National Fund had bought Notre Dame and described the purchase as a great Zionist achievement. The Roman Catholic Church was not going to sit still and allow itself to be identified with Zionist interests, but obviously it would have been a gravely discordant note in all our delicate interdenominational relationships if the case were brought to court – whatever the decision. I therefore went first to President Harman of the Hebrew University, then to the minister of justice, and with him to Prime Minister Golda Meir, and it was finally decided to cancel the purchase and return the property to the Holy See. Notre Dame was returned for the price it had cost, even though prices of real estate had quadrupled during the two intervening years. The Vatican is now restoring the building as a pilgrims' hostel.

The choice of this solution naturally had repercussions in Israeli public opinion. The minister of justice and I were denounced almost as traitors for giving up such a valuable vantage point in Jerusalem. I, on the other hand, felt it was a major investment in goodwill, which can be measured neither in dollars and cents nor in terms of national pride. It is, however, one of the most important ingredients for a flourishing future in this city of three religions and many different peoples.

15 The New-Old Jerusalem

I REMEMBER Jerusalem in the days of the British Mandate : a sleepy little town in the mountains dotted with clusters of houses built of grey Jerusalem stone and capped by red-tiled roofs. It was a mosaic of communities tucked away in hidden courtyards at the end of narrow alleys. Even its bazaars and offices were totally removed from the noise and tempo of modern life. Walking the streets during those years in the forties, I often thought how remarkable it was that a place so central in history – holy to three religions yet so often ravaged by zealous warriors – could be so quiet, so provincial, so at peace with itself. For some Jerusalem has always been home, the place where their ancestors lived, where they grew up, where every house conjures up some personal association. I did not grow up in Jerusalem, but every house meant something to me because it had a history of its own, a special character, a beauty that comes only with time.

For many years I permitted myself the luxury of taking this in as a resident of the city. I certainly never expected to be the mayor and have the responsibility for Jerusalem's preservation and development. The truth is, planning and building Jerusalem is a tremendous burden and the greatest challenge I have faced in my life. Jerusalem is not New York, London, Paris, or even Rome. It is not just a great city or an historical city. It is a place where everyone seems to feel he has a share, a stake – and a say. Because Jerusalem is a city holy to millions, every new house that goes up adds itself to history and thus often becomes controversial. Yet I feel there is also a deep human value in preserving Jerusalem, independent of its political future, because I am overcome by sadness whenever a long-established thing of beauty and character disappears.

In the nineteenth century people hardly hesitated to tear down the city walls of old European capitals in order to build something new in their place. The great Vienna Ringstrasse stands on the ruins of the wall that used to surround the city. It was torn down because it no longer fulfilled a strategic purpose and to make room for great museums and palaces.

Today we feel differently about such things. In 1967 we encountered ancient structures that had been left to crumble under Jordanian rule. The Old City walls themselves would not have lasted much longer. But decay was not the only problem. The division of the city had caused a lot of unfortunate errors and misconceptions. Highrises and buildings like the Intercontinental Hotel on the Mount of Olives were built when the city was divided and no one had a feel for what Jerusalem would look like if it were united again. Now we are trying to do everything possible to restore the perfection of the city as a whole. We must plan with a vision of a new-old Jerusalem, a city of history that is at the same time a growing metropolis in this modern era. It isn't easy.

Planning does not merely mean deciding what to build where. It means deciding what kind of city we will have, how quickly it will grow, what its social patterns will be, how its income will be sustained, how to provide for its quality of life, and what it will look like in the year 2000 and after. The Municipality had always engaged in this field, of course. But when Jerusalem was a divided city, to some extent we were working in limbo. Soon after I became mayor in 1965, I was asked a fundamental question: are we to presume that Jerusalem will one day become a united city – which means, for example, that roads have to be planned from east to west, toward and across the dividing walls? I said yes, without any hesitation, and I believed that somehow I would be proven right. Still, it was hard to go about solid townplanning on the basis of hopes alone. I had no idea that the unification would come so soon. I just felt that it would happen some day, that it was simply on the cards. Then, in 1967, the dream materialized, and all of a sudden I was no longer the mayor of a small Jewish city, the capital of Israel, but of a worldwide center. It was a staggering change, and I knew I must assume a new kind of responsibility and plan with utmost care.

In 1968 I invited an unusual group to form the Jerusalem Committee. It comprised distinguished personalities from all over the world – educators, writers, historians, philosophers, theologians, architects, city planners, and artists – sixty or seventy people in all. This was our way of recognizing the universal character of the city and demonstrating that we were not planning and building just for ourselves. The committee convened for the first time in 1969, and its first session was most impressive. Because of later developments, it is interesting to note that one of its first decisions was to encourage us to dig and carry out archaeological research in order to establish a continuity between the past and planning for the future. We might even have accepted the New York public works slogan: 'Dig we must!' Then, in December 1970, we convened a sub-committee of the Jerusalem Committee, comprising mainly architects and townplanners. I recall a lead article about the best architects in the world that appeared in *Newsweek* a few months later.

Almost every name it mentioned happened to be a member of our sub-committee. They were the city's guests, of course, but they extended their services free of charge. I don't believe any other city in the world could have secured such services. As one of the sub-committee members put it: 'Each one of us has two cities, his own and Jerusalem.'

By that time we had developed a masterplan for the city and submitted it to the sub-committee's members for comments. During their four-day stay in Jerusalem, they tore it to pieces. The members feared we would make the same mistakes they had made in their own cities. Perhaps the most typical experience was that of Göran Sidenbladh, who had been in charge of the townplan of Stockholm. Until a few years earlier, that plan had been regarded as the most noble and courageous experiment in changing an old city into a modern one. And because the Swedes had the great advantages of peace and major resources, they could afford expensive solutions. The townplan's basic principle was that every resident should be able to travel from home to his place of work by car. It turned out to be a principle that could not be realized. The race between road and car cannot be won. When you build major roads, they attract even more cars, and congestion actually increases. At any rate, our masterplan was condemned. (I believe it may have been criticized too sharply. There were some good ideas in it, but even these were poorly presented.) So we decided to restructure the plan and appointed an urban planning group of bright young people.

Meanwhile, as a result of the Jerusalem sub-committee conference, which was followed with universal interest, the world leveled a great deal of criticism at us – some of which was pretty hard to swallow. In fact, most of the complaints continued as if the plans we had already decided to scrap had already been carried out! We were probably the first city that ever voluntarily laid itself open to criticism, and there were times when I thought that we were paying an unfair price. The list of self-appointed experts on city planning sometimes included unexpected entries. The Pope and the Archbishop of Canterbury even came out against highrise apartment houses in new residential areas of the city. I have always believed that these church leaders have a right to express their opinions about the historic Old City and its environs, because this is the Jerusalem dear to many people around the world. But I do not feel that the Pope, the Archbishop, or anybody else has a standing when it comes to construction in new Jerusalem at a considerable distance from the Old City. This is purely an internal matter to be decided by the citizens of Jerusalem alone. Nonetheless, by the time we started making new plans, we had learned that both national and international interests had to be taken into account, and the two often came into sharp conflict. And these, of course, were in addition to the political, religious, and historical considerations that are special to Jerusalem, not to mention the usual aesthetic, commercial, and social factors that go into town-planning everywhere.

Even those 'usual' factors can become rather extraordinary in Jerusalem. Socially, the city is an incredible mosaic. We have a higher percentage of religious Jews and more elderly people, new immigrants, young couples, Moslems, and Christians than any other city in Israel – and they all have to be taken into consideration. After the Six Day War there was a flow of newcomers to the city, and as a result we witnessed an incredible building boom. It was obvious why Jews wanted to return to the Jewish Quarter of the Old City, but the reasons for settling in the new neighborhoods built in areas previously under Jordanian rule were somewhat different. One reason was the desire to secure Mount Scopus by creating a landbridge to that area so that it could never be cut off again, as it had been in 1948. But probably no less important was the fact that housing in Jerusalem was very poor and crowded.

The last large housing development built before 1967 was right on the frontier with Jordan. It was completed in the early 1960s and included close to five hundred apartments. The people who moved in had come to Israel as refugees from Arab countries, and they had few possessions. The apartments were densely crowded, and after a few years some families had three generations living together – grandparents, parents, and an average of five children in an apartment of about five hundred square feet. By 1967 they had been living in such conditions for ten to fifteen years. They also lived facing Jordanian guns on Ammunition Hill, a very strongly fortified Arab position. The apartments had only narrow slit windows that could be covered with heavy iron shutters against the periodic shooting. From time to time somebody was wounded or even killed, and during the Six Day War over a hundred of these apartments were hit and badly damaged. After 1967 new, beautiful houses were built right across the way from this neighborhood. The new apartments were fifty percent larger and were purchased mainly by smaller families, many of them newcomers to the city and to the country. Inevitably this imbalance created resentment among the people who had long suffered from danger and inferior living conditions. More than ever, planning and building became a great social problem, and tensions were steadily rising.

The housing issue coincided with the rise of the 'Black Panther' movement in Israel. The Panthers were young people from the Oriental Jewish communities (mainly Moroccans) who were dissatisfied with their social and economic state. They were inspired by disciples of Saul Alinsky, a radical Chicago social worker, who had imported his theory from the United States. (I believe that the very name 'Black Panthers' was suggested by one of the American social workers in our Social Welfare Department as a good publicity gimmick – and it worked!)

The call for revolutionary action was not really appropriate to our situation in Israel, and the Panthers' demonstrations were short-lived. But their purpose was to dramatize the contrast between different sections of our population, and in this they were more than successful. In fact, there was a time when everyone from the prime minister down to the last Knesset member or Jewish Agency department head felt he was not doing his duty if he hadn't had breakfast or lunch that day with a Panther, and the movement received a great deal of publicity. On the other hand, all the sound and fury only made it more difficult to deal with the practical problems of the day.

There were good reasons why the tensions should have exploded in Jerusalem. All demands for improved conditions had been suppressed before 1967 because we were living on the border in a permanent state of war. Now they came to the fore in an explosive fashion. No one ever denied the fact that the demands of the underprivileged sections of our population were to a great extent justified. So we started working in two directions: improving conditions in established neighborhoods, by enlarging apartments wherever possible, building youth and community centers, laying out playgrounds, opening child-care centers; and building new and better-planned neighborhoods. Both went hand in hand with improving our educational methods in new and better school buildings.

Since we wanted to build a reasonably well-planned metropolis, there was hardly anywhere else to extend the city but into the former Jordanian areas. Thus the government requisitioned considerable tracts that had mainly been Arab owned. It is never pleasant for anyone to have his land expropriated, and although this was uncultivated land, the very fact that compensation was offered by the people the Arabs regarded as 'conquerors' made for resentment. There was no other choice, however. In some cases the owners of the land were unknown; in others the land had never been properly mapped and parceled. Under the old Ottoman land law, tracts were divided among an owner's children and went on to be divided among his children's children. Because detailed mapping was lacking, we came upon areas that belonged jointly to hundreds of descendants of the original owners. Each knew what his percentage of the original tract was, but not where his portion lay. Since the legal position was so confused, Arab countries that had once been a part of the Ottoman Empire had long ago expropriated such land wherever necessary and paid compensation to the individual owners according to each one's share in the property. The Jordanians had not yet made that progressive step, so it was left to us to do so and eventually to pay the compensation. What was definitely excluded from our expropriation plans was agricultural land and built-up areas. Our primary consideration was not to harm individuals. Not a single house or tree was destroyed.

Not that our care helped very much from a political standpoint, as the

Arabs objected in principle to any kind of expropriation (except for schools and roads, which is an established practice anywhere in the world). However, since few individuals suffered, it created less tension than would have been the case otherwise. Moreover, the Municipality fought for the return of all the land originally expropriated from Arab institutions, and this was done. Nonetheless the Arabs in East Jerusalem would like their part of the city to revert to Arab sovereignty, and this cannot come about if the area is geographically cut off from Arab territory by new Jewish suburbs. Many of them believe the frontiers of 1967 will yet be restored. Thus the Arabs do not want to discuss our plans for Jerusalem, because they are opposed to the unification in principle. We have held several debates on questions of planning, sometimes in the presence of foreign journalists. They led nowhere. The true principle is not related to the details of planning, however; the Arabs simply do not want Jews here.

The vehemence of this attitude is matched by the overriding desire of some Jewish nationalist forces to have Jews settle everywhere and throw planning to the winds. Even Ben-Gurion was on their side at one point. I remember a meeting held in our apartment shortly after the 1967 war. Ben-Gurion, still a member of the Knesset then, had asked me to invite representatives of all the parties and high government officials. He held forth passionately, calling for tens of thousands of Jews to settle in East Jerusalem immediately – in huts, tents, helter-skelter – to ensure ourselves, and make it clear to the world, that it would never be taken from us again. It was a blazing Biblical plea, and he persuaded the rest of his audience; they were with him unanimously. But I was against it both on principle and in practice. I could not see any immediate threat to an Israeli Jerusalem. But I thought there was great danger in establishing large camps that would be filled in the initial stages of enthusiasm and deserted soon thereafter. Certainly we had a few years at our disposal in which to create proper communities. Fortunately Ben-Gurion's ideas were so impractical that no one ever tried to implement them. But I did come into sharp conflict with both the Ministry of Housing and members of our own City Council over very similar issues.

One area of serious contention was the area called Nebi Samuel. It is not within the city limits, but people wanted to settle there for several reasons. As usual there were those who believed that by settlement you 'conquer' a piece of land and add it to the Jewish patrimony. But equally important was the fact that the view of Jerusalem from Nebi Samuel is breathtaking. In short, who would not want to live with Jerusalem at his feet! Various pressure groups emerged in favor of settling there : army officers, retired government officials, university professors. But my colleagues and I were categorically opposed to the idea. We wanted to preserve the beautiful hilltop mosque of Nebi Samuel (traditionally the

Tomb of the Prophet Samuel and a familiar landmark for hundreds of years), and keep the area a graceful open space between Jerusalem and Ramallah to the north. Nearby, but at a considerable distance from the mosque, we were building the area of Ramot – also a source of contention, since the Ministry of Housing wanted to cram as many as thirty thousand apartments into the area. We pressured for a reduction, and the plan was finally reduced to about eight thousand apartments. We also argued that Ramot safeguarded the city, but villas in Nebi Samuel would add nothing.

I also fought against the creation of suburbs for the economically well-off as a crime against urban planning. We did not want to repeat the mistakes that had been made with the Scarsdales and White Plainses of New York. I believed that we had a special task to fulfill by integrating Jewish society. In addition, the infrastructure for this 'villa suburb' would have been extremely expensive, and in the end it would have been paid for out of the national purse, not by the individuals who enjoyed the view. Personally, I believe in building the city rather densely and even comparatively high (outside the zone around the Old City), rather than have it sprawl over one hill after the other until it finally meets with Tel Aviv. I can't see why three- or four-story houses are necessarily more beautiful than eight-story buildings.

Altogether, over thirty thousand new housing units have been constructed in Jerusalem since the Six Day War, and this does not include new housing built for the Arab population, whose needs and tastes were both different. Jerusalem's Arabs, particularly those living in the Old City, were housed in severely overcrowded conditions. Building new homes for them was as arduous and complex a task as providing for the tremendous immigration of Jews who arrived over the last decade, although the needs in absolute numbers were much smaller.

First of all, we experimented. Taking several acres of expropriated land, we consulted Israeli-Arab architects from Nazareth and Haifa and built a small housing development of twenty-nine apartments. The price of these apartments was relatively low, and we made special efforts to offer long-term credit and generally to facilitate purchases. But there were still difficulties. The Arabs did not want to move into apartments on expropriated land, and it took some time until all the units were occupied. After that we reduced direct government involvement in Arab housing to a minimum and provided financing for a private Arab construction firm instead. These activities expanded when we found an Arab contractor who could handle large units. The builder, Muhammed Nusseibeh, a brother of Anwar Nusseibeh (a former Jordanian minister of education, minister of war, and ambassador to England), no doubt received approval from his brother and from Amman. The Housing Ministry gave Nusseibeh the same privileged credit facilities that it offers Jewish contractors, and he started out with a unit of a hundred apartments. Then another 150 followed, and more are planned. Our only condition has been that some of these apartments be reserved for city needs. For instance, if we found it necessary to move some Arab tenants still living in the Old City as squatters, these apartments would provide alternative housing.

Then we tried different approaches. For example, we offered mortgages to Arabs who wanted to do their own building. The majority of these people are located in outlying districts where land is readily available and extended families live in one sprawling building, to which more and more rooms could be added. The legal status of most of these mortgages is a little dubious. Had we sent the applicants to a normal Israeli mortgage bank, few would have been able to provide the necessary documents regarding land ownership. We therefore established a special branch of the government mortgage company, which worked in cooperation with the Municipality and gave loans practically on trust alone. Since Arab families often manage to do most of their own construction work, the amount of cash needed was comparatively small. This approach has worked extremely well, and we have provided thousands of such mortgages. As a result, building activity among the Arabs is steadily on the increase, which I take not only as a response to a pragmatic need but also as a sign of well-being and stability. Anyone who thinks that he might be leaving tomorrow or that war might break out and spread its destruction will hesitate to invest in home improvements.

All but one of these building projects in the Arab and Jewish sectors took place outside the walls of the Old City. The single exception was the reconstruction of the Jewish Quarter. In 1967, when the city was reunited, all that remained of the Jewish Quarter were the ruins of houses and synagogues occupied by Arab villagers who had found work in Jerusalem. But it was once a flourishing neighborhood. Around the turn of the century, in fact, the Jewish Quarter was comparatively large, though it shrank as more and more Jews settled in the various parts of Jerusalem outside the Old City. In 1948 the residents of the Quarter fought against the Arab Legion until they ran out of ammunition and water and had to surrender. John Phillips, a *Life Magazine* photographer who was with the Arab Legion in 1948, had photographed the Quarter at the time of the surrender. His pictures show that little destruction had been caused by the fighting itself. But immediately after the surrender, the Quarter was plundered, and even before the end of the war it was practically razed by the Jordanians.

One of our first decisions was to rebuild the Quarter and find alternative housing for the Arab squatters. There were only a few Arab families who had lived in the Quarter for a generation or two, or even longer, and some of these were reluctant to leave. But with these exceptions, all the Arabs in the Jewish Quarter were only too happy to receive ample compensation and settle outside the Old City. They had no special feeling for the place. Nonetheless, the evacuation of Arabs automatically seems to be grounds for an international scandal. The truth of the matter is that we have evacuated many more Jews than Arabs in the course of our townplanning activities. (The renovation of the Yemin Moshe quarter in the new city is just one example.) In addition, the integrated planning of the entire Jewish Quarter made it impossible to allow many Jewish institutions to reinhabit their properties there, but I don't recall any international hue and cry over that 'injustice'. It's a very curious situation. When we moved to improve the lot of Arab families living in substandard housing and rebuild a derelict section of our city, a chorus of voices was raised in protest. But in 1948, when Jews were driven from their homes and the Jewish Quarter was destroyed, the world had nothing to say.

Once we started renovating the Jewish Quarter, I did not want the other quarters of the Old City to remain primitive by comparison. I approached Cabinet ministers for funds but couldn't seem to get very far with them. Finally, with a gift of $200,000 from personal friends abroad to the Jerusalem Foundation, we started work on our own. That initiative demonstrated our determination to try and equalize living standards in all parts of the city as best we can. It finally convinced the government to lend us a helping hand, and since 1973 we have been receiving about $1.5 million a year for this purpose. We have used these funds to renew the infrastructure (sewage and drainage, which sometimes goes back to the fifth century and at best to the nineteenth century) in the Christian and Moslem Quarters, to restore flagstones where repairs had been carried out with asphalt over the past few years, to replace television aerials with a master antenna and cable connections, to bury the telephone cables, and to improve house fronts and streets in the souks. At the present rate, it will take until 1983 or 1984 to complete this ambitious program.

Our aim in rebuilding the Jewish Quarter was to bring back Jewish residents, especially the families who had been driven out in 1948 and now wanted to return. Right after the Six Day War, many Jews felt a strong urge to rush into the Quarter and settle in hastily built, unplanned houses; the important thing was just to be back again. Fortunately, the Municipality succeeded in preventing that. Conditions would only have forced many people to leave again after a short time. Instead we planned the area slowly and carefully in order to preserve, restore and integrate archaeological structures wherever possible and build anew according to proper scale. The plan calls for settling of about six hundred families, in addition to *yeshivot* (religious schools), for a total

Jewish population of about 3,500. (I should mention that at the beginning of the century there were fifteen thousand Jews living in the Jewish Quarter, but obviously living standards have changed and we are not aiming for the same population density that existed then.) At the same time, we decided that before initiating any new construction, we would go down to bedrock and find out what archaeology could teach us about the area. As it turned out, we found remains of almost continuous Jewish habitation since as far back as 600 or 700 B.C. Among the most moving finds were several rather elegant buildings destroyed in A.D. 70, when the Temple was burned by the Romans. Large wooden beams had collapsed in a fire that left thick layers of ash over broken implements and household goods. Sometimes remnants of food were still recognizable among the ruins. You got the tragic feeling of being present at the destruction.

Gradually we intend to restore all these remains, some in vaulted underground rooms so that buildings can be constructed above them. Meanwhile, we have completed the reconstruction of some of the earliest synagogues in the city. They were built by Jews who returned to Jerusalem after their expulsion from Spain in 1492, and they were in continuous use until 1948. The first group of synagogues we reconstructed was the Yohanan Ben Zakkai complex. At the time they were built, around the start of the sixteenth century, an edict was in force that no Jewish building could be taller than an Arab building in the vicinity. Thus in order to create rooms with high ceilings in those synagogues, the builders dug their foundations deep into the ground. They were sunken synagogues, so to say, and that was what practically saved them when the Quarter was bulldozed in 1948.

While clearing the area, an ironic monument was found. Upon removing all the rubble and going deeper than any excavation in the last few centuries, our archaeologists discovered the foundations of a Romanesque church with three apses. After searching through the relevant sources, it became clear that this must be St Mary's of the Germans, a monastery built in the twelfth century when the German knights split from the order of the Hospitalers of St John. This was the monastery where the order of the Teutonic Knights was founded. The order later left Palestine and eventually conquered East Prussia from its Slavic inhabitants – and I don't think I have to elaborate on later developments of German history. So here we had a German church with historical connotations reminding us of both the massacres of the Crusaders (who indiscriminately killed all Jews and Arabs when they took Jerusalem) and the tragic impact of Germany on modern Jewish history. Nevertheless, we decided that as part of the city's past, it should be restored. Some of the more religious Jewish circles in the city objected : 'Why not let it disappear? Why do we need even the remnants of a church on the way to the Western Wall?' These were pointed arguments; but, then again, how could we falsify or change history? Much of the church was restored, although not enough was found to re-create the roof, so we turned it into a walled garden on an alternate route to the Wall.

The most serious reconstruction problem is still before us – the plaza of the Western Wall. We have tried to do away with the name 'Wailing Wall'. I don't know who first changed that adjective in English, but it has always been referred to as the Western Wall in Hebrew. In addition, the very fact that the Wall is ours again for the first time in two thousand years should stop the customary wailing, although many Jews believe that the mourning will only stop when the Temple is rebuilt. Incidentally, I receive about twenty or thirty letters a year, mainly from Fundamentalist Christians of various churches, urging us to build the Temple, because they regard this as a prerequisite for the return of Christ. At press conferences I am often asked whether we plan to rebuild the Temple. I usually reply that according to Jewish tradition, the Temple already exists and will come down from heaven to its proper place when the Messiah comes – and that's a chance everyone has to take.

The Western Wall (which is actually the western retaining wall of Herod's Temple mount) extends over more than 1,200 feet, of which only a very small portion (about a hundred feet) was visible and used for prayer during the last millennium. This portion was widened to over two hundred feet in 1967, when we cleared the area and tore down latrines and other structures actually attached to the Wall. At the same time we also dug down six feet deeper and revealed two more rows of the monumental Herodian stones. Before the area adjacent to the Wall was cleared, the Wall itself could not be seen from afar, and an im-pression of greater height was created when people viewed it from up close. There was also a more intimate relationship with the Wall in the days when worshippers were crowded up against it in a narrow space. I personally have always felt that clearing the area before the Wall was only the first step in the process of reconstruction. Our generation must replan the space so that the approach to the Wall will again assume an element of mystery, surprise, and strong feeling.

Of course, all our work in the Old City has become even more compli-cated because of the unfortunate pronouncements of UNESCO demand-ing a halt to any archaeological excavations in Jerusalem. Ironically enough, most of the digs, which were carried out with exemplary care (particularly where they might have affected the neighboring mosques), have brought to light many Moslem buildings, especially of the Omayyad period. This is an era in Jerusalem's history with few written sources, and the discoveries have therefore revealed much more about the Moslem period in Jerusalem's history than had ever been known before. All considered, it is really difficult to understand why the Arabs are so interested in having us stop digging. The only explanation is the usefulness of the big lie.

Ten years after the reunification of Jerusalem, we don't have 'integrated' Arab-Jewish neighborhoods. But there is no segregation between Jews and Arabs in the law. There is nothing to prevent an Arab from buying or renting an apartment in an otherwise Jewish building or vice versa. It just does not work out that way. If an Arab has children, he will want to send them to an Arab neighborhood school, and he and his wife will want to be near their friends, the mosque, the markets, the very smells and sounds they know. The same is true not only for Jews, but for Armenians and all the other sects and ethnic groups as well. If you had walked into Jaffa Gate a hundred years ago, or three hundred years ago, you would have passed the Armenian Quarter on your right, a Greek Quarter on your left, then a Latin Quarter, and in between smaller Christian groupings – Copts, Abyssinians, Assyrians, and many others. Then you would have come to a large Jewish Quarter and a large Moslem Quarter. No Armenian then, or now, wants to become a Copt or a Greek. No Greek ever moved into the Jewish Quarter. Communities kept themselves meticulously apart. The city was a mosaic, a multicultural society, never a melting pot. Everyone belongs to one community or another, with its separate language and tradition. That is part of Jerusalem's traditional character, and all the new housing will undoubtedly not change it.

Although it is our housing program that has been the subject of headlines, the city administration has also been extremely conscious of the need to plant trees and create green spaces. One of my first actions after assuming office was to begin laying out small green areas and pocket parks all over the city. In our climate and conditions of cramped living space, small parks for children, adolescents, and adults are a major necessity. For eight months out of the year, they are practically an extension of living space – once people grow accustomed to making use of them, and over the years our citizens have come to use them more and more. When all the trees planted in recent years mature, Jerusalem will for the first time be a green city.

Beyond this, we are creating extensive green belts in Jerusalem. For example, I had envisioned creating a national park in the cleared area adjacent to the walls of the Old City to protect that area from the inroads of the modern city. Soon after the Six Day War, I organized a meeting in Prime Minister Eshkol's office with seven or eight Cabinet members and they accepted my proposal, but no action was ever taken to create the park. Nor could I rouse any succeeding government to action. Nonetheless, I refused to abandon the idea, and today work on the national park, which will cover five hundred acres, is well advanced. Where the government did not come through, we were helped by friends abroad, through donations to the Jerusalem Foundation, and also, to our pleasant surprise, by the churches who owned sections of the land in question.

It was an expensive proposition. First of all, we had to acquire the land, most of which was owned by the oldest of the churches in Jerusalem, the Greek Orthodox and the Armenians. These congregations collect a good bit of rent from their properties. But they are not fabulously rich, and they always need money for their educational and social activities, as well as for the maintenance of their churches and monasteries. On the other hand, they are conscious of the city's needs and are interested in fostering its prestige for obvious reasons. So with their cooperation we acquired the land around the Old City and declared it a National Park, which legally prevents any future city administration from ever changing its character. I believe we are the only city in the world that is creating such a central park at present. After all, Hyde Park, the Bois de Bologne, and Central Park were created by preserving green areas, not by buying up building land at extremely high prices and turning it into parks. Together with the Jewish National Fund, we are also creating a second large green belt, on the outskirts of the city, the Jerusalem Forest.

Not all our projects have been on such a large scale, but even the smallest is important to me because it adds to the quality of life in the city. What is special about these smaller parks and playgrounds, besides their benefit to the immediate neighborhoods, is that so many of them are personalized. Just as we opened up our plans for Jerusalem to an international panel, I have tried to open up the development of the city to more than its residents. The instrument for doing so is the Jerusalem Foundation, which was established in New York in 1966. Soon after I was first elected mayor, a few friends there suggested that from time to time I might need funds for some extras – like a research assistant or some work for which I would not want to request a special budgetary allocation. This was the original concept behind the foundation, but it quickly developed into a small, independent fund-raising organization that carries out projects of its own in Jerusalem. Unlike the government and the city, it is not bound by red tape. It is presided over by a board of outstanding citizens who do not have to consider coalition agreements or other political obligations and can objectively judge the real needs of the city. Therefore action can be taken much more speedily, and the results are evident all over the city.

The foundation has several unique features. First of all, it does not have a single paid fund-raising official abroad; all those who give their time work as volunteers. Secondly, even its staff in Jerusalem has remained small and close. The foundation is run by Ruth Cheshin with great devotion, flair, and the deep love for the city of a seventh-generation Jerusalemite. Finally, and most important, the fund-raising activities are carried out right here in Jerusalem, where we show our visitors what is needed. We do not ask for donations *per se*. We offer donors the opportunity to support a specific project, for which he or she pays in full. The donors thus have a feeling that something in the eternal city is their own, that they are a part of it.

One such project that particularly expresses the spirit of Jerusalem originated with a close friend from Dallas, Texas. He once mentioned that he would like to honor a business partner, a Baptist from Austin, and an ecumenical idea occurred to me : why not build a garden on the Mount of Olives (which is now a Moslem neighborhood). The notion of a Jew in Dallas giving money to the Jewish mayor of Jerusalem for a garden in a Moslem neighborhood to honor a Baptist appealed to me immensely. My friend agreed, and in the summer of 1975 the garden was dedicated in the presence of a delegation from Austin. Instead of a heap of refuse, we now have a shady area with beautiful trees where the elderly can relax and smoke their narghiles while the children come noisily down the slide. This is just one of the many small gardens the Jerusalem Foundation has been instrumental in creating. We show it with pride to other 'spiritual citizens' of Jerusalem in the hope of turning them into practical taxpayers through a gift to the foundation.

The story of Mishkenot Sha'ananim is another expression of Jerusalem's true international character. I had long dreamed of opening the city to the world's finest artists and helping them feel at home here. One way of doing this was to provide them with a place they could really think of as home during their stay – a place where they could both relax and continue their work – and we found just the setting in Mishkenot Sha'ananim (which translates into something like 'Serene Dwellings'). Mishkenot is in the neighborhood called Yemin Moshe, which was established by Sir Moses Montefiore a century ago. It was the first Jewish neighborhood in Jerusalem built outside the Old City walls, and when the city was divided in 1948 it was right on the frontier, very vulnerable, and eventually rather neglected. After 1967, when the frontier vanished. Yemin Moshe quickly became a very desirable neighborhood. Mishkenot Sha'ananim, a long, low-strung structure just below the windmill (which is now a small museum containing Montefiore memorabilia), was still its outstanding feature.

If you restore old buildings, you have to give them new content. The Jerusalem Foundation had already done this with the Khan, a Turkish caravanserai that was turned into an intimate theater-restaurant-art gallery-entertainment complex. Mishkenot Sha'ananim needed some thought, and the idea finally crystallized to make it into a guest house for creative artists from outside Jerusalem. The major gift that enabled us to reconstruct the building came from the same Bill Levitt who twenty-five years earlier had come to the aid of our fledgling state. Mishkenot was restored as nine well-designed, well-equipped apartments with a view of the Old City walls and the Valley of Hinnom. We reopened the building in August 1973 with an unforgettable ceremony. Pablo Casals was there, as were Isaac Stern, and Sasha Schneider, Eugene Istomin and Leonard Rose, and, of course, Bill and Simone Levitt and many of their friends. We had chosen a night with a full moon for the outdoor ceremony. It turned out to be the last public concert that Don Pablo ever gave – a very moving and beautiful evening.

This was also the first of many cultural activities at the Jerusalem Music Center. When I was still in the Prime Minister's Office, I supported the initiating of an annual Israel Festival. It was to be mainly a music festival, with some additional theatrical and ballet performances, that would draw famous artists here. Through the Israel Festival I met many outstanding musicians, although I personally had never had a deep understanding of music. The one to whom I grew closest – not only because of his music, but also because of his devotion to Israel – was Isaac Stern. But there were many other outstanding musicians who demonstrated their love for Israel through their art : Casals, who came to Israel regularly; Stravinsky, who composed a special work for the festival on 'The Sacrifice of Isaac'; Sasha Schneider, violinist, conductor, and the organizer of the Casals festivals; Artur Rubinstein, Leonard Bernstein, Gina Bachauer, and many, many others.

One moving experience I remember was when Sasha suggested that we go and test the ruins of the Roman amphitheater in Caesarea as a possible site for a music festival. What was supposed to be a test turned out to be a gala evening. Casals, Stern, and the glorious Budapest Quartet, with Sasha Schneider, all trooped along, and Stern, Rose, and Istomin played. A few hundred guests were sitting on the rocks that once had been the elegant seats of the amphitheater. An Arab family had pried off the remaining pieces of marble and burned them into gypsum over the last few decades, so the seating was very uncomfortable, but the acoustics were absolutely perfect. With the sea as a backdrop, that quiet hour before sunset – the hour for which the theater was really created – provided an atmosphere never fully recaptured by the evening performances at Caesarea, even in the beautifully restored theater with the wind blowing off the water late at night.

There is a direct line from this experience to the excellent music center that has now been created next to Mishkenot Sha'ananim. This time the dream was Isaac Stern's. He had begun to fear the gradual disappearance of the great traditions of music brought to Israel by European musicians who fled from the Nazis and, more recently, by

Russian musicians. The answer, he felt, was to improve our own teaching methods and even attract teachers and pupils from outside the country. Isaac visualized a particularly intensive and high-level technique of teaching music and recording the lessons on color videotape. Thus not only the pupils and teachers present, but people involved in musical education all over the world would benefit from it. He was able to persuade the English Rothschilds to support his idea. The program started with Casals teaching at the Khan Theater. Since then, the Jerusalem Music Center has been completed, and the results are exciting and impressive, particularly as the technical equipment is of the highest quality. The interviews we have recorded with the great musicians of our time will remain documents of permanent importance.

Among the guests we have hosted at Mishkenot since its opening are Artur Rubinstein, Isaac Stern, Isaiah Berlin, Simone de Beauvoir, Alexander Calder, Robert Rauschenberg, Bernard Lewis, John Hersey, and many others. Saul Bellow stayed there for a few months and subsequently wrote a book about his visit, *To Jerusalem and Back*, which appeared shortly after he was awarded the Nobel Prize. I was particularly impressed with Bellow's argument with Sartre and with the stand of the New Left against Zionism. I also believe this was the first time that Bellow expressed his concern and identification with Israel in his writings. Probably our most unusual guest, however, was the Egyptian writer Sana Hassan, who requested and received an entry permit in order to write a book about Israel. She was a long-time guest at Mishkenot, and though she did not hide her personal views and criticism of Israel, she was received everywhere with great interest. (It is not often that we host citizens of our belligerent neighbors.) Mishkenot has added an entirely new dimension to Jerusalem. I am confident that in the long run it will have a valuable influence both on Jerusalem and its guests, for this is a marriage between great talent and the atmosphere of the city.

Another means we have developed to express the universality of Jerusalem is through the biennial Jerusalem International Book Fair. It is one of the nicest events we have, and has had consistently strong drawing power for writers, publishers, and agents from all over the world. The first one, held on a very minor scale but based on a good idea, took place in 1963, before I became mayor. Since then the book fairs have been held regularly and have grown larger each time. Though our fair is still far behind the great Frankfurt Book Fair, it is nonetheless second in volume and stands well ahead of all the little book fairs that spring up here and there and then vanish again. And unlike the many book fairs that are closed to the public, the Jerusalem fair is also a major cultural event for our citizens, who faithfully flock to Jerusalem from all over the country and visit the stalls by the thousands. Our foreign participants never seem to get over the sight of the crowds; but as the People of the Book, I guess we take that kind of interest for granted.

At the time of the Fair, the Municipality confers the Jerusalem Prize, a literary award in the field of *belles lettres*, philosophy, and research given to an author whose writings express the theme of the 'Freedom of the Individual in Society'. The recipient is selected by an independent jury of writers and scholars, and the first recipient was Bertrand Russell. Since then we have wandered all over the globe, as far as Borges in Argentina and Ignazio Silone in Italy, as well as André Schwarz-Bart, Max Frisch, Eugene Ionesco, and Octavio Paz. In 1975 the judges chose Simone de Beauvoir as the recipient. By the usual procedure, the prize was offered to her without publicity, and only after she had accepted it and agreed to come to Jerusalem in person to receive it (which is one of the conditions) did we announce the award.

Simone de Beauvoir is the favorite of the New Left, which, with few exceptions, is sharply anti-Israel. So when she came here and made a moving speech supporting the unity of Jerusalem – an appeal phrased in much stronger words than she had originally intended, following a day-and-a-half tour of the city – it made a strong impression on the world. Accompanying her on the visit was Claude Lanzmann, who persuaded her to accept the prize. (He had been Sartre's literary secretary for many years and is now a documentary-film producer.) He had very rarely seen Simone de Beauvoir as emotionally affected as she was by her first visit to Jerusalem.

A stay at Mishkenot or receiving the Jerusalem Prize tends to be a rather personal affair between the artist and the magic of Jerusalem. But I also try to bring over artists who will share their special talents with the people of the city. Admittedly, it's a long trip to Jerusalem for an appearance or two, but one request that few entertainers can turn down is a benefit concert in the city. And that's how we finally got Frank Sinatra to come back. I had met Sinatra for the first time in 1962, when he came to Israel on a concert tour, and again in 1965, when he came for the filming of *Cast a Giant Shadow*. Since I became mayor, I had been trying to persuade him to return and give a benefit concert, and while he agreed in principle, he never gave a definite date. In 1972, when I was in Los Angeles, I ran into him playing golf with Spiro Agnew at the Hillcrest Country Club in Beverly Hills (mainly a Jewish club, by the way), where he is a member. Again Frank and I talked about his coming to Jerusalem, but again nothing definite was set.

Incidentally, during that same visit to the States, I was a guest on the Johnny Carson Show, together with Mayor John Lindsay. When I entered the waiting room, I saw a good-looking black man sitting there. Someone whispered to me, 'Do you know who that is? Muhammad

Ali.' Not only did I know who he was, but our son, Amos, admires him more than any other person alive. Before he went on camera, we were introduced. Ali seemed quite moved, and he embraced me and said, 'I always wanted to meet the mayor of Jerusalem!' Three years have passed since then, but people still approach me and say, 'I saw you on the Johnny Carson Show!' Apparently this is the best possible way to become known in the United States – or at least much better than building twenty schools and keeping the streets of Jerusalem clean!

At any rate, with the help of Mickey Rudin, a mutual friend and Sinatra's lawyer, Frank finally came to Jerusalem in November 1975 to give two performances. All proceeds were donated toward cultural activities for Jewish and Arab schoolchildren, and needless to say the concerts were a fantastic success. After the first one, we gave a reception in Frank's honor. He kindly walked around and shook the hand of everyone I introduced him to. Then after dinner we sat down to a private Thanksgiving Day meal in his hotel suite.

During the dinner Frank told a story that dates back to 1948, when he was appearing at the Copacabana. Of course, he didn't know then that above the Copa was the now-defunct Hotel Fourteen, where we had our Haganah mission headquarters. A Jewish acquaintance approached him after a performance and asked him to take a briefcase down to a certain pier in Brooklyn and hand it to the captain of a boat. He was told to take the third taxi in the line down the street. Since it was 4:30 in the morning, he knew that it must have something to do with Israel's War of Independence, so he agreed gladly, went down to the pier, handed it over, and watched the ship sail. When Frank returned to the Longchamps restaurant on Madison Avenue about 6 A.M., some of his fellow entertainers who were still there teased him about his 'date'. It was far from the kind of date they had in mind. Since we had to get the money to the ship urgently and knew we were all watched, we turned the task to someone who wouldn't attract any attention – Frank Sinatra!

Years later, when he came to Jerusalem for the first time in 1962, Frank called on Ben-Gurion at the Prime Minister's Office. The prime minister looked at him and, characteristically, asked, 'What are you doing here?' Then he thanked Frank for getting a shipload of arms to Israel. At first Sinatra had no idea what Ben-Gurion was talking about. Only after leaving the Prime Minister's Office did he remember the long-forgotten incident and realize that in the suitcase was a payment, in cash, for shipping arms and ammunition to Israel.

Frank Sinatra is just one of the many gifted entertainers who have come to Jerusalem since I've been mayor. I am constantly trying to attract people who stand out not only by virtue of their talent but because of the glamor surrounding them. These visits are important as a counterweight to the wide publicity given to the occasional terrorist incident in Jerusalem. Since a visit by Sinatra or Elizabeth Taylor gets almost as much coverage, their very presence in Jerusalem shows people abroad that they can come here too, that life in Jerusalem is not dominated by bombings or by the tension between Arabs and Jews. I believe that paying attention to Jerusalem's image abroad and the psychological mood in the city is as important an element of our 'masterplan' as all the blueprints and development schemes. Steeped though it is in the past, Jerusalem is not a museum, and we will continue to work hard to keep it open and vibrant for citizens and visitors alike.

16 Toward the Future

On October 6, 1973, the Yom Kippur War began with a simultaneous attack by Egypt and Syria. The following day I went around the Old City with some colleagues from the Municipality. We did not know what to expect, but as we walked from one Arab restaurant and coffee house to another, the tension was obvious. Nevertheless, there were no incidents of violence, nor was there any personal display of hostility. Unlike 1967, the war did not touch Jerusalem physically and the city itself did not suffer this time. But we felt the tension and the losses on the front deeply, since it was a Jerusalem reserve brigade stationed on the Suez Canal that bore the brunt of the attack, and the number of casualties – mostly middle-aged men and almost all fathers of families – was particularly high.

Then the mood in the Arab sector shifted somewhat. Sensing that a great Arab victory was at hand, the Arabs became somewhat arrogant during the first days of the war. On the second or third day of the war, when the news was particularly critical, an Arab employed in a West Jerusalem hotel flung curses at his Jewish manager, stormed out, and never returned. The manager, obviously shaken by the incident, came to tell me the story. 'I've pampered this man,' he said. 'Look how much he earned and how well he was treated. And now he has shown his real colors!' I personally never had illusions about such things. I had never thought that the Arabs especially liked us. In fact, I was certain that the moment the Arabs of Jerusalem believed they could get rid of us, they would do so. Certainly improved economic conditions carry less weight than national feelings.

Although such unimportant incidents stopped after a few days, for the first time since 1948 the Arabs felt that Israel was not invincible. They had believed the Israelis would be defeated eventually, but had not expected a development like the initial success of the Arab armies in the immediate future. The shift in mood made me think of an incident with Mahmud Abu Zuluf, the publisher of *El Kuds* (an Arabic daily published in Jerusalem). A refugee from Jaffa, he had lived in East Jerusalem

under Jordanian rule, and once or twice his paper was shut down and he
was arrested for his criticism of Hussein's regime. But Abu Zuluf continued publishing his paper after the Six Day War. Being a man of
conviction and no collaborator, his articles often do not please us. But I
believe the very fact that freedom of the press extends to such papers in
Israel is of great importance to Arab-Israeli coexistence, particularly as
Israel is the only country in the Middle East with a free Arab press.

I maintain a cordial relationship with Abu Zuluf. One afternoon in
1970, he was at our home together with Ben-Gurion. They had met once
before – for an interview in Cairo in 1946 – and they picked up right
where they had left off a quarter of a century earlier. Ben-Gurion
repeated the opinion he had expressed in 1946 that peace would be
achieved not in his own lifetime, but in the lifetime of Abu Zuluf, who
was a much younger man. The longer it would take, Ben-Gurion said,
the harder the peace terms would be on the Arabs.

Some time later, after the death of the mufti of Jerusalem, Haj Amin
el-Husseini (whose violent policies had brought about the death of more
Arabs than Jews or Englishmen and who had been living in Beirut since
1948), Abu Zuluf published an article criticizing him. A few days later,
in another article, he contended that the future of the Palestinians should
be decided by the Arabs who had remained in Palestine (a million
people), though they were now living under occupation, and not by
Palestinians living abroad. His article was criticized a few times by the
el-Fatah radio, and one night his car was set on fire. Abu Zuluf came to
me the next morning to complain : 'I have six children. Today it is my
car, tomorrow it may be my son who will come under attack. If you
cannot protect me, how can I continue to write freely? Why don't the
police prevent terror?' This was before the 1973 war, when the Arabs
felt that we Israelis were all but omnipotent. I don't think that Abu
Zuluf would come to us today asking for protection from Arab terror.

For years the Palestinians had taken every day as it came, hoping that
others – the U.N., the Russians, the Americans, the Arab countries –
would solve the problems of Jerusalem and return the city to them. Now
they not only began to believe more in the strength of the Arab countries
but they felt themselves a part of it. They were so taken up by the Arab
euphoria of the early days of battle that they failed to see the real lesson
of the war : Egypt and Syria were defeated on the battlefield more
decisively than they had been in the Six Day War, when the surprise
had been on our side. Because they turned a blind eye to reality, a new
assertiveness developed among the Arabs, but it has had no effect on
daily life in the city. As before, they would take no action on their own.
On the contrary, they felt they should stay put, develop the economy of
the city so that no Arab would emigrate because of lack of work, and see
to it that the Arab character of their part of the city was preserved. This

was their historic task. It was a comfortable philosophy that did not place any particular demands on them, and they could continue to live a comparatively pleasant life while fulfilling their patriotic duty.

At the same time, the Arabs of Jerusalem find themselves in a difficult predicament. Certainly they do not desire Israeli rule, but neither do they particularly like King Hussein, who had killed many Palestinians in 1970 and had treated Jerusalem shabbily throughout the years. They like Yassir Arafat even less, because they remember his forerunner, the mufti of Jerusalem, and are aware of what happened in Algeria when Boumedienne marched in with a small well-armed force and eliminated Ben Bella and Farhat Abbas, the very men who had freed the country from French rule. In an ironic fashion, therefore, Israeli rule in East Jerusalem is almost a convenience for its Arab inhabitants – at least inasmuch as none of the other alternatives appear to be particularly attractive.

As a consequence of the war, our earlier timetable was shattered; and had we prevented the war, another five or ten years might have been at our disposal to carry out a peaceful process of integration. This period would have been of inestimable importance. I am a sincere believer in gradualism because people become accustomed to new situations slowly and change their views with the passing of time and accumulation of experience. It is the upheaval of unexpected events that often makes them take 'shelter' in old and 'comfortable' views and tends to make them rigid. For example, if not for the El-Aksa fire in 1969, we would probably have had Arab candidates running for the City Council two months later. Although that might have brought about many uncomfortable moments – because the Arab councilors would undoubtedly have had to start every speech by asserting that they did not accept the unification of the city and that they were loyal to the Arab nationalist cause – in the long run it would have been preferable to the policy of paternalism we have been forced to adopt. As things stand, we must try to analyze Arab needs and find reasonable solutions to them. We attempt to represent their interests without having been elected by them, and this situation cannot last forever. Again, if not for the Yom Kippur War, we would probably have had a good representation of the Arabs on the council after the 1973 elections. Equally important, more Jewish-Arab business partnerships and joint enterprises would have developed, and that would surely have served as an additional counterweight to extremism. With the Yom Kippur War, and especially with the new role of oil in the world, I do not think we can now expect such developments for a very long time.

Spirits had taken a radical turn not only in the Arab sector. In fact, the mood of the whole country was out of sorts in one way or another during that time. Many were so deep in mourning for the war dead they failed to see we had scored a military victory, not suffered a defeat. There was also a severe drop in confidence in the nation's leadership as a result of our being caught off guard – not only in terms of the actual surprise attack, but also regarding the assessment of the Arabs' strength and ability. Then, in the midst of it all, we were deprived even of the symbol of decisive leadership in days gone by. On December 1, 1973, Ben-Gurion passed away at the age of eighty-six.

A week or two before Ben-Gurion died, Tamar and I had visited him in the hospital. I was not quite certain whether or not he recognized me. During his last year, after his memory had started failing, he acquired an extremely clever trick to hide this disability by speaking in generalities. That's just what happened during our visit. A few weeks earlier the family and a few friends had celebrated his birthday at his home in Tel Aviv. Ben-Gurion was, of course, aware of the war, but did not refer to it or to its outcome, and we could not tell how he felt about the situation. Two weeks later, at the hospital, his condition had obviously deteriorated, and it was a very sad visit. Before I left, he looked at me and there was suddenly a helpless smile on his face, as if he wanted to say, 'Well, so this is the end of it all.' I was terribly shaken as I walked out.

A few days later, Chaim Yisraeli, who for many years headed the defense minister's private office and was close to all his superiors, but particularly to Ben-Gurion, called to tell me it was all over : Ben-Gurion was dead. Naturally, I was prepared for Ben-Gurion's death. Watching him lose his tremendous awareness and become only half a being over the previous months was almost intolerable. In a way I had wished it would end already, yet coming just at that time, Ben-Gurion's death seemed to be like some cosmic trick to pour salt on our wounds. The nation was facing one of its worst crises; people were uncertain and confused; and the one man in whom so many had confidence, who had always found the right way, was gone.

On the day of the funeral, after Ben-Gurion's body had been lying in state outside the Knesset for almost twenty-four hours, I passed by in the early hours of the morning. During the previous day and night, tens of thousands had passed, young and old. It was as if they suddenly felt how much they lacked a leader like Ben-Gurion. They longed for what now seemed to be the good old days, whether they had really been so good or not.

The funeral took place on a cold morning, and everybody was there. I remember Dayan standing by himself, almost an outcast. Tamar, who couldn't bear it, walked over to say hello as usual. I have known Dayan since 1935 and have been fairly friendly with him. In the years when I traveled to Tel Aviv often, I enjoyed spending evenings at his home, and both Tamar and I spent many hours with Moshe and his wife talking of everything from Cabinet ministers to archaeology. Nonetheless, I would not describe our relationship as close. I don't think that anybody is really close to Dayan. But we certainly had a good understanding. Perhaps one trait we share in common is not being cowed by convention and paying little attention to what people say about us, but Dayan is more extreme in this sense than I. In fact, I believe his disregard for public sensitivities has sometimes led him astray and could on some occasions turn out to be a serious liability for him. We also had in common a close relationship with Ben-Gurion, something that bound many people together.

I have always had great respect for Dayan. He understands both Arabs and general world affairs better than anybody else in our political arena; he is both more pragmatic and more innovative than our other politicians; and he is not bound by preconceptions. When new problems arise, he seeks new solutions, while most others just apply the old formulas over and over again, whether they fit the new situation or not. Long before the 1973 war, Dayan felt – and said at closed sessions – that we were pushing Sadat into a corner from which only a war would extricate him.

Nevertheless, he failed to take the action that his own reading of the situation demanded, and because of his loyalty to the prime minister, he did not carry his argument about Egypt into the open. Then, despite his generally acute perception just before the 1973 war itself, he failed to foresee what would come the next day or the day after that. But I think that his most unfortunate mistake – and the one which did the most harm to his career – was that after the war started, and our lack of preparedness had become obvious, he did not immediately admit to the errors made or ask for a proper investigation of the blunders as soon as possible. Later he let his chief of staff take all the blame, although to anyone not concerned with legal niceties, there was no real difference between parliamentary responsibility and direct personal responsibility.

It is very sad that the one man who showed such outstanding leadership brought about his own temporary political eclipse. On the third or fourth day of the war, when I first realized that we were not going to overcome the Arab forces quickly, I telephoned Dayan. As I could not get through to him directly, I spoke twice, on two consecutive days, with his aides. Through them I suggested that he publicly acknowledge his mistakes, as well as his responsibility, immediately and undertake that the whole matter would be thoroughly investigated after the war. I think this was a widespread feeling, and for me it was an obvious step to bring it to his attention. But Dayan apparently did not accept the idea, and an able man lost the confidence of the people, which had been almost universal.

This was not my only difference with him. Dayan believed in our rights to the historical Land of Israel and chose to place aside the eventual dangers to democracy in absorbing the million West Bank Arabs into our society. Once, while walking out of the King David Hotel together, I asked him what would happen to morale if the nation was led to believe that we could keep the West Bank and we were then forced to give it up. Dayan, then at the pinnacle of his popularity, was not worried. We were growing less dependent on outside sources for arms, and he was therefore less concerned about international pressures. But even if we would have to relinquish territories, he believed that the people would remain loyal to their leaders.

During this same period, efforts to achieve some kind of understanding between the confrontation states were initiated by Secretary of State Kissinger. I requested an appointment with him during his second shuttle mission. I have known Kissinger for years. We had met several times in Jerusalem, when he came to lecture in the late 1960s, and had become friendly enough to start corresponding. He invited me to visit him but I was so preoccupied with daily Jerusalem affairs that I never took time off to accept his invitations. Then, with the changes in the political mood brought about by the Yom Kippur War, I wanted to discuss the Jerusalem issue with Kissinger personally.

Since the war, I think the whole subject of Kissinger has become somewhat of a red herring in Israel. Where our government and people faltered in their grasp of a clear-cut policy, it seemed easier to cover up the confusion by shifting the spotlight onto Kissinger and portraying him as the source of our problems. I truly believe that he wishes us well. That does not mean that our conceptions were always identical or that he was not liable to make mistakes – and sometimes serious ones. But that is not really the point. Much of the criticism of Kissinger here in Israel derived from a distorted conception of the man and his role. Many parochial-minded people would have liked him to act first as a Jew and only after that as secretary of state of the United States. They suffered from the 'Queen Esther syndrome' : like Queen Esther of old, they believed, Kissinger had been sent by providence to help the Jewish state at a critical point in its history – but he was not fulfilling their expectations. A number of people on our political Right have even taken this complaint to the extreme and portray Kissinger as a self-hating Jew!

The outcome, of course, was to divert attention from the true, and intricate, issues of the negotiations by making Dr Kissinger himself the issue. Yet because the fundamental subjects touched on during the shuttle negotiations are so difficult for many people here to face, I can see why the 'diversionary tactic' worked. Given time and perspective, however, I'm sure that Israelis will develop a clearer understanding of Kissinger and what he tried to do. I personally believe that he put up a fight for us whenever he reasonably could, considering the fact that he was a high government official of a country with global responsibilities.

I went to see Kissinger at the King David Hotel. We walked out on the terrace of his suite and, while showing him the view from there, I tried to explain to him the problems of Jerusalem. I hoped to get from him confirmation that he intended to deal with the question of Jerusalem at the end of the negotiating process, not the beginning. As I expected, he agreed. It was a wise decision, for Jerusalem will not be an easy subject to tackle and, taken first, might have sabotaged interim agreements between Israel and the Arabs.

For that very reason, it seems that everyone who is concerned with the Middle East worries about the future of Jerusalem. To some the problem seems to be the insurmountable obstacle on which peace will eventually flounder. Even if progress is made, how can the fundamental differences be reconciled? I tend to think that this view is somewhat alarmist. People tend to forget that, after all, the Jerusalem 'problem' was a subject of discussion long before the unification in 1967. The first known census in the city's history was taken in 1870, and at least since then there has been a Jewish majority in Jerusalem. It is on record that in 1947 the United Nations decided that Jerusalem was to be transformed into an international city belonging to neither of the two neighboring countries in whose territory it lay. But the U.N. never implemented its decision, and by the early 1950s it was clear that for all practical purposes the subject was a dead letter. Anyway, internationalization was a paper solution and at odds with reality. After all, none of the international cities created in the past worked. Danzig, if anything, brought on World War Two; Trieste would have led to a war between Yugoslavia and Italy had its international status not been cancelled in order to divide it up between the two countries.

In 1967 the internationalization idea was dragged out of the U.N. archives. But it was a short-lived proposal for a variety of reasons. One was that the Vatican, which had been an original sponsor of internationalization in 1948, suddenly realized that world conditions had radically changed. Internationalization would no longer mean that Catholics, or even Christians, would run the city. The U.N. is now in the hands of the Third World, and an international committee would now consist mainly of non-Christians who have no interest in the Holy Places. Besides, the churches in Jerusalem have learned that never before did they enjoy such true freedom of worship and education and less interference in their affairs. Never in recent memory have they received more practical help from the authorities, particularly the Municipality, and this at a time when greater pressure is being placed on the Christian minorities by a more aggressive Arab nationalism all over the Middle East.

Another reason why the call for internationalization faded was that statesmen had become a little more sophisticated. They realized that the city needed a real administration, not an international bureaucracy that would be unable to decide anything. The citizens would be the first to suffer, and the city would inevitably face neglect. Who would govern Jerusalem? A Chinese, a Nepalese, a Nigerian, a Swede, and an Argentinian? Each member of such a council would have to get confirmation from his Foreign Office for every change in a sewage pipe. It would be like the situation that used to exist in the Church of the Holy Sepulchre, where no one could hammer in a new nail before negotiating with all the churches that have a share in the site. An even worse and more topical comparison would be with the United Nations itself. Heaven forbid that Jerusalem should be as shabbily treated as the U.N. treats the world's problems.

Though the crusade for internationalization has pretty much been abandoned, during 1975 I became aware of several studies and other proposals that were being prepared in connection with Jerusalem. Some were just reformulations of older ideas. Lord Caradon, who had been the British representative in the United Nations at the time of the Six Day War and had submitted the famous Resolution 242, came to Jerusalem on several occasions. I had known him for many years, since the time he was British district officer in Netanya and later in Nablus. We had also appeared together in New York, while he was still at the United Nations, before the Council on Foreign Relations and similar forums. So it was natural for him to call whenever he came to Jerusalem.

One day he telephoned and asked to pay a visit. I suggested that we drive around the city for an hour or two. In the Old City I showed him the remnants of the destroyed Jewish Quarter and the start of its restoration. I pointed out the achievements of which we were proud, from the restoration of the old churches to newly created parks around the city. I also showed him the new housing for Arabs that we had initiated and other projects I felt might interest him. But this did not change his opinion that Jerusalem should be divided along the pre-1967 border into two cities, one section under Arab administration and one under the Jews. Of course, this time there would be no barbed wire or dividing walls. The Arab sector would presumably be under the rule of the peaceable Arafat. I think this is a naive belief, at best. In my office I keep a photo of the street near City Hall taken at the moment the dividing wall was toppled on June 29, 1967. Jerusalem Arabs say that they want one open city but divided sovereignty. This in itself is a most complicated if not impossible concept. But I have no doubt that in such a case Arab nationalism would bring back the walls, the minefields, and the barbed wire – and with them the saddest chapter in Jerusalem's history.

Lord Caradon later published a brochure called *Jerusalem Proposals,* which he sent to me. The pamphlet had a chapter filled with praise for what the present city administration, and I personally, were doing for

Jerusalem. It even included a letter of mine explaining that the post-1967 changes were irreversible. Yet inclusion of a chapter detailing my approach to Jerusalem's future may have helped to make Lord Caradon appear 'even-handed', while his supposed objectivity was actually a one-sided advocacy of the Arab position, both regarding Jerusalem and the Palestinian problem in general. His basic contention was that the Jerusalem issue had to be solved now, immediately. He was firmly convinced that Jerusalem would be a major stumbling block to peace, and it was not worthwhile making progress on any other front if it were all to break down in the end over the most difficult issue.

Strange that it never occurred to an experienced diplomat like Lord Caradon that the very chance to make progress on any other front might be a practical first step. After all, it would demonstrate to both sides that it is truly possible to sit down at a negotiating table and reach solutions together. Israel and the Arab states have had precious little experience with that process – and that almost thirty years ago during the Armistice negotiations – so that some people on both sides have begun to doubt whether negotiating is actually feasible. For the present, this is really the major obstacle to overcome. But putting the most difficult issue at the head of the list would probably just reinforce the rigid and defensive positions at the extreme. I'm afraid that Lord Caradon's proposal is an invitation for us all to bang our heads against the wall, and I think that both sides to this dispute have already been battered enough.

More complex than Lord Caradon's brochure were several studies prepared by learned political scientists for institutions in the United States and Europe. They did not advocate that the future of Jerusalem be negotiated immediately but wanted to prepare suggestions that could be ready at hand whenever the political atmosphere dictated the time was ripe to face the issue. Since the problem of Jerusalem will be raised in the not-too-distant future – assuming progress is made toward a stable situation in the Middle East – I believed that we, too, should prepare ourselves for that day. This is not necessarily a job for the city. I felt that our government should deal with it, or that a private group in Israel should be commissioned to prepare studies similar to those done abroad. But every time I suggested that we prepare papers on our own position for future negotiation, the government ministers shied away: 'This is too hot a potato to touch. We have enough problems at the moment with Sinai, the Golan, and the West Bank, not to mention domestic problems. We can't add Jerusalem to them.'

I stood my ground, however. The fact that bodies like the Brookings Institute, the Aspen Institute, and others started thinking about the future of Jerusalem convinced me that we should at least have some basic facts ready, bricks from which we could eventually build a plan of our own. Luckily I received the modest financial support needed for such a project from friends, and I was able to invite a varied group of academics to supervise research on a number of Jerusalem's problems. Rather than ask them to draw up a definite plan for the future, we have asked them to research the many solutions that were suggested for Jerusalem in the past as well as the experiences of other cities with problems similar to ours and the solutions they have adopted. It's a start toward developing options that can be discussed when the time to map out Jerusalem's future is at hand.

I reject the argument of those who say that if you indicate what you *might* be willing to give, you are assuming a weaker bargaining position because your offer will be taken for granted and negotiations will start from there. Today, of course, many have come to share my belief that we wasted opportunities immediately after the Six Day War. Having squandered our assets and diplomatic possibilities, we now have to make up for them by an unconventional kind of open diplomacy. In 1968–9, the notion that most of the West Bank and the Gaza Strip would be returned was still prevalent in Israel. While some wanted the right for Jews to settle in places like Hebron, the vast majority of Israelis displayed a basic readiness to relinquish political sovereignty over practically all the territories we had occupied in 1967. Israel's only real problem was secure borders. Over the last decade, however, this mood has shifted, and as a result of Arab intransigence even over direct negotiations and of the drastic change in our political situation in 1973, more extreme opinions have taken root, particularly among very vocal groups of young people and the religious circles. Inside Israel, the question of territories has become a very emotional issue that will be difficult to deal with.

While everyone in the state agreed from the beginning that Jerusalem would remain united and the capital of Israel, the *Jerusalem Post* reported, correctly, that in April 1969 I suggested to the Foreign Press Club – as a personal idea – that when peace was achieved, one possibility to consider was the notion of a Greater Jerusalem. (I had found such a plan in the drawers of the previous Jordanian administration, and their map of Jerusalem extended from Ramallah in the north to Bethlehem in the south.) This idea was based on the assumption that the major part of the West Bank would be returned – a course that seemed very likely before terrorism had started and before the Yom Kippur War brought about its own changes. I suggested that part of this Greater Jerusalem might be under Arab sovereignty – even an Arab capital (though Hussein had chosen to make Amman, not Jerusalem, his seat of government). Yet the attack on me then for such a far-reaching proposition (the complications of which I fully understood) was much milder than the fervent criticism triggered by an innocent word I threw out a few years later.

In 1975 I spoke at a congress of international political correspondents and expressed the belief that any solution we find – although within the framework of Jerusalem's present boundaries and status as the capital of Israel – will entail difficult and painful decisions for the Jews. By that I meant that much of what had already been granted to Jerusalem's Arabs would become self-imposed infringements on our absolute sovereignty if we were to formulate it into law. Comparing reactions to suggestions I make now to those made immediately after 1967, I have no doubt that we are moving toward extremism and polarization of opinions. The reason may be that since the Yom Kippur War our people feel more vulnerable and thus instinctively want to hold on to every particle.

Ironically enough, Jerusalem's unique status is not yet fully recognized by our own government and laws. I believe there must be a special law for Jerusalem defining its unique status as the capital of Israel, giving the Municipality a wider range of authority in matters concerning the city, and establishing a special capital grant in the national budget. Jerusalem is not just another city and cannot be treated as such. In other countries, capital cities are dealt with in a special way. Washington is run and financed differently from other cities in the United States; so are Canberra, Ottawa, and The Hague. These cities have a kind of 'federal' status. 'Federal' may not be the right word for Jerusalem, because it immediately suggests a federation between Israel and Jordan, whereby Jerusalem could be the capital of both. But what I mean is a real chance for all the minorities to be represented on the City Council. The Moslems and the various Christian groups would participate on the council by statute, not only by virtue of elections (which may be influenced by external pressures and therefore even result in an electoral boycott).

For a long time to come, Moslems will not recognize Israel as the legitimate ruler of Jerusalem. Nor will Christians officially do so for reasons based on religious dogma. Some Christians believe that they are the successors of the Jews, to whom the return to the Holy Land was promised by the Lord. More important, their non-recognition stems out of concern for their brethren in Arab countries. But things might be different if we had a law similar to the one that served Lebanon well for fifty years. Such a statute would determine a definite ratio between Jewish, Moslem, and Christian representation on the City Council, regardless of how many voters in each of these groups go to the polls. (Only the Knesset, of course, could pass such legislation.) We would then have a more representative council and could establish greater unity in the city. I believe that Moslem and Christian leaders could more easily accept such appointments than take the initiative and compete directly in the city elections.

We have so far carried out some far-reaching steps in the direction of autonomy for the Arabs of Jerusalem. Israeli citizenship has not been forced on them, and ninety-nine percent of them have not exercised their right to opt for Israeli citizenship. We have continued Arab education in Jerusalem according to a curriculum based on the one drawn up by the Arab League (with the addition of the Hebrew language and a basic knowledge of Israeli civics). Arab residents of Jerusalem who hold Jordanian passports can travel across the bridges to Jordan any morning, without having to ask for permits, and their relatives can likewise visit them in Jerusalem. They can enter into partnerships with enemy sub-jects, and they are in full charge of administering the Temple Mount, even if they do not hold sovereignty over it. These are just examples of arrangements we have instituted to make their life as a community possible. There are no barriers between Jerusalem's Arabs and the wider Arab world. They are part of it, and the initial fear that they would be cut off from it has disappeared. But these administrative arrangements should be anchored in Israeli law. They should not be offered as temporary benevolent gestures that may disappear with a change in government.

I believe that the creation of boroughs is a necessity for the recently established Jewish suburbs, and at the same time a system of boroughs might provide possibilities for Arab self-government within Israel's capital. I can imagine 100,000 Jerusalem Arabs some years from now living in a geographically defined borough where to a very large extent they run their own affairs, much as a borough in London does. (The boroughs of New York are nominal and to some extent political, but the boroughs of London have large independent budgets and there is a clear division of labor between the thirty-two boroughs and the Greater London Council.) There is an historical precedent for this arrangement. In Ottoman times ethnic communities were organized in the *millet*, a concept that was not bound by geography. The Jews were a *millet*, the Armenians were a *millet*, the Maronites were a *millet*, and so on. Wherever they lived, they belonged to this framework and were governed by it. The *millet* had jurisdiction over personal status and a variety of other matters. Since this notion is not alien to the Middle East, it could be reintroduced, or a combination between a *millet* and a borough could be devised. My attempts in 1969 and 1970 to convince the Cabinet to consider the idea of boroughs were unsuccessful. Today I believe the Arabs would no longer be agreeable to it. It's a pity, because I am convinced that the boroughs would have consolidated the city, rather than divided it, as some of the opponents of the system maintained.

I believe that there are probably more viable solutions to Jerusalem's political problems than most people suspect. The major task is to apply ourselves to formulating them, and there is much room for imagination as well as solid analysis. One thing, however, must be clear to all at the outset. What may appear as the easiest and most clear-cut answer — dividing the city in two again — is not only politically unacceptable to us, but the most destructive thing anyone could do to Jerusalem.

Today Jerusalem is a beautiful city, and I often wish I could take people back in time and show them the city before 1967: the sadness of no-man's land, the walls, the barbed wire, the deserted streets, and deteriorating areas along the frontier. For whatever reason, this city has only flourished under the Jews. Nobody else ever paid a great deal of attention to Jerusalem. The Crusaders had a high regard for the city and were willing to sacrifice their lives for it. The British had a historic feeling for it. But only under the Jews — both in ancient and modern times — has it been the capital of a nation. When the Arabs had the choice, they bypassed Jerusalem and built Ramle as their capital — for the brief period they had a capital in this country at all. They never really developed Jerusalem and grew much attached to it only when others ruled it. The Arabs expressed their passion for Jerusalem when the Crusaders ruled it and again since we have governed it. In between, there was very little feeling for the city, and it suffered conspicuous neglect.

In contrast to the Christians and Moslems, the Jews do not really have Holy Places. Tradition attaches itself to sites, and, of course, no place is more revered by this tradition than the Western Wall, the only physical remnant of the Temple Mount. But it is Jerusalem, the city as a whole, that is mentioned in our prayers. Jerusalem, the embodiment of glory, the source of all joy, wisdom, and the law, is holy to the Jews. It is the city itself — temporal as well as spiritual — that is important, not any individual place. In fact, it is the soul and the heart of the Jewish people. A body can live without a limb; it cannot live without its head, heart, and soul. For all that, if the Jordanians had heeded our warnings in June 1967 and had not started shelling the city, Jerusalem would have remained divided, and we would have continued to pray for its unification. But now the unity of Jerusalem is an irreversible historic fact. The shock of the Yom Kippur War, which we still have not overcome, is nothing compared to the trauma that the Jews of Israel and the Diaspora would experience if Jerusalem were divided again. I cannot imagine how the Jewish people and the State of Israel could survive such a blow intact.

In the summer of 1976, when I spent a week at the Aspen Institute of Humanistic Studies, someone from the local Jewish community called to invite Tamar and me to the Friday evening service. It turned out not to be in a synagogue but in a church. The first person I met there was the local minister, who wore both a Jewish star and a cross around his neck. He had studied all the songs for the various Jewish holidays and was acting as the congregation's cantor. Not a single ritual during these

Friday evening prayers was performed in the accepted traditional manner. Not only did the service take place in a church, but men and women took turns reading the Torah, which has always been an exclusively male prerogative and is performed on Saturday morning. The congregation had recently had its first circumcision ceremony, performed by a Jewish doctor from the Aspen hospital who specialized in repairing the damage caused by ski accidents. And at about the same time, the community also celebrated its first *bar mitzvah*, also under very unusual circumstances. But for all the deviations in detail, Tamar and I were completely taken by their tremendous desire to preserve their Jewish identity. They want to learn more and more about their own tradition and keep the faith. Yet I doubt very much whether this would happen without Israel. Many people came to that particular service because it took place a few days after the Entebbe rescue operation. The week before, attendance had been only about a third.

The Aspen community may not be wholly typical of Diaspora Jewry today, but that encounter made me stop and think that if the hopes created by Zionists during the last century and pinned on the State of Israel in the last three decades should be dashed, if the vision supported by a united Jerusalem should vanish, it would crush the faith of many Jews. It is for that reason that we cannot compromise on the unity of this city. Certainly no Israeli government could live with the consequences. And any attempt to shatter its unity would probably lead to war. I am deeply convinced that within the united city, the capital of Israel, we can fashion solutions to all the problems of the three religions and the two peoples. And as long as I am mayor, at least, that aim will be our top priority.

Epilogue

I sometimes have arguments with Tamar about my task as mayor. She thinks I devote too much time to receiving foreign journalists and other visitors, fund-raising, and public relations in the cause of Jerusalem's image abroad and that all this is at the expense of the city's day-to-day problems. There is something to this. But the fact is that everyone prefers doing what he does well, and I believe that having eighty or a hundred large and small parks in Jerusalem (as a result of my fund-raising) adds to the well-being of the city no less than some programs we could develop through our various municipal departments – and for which no money would be available. Nonetheless, I listen to Tamar's comments carefully because, in addition to being my wife, she is a very special person. I can think of few people with as much good sense as she. Tamar can analyze a problem, consider all its aspects, and reach a well-considered solution. She also understands how little fame and fortune are worth. My being in public life has never appealed to her, but because of her conviction that my work was worthwhile, she has always given me full support, leaving all the limelight to me.

Certainly I could not have worked as I did all these years had Tamar not borne the brunt of seeing that our house remained a home. She not only took care of the children and the day-to-day running of the household, but I could bring home a dozen or two guests without prior notice and know that they would receive a warm welcome in a most pleasant atmosphere. Since I've become mayor, our house has become almost a branch of the Municipality, and Tamar does the work of an assistant or two. She takes countless phone calls from irate citizens and always talks to them with patience – which is more than I can always do. But that's not the end of it. Then she does everything possible to help solve each individual problem. Nonetheless, she thinks I am always overworking. Even if I am near exhaustion, there is always something else to be done for Jerusalem. I have little time left for the family. Often the only time Tamar and I are alone together is over breakfast at a dawn or pre-dawn hour.

I know the years of mayoralty have brought a change in me. Until then I had always worked under someone else's authority, most of the time Ben-Gurion's. There was someone above me to authorize, to take responsibility and criticism, and to receive credit. When I was elected mayor I suddenly found myself on my own, and very often – particularly during the first couple of years – with no one to turn to for support. It was a difficult period, and it made me more aware of the burdens of leadership. There are also consequences. I am all too well known for my temper, which expresses itself in many ways, from snapping at my fellow city councilors to shouting mercilessly at my secretaries (though I am convinced that no one any longer takes my shouting seriously). And while I have not broken any glass table tops in the past ten years, I sometimes toss the first thing that comes to hand.

An American friend had given me a beautiful, heavy glass ash tray and I put it on the desk in my office. Then it disappeared mysteriously. A few days later I discovered it in our living room at home. 'Your secretary sent it,' Tamar explained. 'She said she'd feel safer with it here.' American-born Shulamith Eisner, who assists me with unequalled efficiency in my correspondence with friends all over the world and is my invaluable right hand at the museum, either walks out of the room whenever I throw a temper tantrum or else screams back at me. This way we both get it out of our systems, which is the only explanation why we haven't developed ulcers in all these years.

Some of the expressions I have used amidst fury have pursued me to this day. During the first Black Panther demonstration outside City Hall – with more journalists and sympathizers than actual Panthers – the demonstrators marched all over the newly planted grass outside the building. My shouting 'Get off the grass!' is still regarded as a great anti-social expletive, and from time to time – sometimes in jest and sometimes in dead earnest – it's thrown back in my face. I know my temper certainly does not help me, even if I reason that it is better to let it out than to have it eat away at my insides. Of course, I often have rational explanations for my shouting. At the time of the grass episode, we were desperately trying to teach Jerusalemites to respect the first few gardens that had been created in the city; and today the parks and the gardens are enjoyed by all with hardly any vandalism. I also believe there should be an eleventh commandment, only for mayors: 'Thou shalt not be patient.' A mayor who is patient is lost. In any city, much has to be done immediately to avoid problems in the future, and it is more important, easier, and cheaper, to avoid problems than to solve them. A mayor cannot always get support for such preventative medicine from the budget committee or the regional or national government. But if he is convinced something has to be done, he must do it as quickly as possible – by any means at his disposal – or he will regret it.

Another consequence I've faced in the last decade is that every year since becoming mayor, I've added on two pounds. It is obviously a professional disease. The subject of my weight is a constant concern to everyone – but me. I enjoy good food, and I see absolutely no advantages in dieting. Several years ago, right after we opened the museum, I was in New York and learned that a good friend of mine had had a heart attack and was hospitalized. I went to visit him, and the first comment he made was, 'Teddy, you're so fat that you're going to have a heart attack and die.' I told him that if I had a heart attack, it would only be because of my concern for the financial difficulties of the museum. Then and there he made a deal: if I lost forty pounds, he would make a contribution to the museum. Even this tempting offer didn't work. I simply did not lose weight. But to his credit, my friend made his donation to the museum and followed it with more.

I am also often asked how I manage to keep the hours I do, reaching the office at 6:30 A.M. and often on the go till long past midnight. It's simple: I take catnaps during the day (though not always at the most appropriate times). I have the 'ability' to fall asleep at meetings, at ceremonial occasions, while listening to opening addresses at conferences, or while sitting on a dais between the prime minister and a foreign dignitary. Tamar has spent many an hour surreptitiously poking me in a vain attempt to keep me awake. But by now everyone is accustomed to this little quirk and it is taken as 'my style'. In fact, people now comment when I do *not* fall asleep at a public function.

My short naps also have something to do with the fact that I am on principle opposed to long speeches, particularly at ceremonial affairs. I don't believe anyone listens to them; they are just a set-piece we all feel obliged to go through. With the exception of perhaps one main speech at every such occasion, which is given by a president, prime minister, or chairman of an organization, greetings should be very, very short. I've held to this rule from the day I became mayor. Sometimes I have been able to bring a speech down to the grotesque of half a minute, and to some extent I think this talent has made an impact. Quite a number of people have begun to follow my example, and ceremonies and speeches – which used to be a national pastime in Israel – have now become a bit shorter. If I should go down in history, it should be for this.

Since becoming mayor, I have been offered – and refused – all kinds of jobs, some of them rather attractive. When I was offered the presidency of the Weizmann Institute, for which Marcus Sieff and Dave Ginsburg were particularly pressing, I felt that such a position should be held by someone with a scientific background, even if it is very much a public-relations and fund-raising assignment. Another position suggested to me was the chairmanship of the Jewish Agency. After Pinhas Sapir's death, a few friends suggested that I offer my candidacy. Again

I refused, partly because I felt that the Agency had to be thoroughly reorganized, and that kind of job – which could take eight or ten years – should be undertaken by a person considerably younger than I.

I must admit, however, that there was another major consideration. It would have been very, very hard for me to leave my post in Jerusalem. Whenever the option arose, I would think not only of my obligation to the city (after all, no one is indispensable), but of how much I personally derive from Jerusalem, and the balance always seems to work out in my favor. If I look back through the years, most of my actions were in fact reactions to a particular set of circumstances or to a pressing problem. But there have been instances of real constructive initiative. The two outstanding examples are the development of the Israel Museum and the Jerusalem Foundation.

The country and the city could have continued without the museum. But it is nonetheless a project that has surpassed our most optimistic dreams. The hours I spend in my small office there dealing with its affairs transport me into another world and make me forget my mayoral burdens. The museum is one of my few sources of relaxation, especially when I manage to get some minutes in the galleries as well. Likewise, Jerusalem existed for thousands of years without a foundation through which friends of the city all over the world could participate in its development. It was not easy creating such an instrument in the face of political opposition. But no one can deny today what it has accomplished in its educational, cultural, and artistic activities; in its restoration of historical sites and in greening and beautifying the city; or how its social services have helped to bring Arabs and Jews together. The list goes on and on. In fact, with comparatively little money, the Jerusalem Foundation has achieved great positive changes and substantial progress. Clearly, I derive more satisfaction and pleasure from these two institutions than from anything else in which my work involves me. Some of my activities before I became mayor seemed to have prepared me for this particular job at this particular time, almost as if it had been planned. And though people tell me that Jerusalem is lucky to have me, I know that the exact opposite is true : it is my great fortune that I ran into Jerusalem. Being mayor is the most varied, absorbing, sometimes aggravating, but still the most satisfying job in the world, and while I'm at it, I'll work as hard as I can, eat as much as I want, and shout at whomever I please.

On the whole, I am not a great optimist. I always see black clouds – nationally, historically, and even personally. If we lose track of a member of the family for a few hours, I always imagine some disaster. I don't talk about it, but it is definitely in the back of my mind. Such an outlook does not preclude my enjoying life, but there is no doubt of this fatalistic streak in my character. Seeing the mistakes we were making right at the beginning of our statehood, I thought: how can we possibly pull through? But we did. Now our problems are even more difficult, and our management of them has grown less competent. Firm leadership has been missing for years, and because successive government did not inform the people of the true state of affairs – both foreign and domestic – we have been living in a fool's paradise. The yearning for strong leadership was perhaps the strongest common denominator of the Israeli electorate – irrespective of political convictions – before the 1977 elections. There is no doubt that Mr Begin answered this desire, and the result of his election was a widespread upsurge of confidence and hope. Personally, I am apprehensive about some of the major goals and means of this government. If I could believe that the inclusion of a million additional Arabs in Israel, by whatever formula, would be less risky than even an unsatisfactory frontier; that fine oratory could make up for unremediable differences between us and our few friends in the world; or that mysticism and sincere religious beliefs could overcome political and demographic facts, I would rest more easily. As things stand, I can only hope that whatever the future brings, Jerusalem will remain a thriving and united city and Israel will continue to overcome whatever difficulties it may have to confront.

When the Arabs are building their strength and flexing their muscles more and more, and it appears as if the Americans and the Russians will eventually come down on us – separately or jointly – it may seem irrelevant to be thinking of another playground, or another community center for the city. I am not so certain that I am always right, but I am certain about our consistency and continuity. We cannot stop building Jerusalem because of changes or dangers that the future may hold, any more than we can sacrifice any future cultural or aesthetic needs to present convenience.

Once, when I was touring the city with an American columnist, he asked me whether I didn't find all this furious activity a little futile. 'At worst,' I said, 'we are like ants building the most beautiful ant heap that was ever created, and we hope it will continue to exist undisturbed. But who knows? Maybe a man with a stick will come along, poke it into our masterpiece, and part of it will be destroyed. If so, here we are, like ants. And we will build it again and again, as well and as beautifully as we know how.'

Index